ECODEMIA

ECODEMIA

Campus Environmental Stewardship
at the Turn of the 21st Century

Lessons in Smart Management from Administrators, Staff, and Students

by Julian Keniry

NATIONAL WILDLIFE FEDERATION

The **National Wildlife Federation** is the Nation's largest conservation education organization whose mission is to educate, inspire, and assist individuals and organizations of diverse cultures to conserve wildlife and other natural resources and to protect the Earth's environment in order to achieve a peaceful, equitable, and sustainable future.

National Wildlife Federation
1400 16th Street, N.W.
Washington, D.C. 20036

Jay D. Hair, *President*
William W. Howard, *Executive Vice President*
Lynn Greenwalt, *Vice President and Special Assistant to the President*
Nick Keller, *Director, Campus Outreach*
Julian Keniry, *National Coordinator, Campus Ecology*

ISBN 0-945051-57-3

Cover and interior design by Cutting Edge Graphics.
Cover photograph courtesy of *Duke Magazine*.

Printed on recycled paper with soy-based inks. For more information about the closed-loop recycled paper used for this book, see the inside front cover.

*Dedicated to the staff, student, and faculty participants
in the Aggie REPLANT Program
of Texas A&M University,
and to the memory and vision of its founder,
Scott Harris Hantman.*

CONTENTS

A bibliography and a list of contacts for networking appear at the end of each chapter.

PREFACE

by Jay D. Hair
President, National Wildlife Federation

Ecodemia is the story of how America's colleges and universities are changing their day-to-day operations in response to a growing environmental awareness. These institutions have long helped to shape conservation initiatives. The leaders they have produced have made many of the most significant contributions to conservation history. Today, many campuses are adding a chapter to that history by demonstrating the compatibility of fiscally sound institutional management with pollution prevention and the protection of biological diversity.

The National Wildlife Federation, the nation's largest conservation education organization, created its Campus Outreach Division to assist college students in educating themselves and their schools on the issues of sustainable development. Since Earth Day 1990, the Federation has worked with over one-third of the institutions of higher learning in the United States. As our staff has assisted campus leaders, they have also brought ideas and innovations back to the Federation's Environmental Quality Task Force, where efforts to improve our own environmental profile often parallel those of colleges and universities. *Ecodemia* is a product of these joint endeavors.

Individuals, institutions and local governments across the country are struggling to improve the economic viability of their communities while protecting wildlife, natural resources, and public health. Although the federal government will continue to play a crucial role in environmental protection, with increasing urgency solutions to environmental problems must be crafted and perfected at the local level. Institutions of higher learning, where visionary thinking often rubs against the daily demands of institutional life, are uniquely positioned to help invent the greener communities needed for the next century.

Ecodemia will assist students, faculty and staff across the country to develop environmentally sound campuses and communities.

> Today, many campuses are demonstrating the compatibility of fiscally sound institutional management with pollution prevention and the protection of biological diversity.

FOREWORD

by David W. Orr

A revolution in education is underway. Its leaders are a most unlikely sort: student activists, grounds managers, recycling directors, institutional purchasing agents, food service managers, and energy efficiency coordinators. Together they are beginning to change the way educational institutions work relative to their regional ecologies and economies. More importantly, they are changing the way many members of the academic community think about their responsibilities in a world awash with seemingly unsolvable ecological problems. Whether recycling programs at the University of Colorado, the use of native perennials in campus landscaping at Nebraska Wesleyan, or campus purchasing at Rutgers University, the evidence presented in *Ecodemia* documents the fact that creative and ecologically smart management can:

- reduce institutional operating costs;
- improve the quality of services ranging from food served in dining halls to lighting;
- reduce waste and ecological impacts; and help to
- rejuvenate local economies.

The fact that it is also the right thing to do is either an added bonus or the heart of the matter depending on your point of view. In either case, the larger message of *Ecodemia* is one of hope. Seemingly unsolvable global problems are often very solvable if approached at the right scale and with sufficient commitment. And what contemporary institutions are better situated to take the lead in solving problems than colleges and universities? While Congress, for example, seems incapable of formulating a farsighted and economically smart policy to promote energy efficiency, administrators at SUNY Buffalo have developed their own. As a result the university will save $3.2 million per year equal to 15 percent of the present energy budget.[1] They will also substantially reduce institutional contributions to global warming, acid rain, and national cynicism. By decisive action they have demonstrated to students, faculty, and the public at large that

> What contemporary institutions are better situated to take the lead in solving problems than colleges and universities?

---

1. Joye Mercer, "$18-Million Effort to Save Energy," *Chronicle of Higher Education* (December 14, 1994), p. A-33.

the future does not have to be bleak and that with sufficient leadership large institutions can act responsibly.

The author of *Ecodemia* has described a number of encouraging instances in which administrators and students alike are changing institutional policies for food, energy, materials, water, landscaping, transportation, and waste. This is not the end of the story, however, but its beginning. Immediately ahead are large questions about how 3,000 colleges and universities spend an estimated $150 billion, and how they invest another $75 billion in endowment funds. A fraction of those monies, spent or invested with foresight and ecological intelligence, could help lay the foundation for sustainable economic development. Here, too, are opportunities to do well while doing good.

It is possible, however, to envision educational institutions that operate with great ecological sensitivity and efficiency and still turn out graduates who are, in Wendell Berry's words, "itinerant professional vandals." The stock-in-trade of educational institutions is the art of good thinking, which now requires a wide-angled view of the world and a long-term perspective. These, however, cannot be taught in an exclusively discipline-centric setting. The logic behind *Ecodemia*, accordingly must be extended to the realm of curriculum.

To meet the challenges of the 21st century, the present generation of students must learn how to:

- run civilization on sunshine;
- stabilize then reduce global population;
- protect remaining biological diversity;
- prevent pollution;
- manage agriculture and forests sustainably;
- repair ecosystems damaged in the industrial era; and
- do all of these things while improving basic equity and fairness.

These tasks will require, among other things, mastery of skills such as systems analysis, full-cost accounting, ecological engineering, restoration ecology, ecological design arts, and conservation biology. Moreover, the coming generation will have to be smarter about technology than previous generations have been. And they will need a degree of foresight humankind has seldom, if ever, shown. In historian Paul Kennedy's words: "nothing less than the re-education of humankind will do."[2] That, however, will require rethinking the purposes, process, and structure of education and a more liberal approach to the liberal arts.

> The stock-in-trade of educational institutions is the art of good thinking, which now requires a wide-angled view of the world and a long-term perspective.

2. Paul Kennedy, *Preparing for the Twenty-First Century* (New York: Random House, 1993), p. 331.

Like reforming campus resource policies, curriculum change, too, represents an opportunity. In this instance it is an opportunity to rejuvenate disciplines, enliven curriculum, develop interdisciplinary courses and projects, and rise above the idea that education is mostly about preparing young people for careers in the industrial economy. And like the cases described here, these changes will require bold visionary leadership.

David W. Orr is professor and chair of Environmental Studies at Oberlin College and author of Ecological Literacy *(State University of New York Press, 1992), and* Earth in Mind *(Island Press, 1994).*

ACKNOWLEDGMENTS

Thank you to those who, because of your appreciation of the role higher education plays in securing a sustainable future, lent indispensable support to this project: John Behm, Jacqui Bonomo, Alric Clay, Fred Cornelius, Curtis Croley, Michael Crook, Cameron Davis, Frank DiCicco, Archie Dodson, Tim Eder, Marilyn Emery, Jay Hair, Bill Howard, Jim Irwin, Phil Kavits, Rayne Lamey, Sharon Levy, Bill Line, Jaime Matyas, Russ McLaughlin, Ben McNitt, Margaret Mellon, Melissa Murray, Chuck Paquette, Suzanne Sacco, Gary San Julian, Stephanie Sklar, Craig Tufts, Mark Van Putten, Mark Wexler and, most especially, Nick Keller, whose dedication to the campus environmental movement, to students, and to his staff makes all things possible. ❧ Gratitude is also extended to James Allison, Philip Arnold, Greg Asay, Kathryn Atkins, Masankho Banda, Adam Berrey, Craig Bowman, Courtney Brown, Kristen Brown, Robert Byrne, Karan Capoor, Amy Casselberry, Sarah Creighton, Anthony Cortese, Yewande Dada, Chris Fox, Larry Freeman, Dana Hollish, Daniel Einstein, Denis Hayes, Robyn Hurwitz, Beth Ising, Michael Kenney, Ann Krumboltz, Gail and Richard Liebig, Jeff Lynass, Lisa Maloney, Vicki Mangin, Don Oldershaw, Dianne Russell, Lisa Schreibman, Monica Spann, Tim Stevens, Ben Strauss, Brian Trelstad, Mark Troy, David White, Karen White, Lisa Yee, and Miya Yoshitani for support and inspiration. ❧ By reviewing drafts and helping with photos and other aspects of production, Nicole Holt, Michael Heiman, Tom Kelly, Erin McKeown, Neil Michaud, Angie Newsome, Lisa Pope, Walter Simpson, Elena Takaki, Kurt Teichert, and especially, Mehrdad Azemun, Laura Hickey, Fritz Myer, Chris Soto, and Charlene Vivian have added immeasurably to the vitality of this book. ❧ To David Orr, April Smith, and David Eagan—who not only assisted with this project, but have provided the campus environmental stewardship movement with much of its vision, framework, and grounding philosophy—we are deeply grateful and indebted. ❧ For her remarkable ability to translate our vision to the page and her dedication to our work in general, heartfelt thanks to Sally James of Cutting Edge Graphics. ❧ Finally, to the higher education staff, administrators, students, and faculty featured here, we are honored to have worked with you, look forward to continued collaboration, and thank you both for your laborious assistance with this text and, most importantly, for helping to define and envision a sustainable future.

Julian Keniry
May 1995

INTRODUCTION

In addition to dramatically reducing resource consumption and costs, environmental initiatives boost morale. They foster teamwork among scientists, administrators, interns, and others who might otherwise have little contact. They provide a forum for employees and students eager to participate in the decision-making process. *Ecodemia* is about both the tangible and the intangible benefits of greening our institutions.

But more than anything, it is about the people behind the change. Teamwork is crucial, as we have learned from more than 70 interviews with staff and administrators conducted for this book, and from the 1,200 student environmental projects registered with the Campus Ecology Program since 1989. At the same time, it takes dedicated, creative individuals to form an effective team. On any campus, as at any institution, these individuals are just as likely to come from the landscaping department, the library, or the food service as they are to come from the environmental studies department or solid waste division. A "green" job, it appears, depends far less on its official title than on the initiative of the person who holds it.

Although the contributions of faculty and students are discussed in every chapter, *Ecodemia* highlights the work of campus staff and administrators. This is not because the contributions of any one group outweigh those of another; this is not the case. Ultimately, though, staff and administrators are accountable for most operational decisions. And it is they who implement most of the procedural changes behind environmental reforms, altering contract language, substituting products, arranging financing, redesigning equipment, and so on.

Faculty provide vital technical assistance and, through their writings and lectures, inspire other staff and students. Students assist with research and labor and quite often provide the critical mandate for change. But while faculty become acknowledged experts and students make headlines for constructing media-genic "trash monsters" and "quad landfills," it is the purchasers, facilities and personnel managers, housekeepers, office services personnel, and other staff who actually manage most of the vexing logistics—accepting the blame when approaches fail, but receiving little credit when they succeed.

The National Wildlife Federation's focus on administrative initiatives is part of a larger effort to support the staff who are working to improve the environmental profile of their institutions. In this effort, we join the environmental task

A "green" job depends far less on its official title than on the initiative of the person who holds it.

In part, this book arose in response to students' demand for case studies of successful, broad-based campus efforts they could point to when soliciting staff and administration support for new projects.

forces of several associations of higher education, including the National Association of College Stores, the National Association of College and University Food Services, and the National Association of College and University Business Officers. It is significant that staff and administrators had strong representation at the student-organized "Campus Earth Summit" held at Yale University in February 1994, where staff helped formulate the *Blueprint for a Green Campus* published by the Heinz Family Foundation in December 1994. Students recognize that staff and administrators are a vital part of the movement for a sustainable future.

Aware that the momentum for change at some institutions will be held in check if their interest is perceived as fleeting, students are beginning to organize beyond their own limited tenure by creating environmental coordinator positions for themselves, training students in succeeding classes, and working with more permanent staff and faculty. In part, this book arose in response to students' considerable demand for case studies of successful, broad-based campus efforts they could point to when soliciting staff and administration support for new projects. The pragmatic approach of investing staff, doing research, and providing incentives is well-respected by most students who contact us. Laundry lists of ideas make useful planning tools, but students know that campus administrators need real-life examples, cost-benefit analyses, and ways to work within serious constraints on time and resources.

For their part, the administrators behind successful ecological initiatives are working more closely with students, blurring the distinctions between the educational mission of the university and its business practices, as well as those between "The System" and the student body. As a result, students are gaining hands-on experience in a range of environmental fields. They are also working with staff to design a new generation of stewardship programs based on their understanding of steps necessary to elicit and sustain student support.

Though it is the product of six years of broad outreach, intermittent surveying, and more than 100 hours spent interviewing staff, this book undoubtedly leaves many inspirational stories untold. And it cannot be claimed that the programs described here represent the only or the best solutions. Evaluating departmental programs, like the larger issue of institutional commitment to environmental responsibility, is subjective. Chapter 9, Evaluating Campus Stewardship Programs, describes some criteria which have guided this study and others, and examines broader issues, such as the roles and responsibilities of upper-level management and the institutionalization of environmentally sound practices.

The rest of this book is organized by the administrative and operational areas which most influence the use of resources and the generation of waste on campuses. The sections move from the "mouth" and "belly" of the system, where resources are introduced and used—Purchasing, Landscaping, Transportation, Energy, Dining, Communication Services—to the "hind end," where wastes must be managed in the most environmentally sound way possible—Solid Waste Reduction and Hazardous Waste Minimization.

The chapters provide an overview of how campuses tend to fare on each issue, and then focus in greater depth on a handful of outstanding programs. Description of existing programs (letting the story of "what is" lead the reader to "what could or should be") was favored over prescription. Stories from campuses of all types (four-year, two-year, public, and private) will show some of the ways that individuals, and the teams they formed, have changed their colleges and universities for the better.

Ecodemia is about the significance in humble acts. Every initiative described here has far-reaching implications, yet all started modestly; small steps like recycling aluminum cans almost invariably lead to larger ones, such as revising purchasing specifications. Most of the efforts featured here have, over the last several years, grown well beyond their initial stages. Some programs, such as Harvard University's "Shared Responsibility" campaign achieved most objectives within a short two-to-five-year period; other programs, such as the integrated pest management program at Seattle University, have seasoned over more than a decade. If there is one lasting lesson these programs impart, it is that making the transition to a sustainable future requires dedication, patience, courage, and persistence.

Every initiative described here has far-reaching implications, yet all started modestly.

CHAPTER 1

University Purchasing and Campus Stores

E ven small campuses are large when it comes to buying power. Because of the dollars they spend and the quantities they purchase, institutions of higher education can play a key role in building the market for environmentally friendly goods and services.[1] New jobs, lowered prices, and environmental protection are just a few of the benefits that accrue to a campus and its surrounding community when it chooses to use this leverage.

Because purchasing marks the entry of most goods and services into the campus system, this gateway is also one of the best sites for environmental innovation. Through careful purchasing, university procurement staff can support a range of environmental practices, including *source reduction* (buying less of what will eventually become waste), *waste stream diversion* (assuring that what was once discarded is now used longer, recycled, or reused), *recycling* (an approach that now reaches far beyond paper, bottles, and cans), and *closing the loop* by buying goods made from recycled materials. In the details of procurement contracts lie a potential blueprint for a new type of institution, one that purchases less, uses differently, and casts much less away.

While a few campuses can truly be said to drive the market for more earth-friendly products, most institutions are struggling in a changing world. As terms such as "post-consumer," "soy-based," "nontoxic," "organic," "recyclable," "biodegradable," "totally chlorine-free," and so on, enter the lexicon of advertising, purchasers

Kevin Lyons has encouraged Rutgers to incorporate recycled material into a broad array of projects, including the plastic in this deck.

---

[1] Higher education expenditures in the U.S. exceeded $186 billion in 1992–93 (*Digest of Educational Statistics*, U.S. Dept. of Education); college students spent another $45 billion and college bookstore sales in the U.S. reached $6.5 billion in the same year (Campus Promotion Network, Inc.). A bibliography at the end of each chapter contains complete information on materials cited in footnotes.

on most campuses are striving to keep abreast of new definitions and technologies. Integrating higher environmental standards into hundreds of contracts, distinguishing false claims from real, and selecting new products can be baffling, time-consuming propositions.

In the face of these challenges, Rutgers University's Procurement and Contracting Department, the University of Minnesota's Lab Services, and campus bookstores at numerous institutions have established promising precedents. This chapter explores their use of purchasing and contracting as a creative medium for reducing waste, minimizing hazards, and increasing the use of recycled materials.

Where procurement efforts are autonomous, they are featured in separate chapters in this book. Dining, transportation, energy, solid waste, and hazardous waste minimization chapters all include information of relevance to those interested in "buying green." Office equipment purchasing, a relatively new area of environmental concern, is explored along with printing issues in Chapter 6, Communication Services.

❧ PROACTIVE PROCUREMENT AT RUTGERS

Kevin Lyons has a unique niche in the campus environmental movement. As the senior buyer for Rutgers (one of the nation's largest universities) and a committed activist, he has lent his buying insights to many working groups, helping them translate wish lists into pragmatic plans. The Campus Earth Summit held at Yale University in February 1994, Tufts' Greening Academia Conference the following month, EPA-sponsored recycled products conferences, and numerous local forums have benefited from his expertise.

Nowhere are his skills more apparent, however, than on his own campus, where the central purchasing office enjoys extremely broad jurisdiction, providing contract support to one of the largest on-campus housing facilities in the nation and more than 700 academic and administrative buildings.

The Rutgers "environmental economic" effort, as Lyons calls it, began in 1988, partially in response to the enactment in 1987 of the New Jersey Source Separation and Recycling Act, which

CAMPUS EARTH SUMMIT ESTABLISHES PURCHASING PRINCIPLES

Four hundred and fifty-five students, faculty and staff from 22 countries, six continents, and 50 states developed the following mandate at the Campus Earth Summit held at Yale University in February 1994: 1) Include environmentally sensitive specifications in all university goods and services contracts. 2) Purchase products with high recycled content, produced in an environmentally sustainable manner, which demonstrate maximum durability or biodegradability, repairability, energy-efficiency, nontoxicity, and recyclability, as an individual institution and through cooperative agreements with other universities and other large institutions. 3) Require every department and program to meet university-wide purchasing standards. Additional recommendations for institutional purchasing are outlined in *Blueprint for a Green Campus*.

requires that state institutions divert 60 percent of their waste stream by 1995. Initial efforts to meet this goal blossomed into a comprehensive program to reduce waste and support recycled products, says Lyons, when "it became apparent that these activities were not only environmentally responsible but cost-effective as well . . . . Cost-savings, more than any other factor, have driven us to exceed compliance rates and, ultimately, to help build the market for recycled materials."

Since 1988, purchasing staff have worked actively with vendors to adapt bid specifications and contracts, and with the campus community to encourage education and behavioral change. Lyons says the transformation necessitated moving beyond standard purchasing and contracting procedures, in which "various departments send you everything you need to go out and bid, and you simply place standard contract language on top of it."

Today, "public awareness clauses" attached to requests for proposals and contracts announce Rutgers' interest in working with vendors who can support the university's toughened environmental standards. The recycling and waste-hauling contract was the first to hold a contractor responsible for helping Rutgers meet its waste reduction goals. It required the hauler to place educational advertisements in campus publications; provide information on the latest industry trends, products, and recycling markets; suggest programs and policies to increase support among campus personnel; and provide case studies of successful programs at other institutions.

Northwestern University's Recycling Coordinator Kimberly Huber received help from Lyons in designing her own requests for proposals. In an April 1993 letter to Lyons, she writes that when she was first introduced to Rutgers' system of contract preparation, she was "amazed by the demands and requirements placed on prospective bidders; and was even further amazed by the problem-solving results [Rutgers] accomplished through such requirements." In her research, she writes, she had found very few institutions operating under "such a progressive system of accountability and demands."

Creating New Specifications

Because meeting environmental standards had not traditionally been a prerequisite for awarding most contracts, Lyons had little precedent for developing new product specifications. Researching and writing new standards for paper alone required hours of volunteer time from staff and students. Lyons "spent months," he says, "researching the paper mills and copier companies, interviewing and surveying departments, and testing and evaluating" recycled paper before developing the exacting standards that now serve Rutgers.

> Lyons spent months researching paper mills and copy companies, and surveying departments, before drafting Rutgers' exacting specifications for recycled paper.

By holding round-table forums and visiting companies, Lyons got vendors to help revise the specifications. Such a cooperative approach encourages vendors to share information and do research they might skip were Lyons to work with them on a one-to-one basis. Lyons has also sent extensive mailings to contractors, encouraging them to promote "environmentally sensitive packaging, return packaging, and recycled-content parts or products." (See sample letter at right.) Contractors are asked to inform Rutgers of such initiatives, says Lyons, partly to keep the university abreast of its environmental impact beyond campus boundaries. Responses so far have come from vendors of paper and tissue, construction, lawn care, and photographic products. Lyons says the university's environmental goals have been well served by the competition inherent in bidding for large university contracts.

For purchasers without the resources to design new specifications, Lyons suggests an alternate plan: send out a Request for Information (RFI) on the alternative products under consideration, be it energy-efficient office equipment or recycled paper, before sending out Requests for Proposals (RFPs) or Requests for Quotes (RFQs). "Sending out an RFI can help [purchasers] obtain from vendors themselves much of the information necessary for formulating a specification," says Lyons.

If the RFI responses are not sufficient, Lyons suggests following up with RFPs, letting vendors propose a package. "They should then have their purchasing committee evaluate the packages and select the one that is in the best interests of their school." Only when purchasers feel confident in their specifications, says Lyons, should they send out an RFQ. Once written, the specifications should be reevaluated periodically. "Campuses should write and update purchasing standards," suggests Lyons, "as their environmental concerns and expertise evolve."

Reducing Waste and Buying Recycled

Accelerating waste reduction efforts at Rutgers meant targeting companies that make frequent, large deliveries. Lyons tailored a separate mailing to these vendors, announcing the university's interest in returning packaging materials to suppliers for reuse. Lyons asked them to supply a printout of all departments receiving regular shipments, submit a "packaging and shipping materials reuse and reduction plan," and outline any costs to be incurred by the university.

Lyons also identifies troublesome items in the waste stream and contracts with separate waste handlers when necessary. Fluorescent lamps and ballasts are one example. In early 1995, Lyons contracted with a New Jersey company that drains toxic polychlorinated-biphenyl (PCB) from ballasts, strips reusable parts, and recycles lamp tube glass.

Rutgers' largest vendors are required to develop packaging and shipping material reuse and reduction plans.

Construction activities at Rutgers provide a wide avenue for recycled materials and products that "close the loop." Rutgers "has incorporated a significant amount of environmental contract language into road and parking lot repaving contracts," says Lyons, "and is even trying out a couple of recycled decks." Lyons has also introduced recycled ceiling tiles, wall boards, insulation, plastic lumber, roofing products, snow fences, and parking bumpers to the campus.

Lyons tests new products and introduces them to potential users before initiating contracts. Testing recycled bumpers, for example, helped Lyons and staff avoid a parking lot full of cracked bumpers. When, in winter, sample bumpers cracked around the iron rods staking them to the ground, Lyons and the staff of the Rutgers Center for Plastic Recycling Research found that drilling larger, oval holes would allow the bumpers room to expand and contract through the

A letter to Rutgers' vendors encouraging earth-friendly practices (left) prompted the reply below, among others.

THE STATE UNIVERSITY OF NEW JERSEY
RUTGERS

UNIVERSITY PROCUREMENT AND CONTRACTING · PO BOX 6999 · PISCATAWAY NJ · 08855-6999
(908)932-3000 · FAX (908)932-4712

September 1, 1993

Dear Valued Contractor,

Rutgers-The State University of New Jersey has encouraged a high level of environmental awareness to all its Faculty, Students and Staff. We would like the vendors who do business with the University to contribute to these standards also.

You may already be contributing to these efforts; by way of environmentally sensitive packaging, return packaging, recycled content parts or products.

To this end, we encourage and support all initiatives your firm has to share with Rutgers University in regards to environmental preservation.

Please write to me and let me know how your firm has benefitted the University's goal to reduce landfill waste or increase recycling. This information will be shared with the Faculty, Staff and Students.

You may forward to: Kevin Lyons, Senior Buyer and Chair, Rutgers University Recycling and Source Reduction Committee, Procurement and Contracting Division, P.O. Box 6999, Piscataway, NJ 08854, 908-932-5192.

Sincerely,

Kevin Lyons
Senior Buyer
Chair, Recycling and
Source Reduction Committee

c: John Baron, Jr.

Grant· Grant Supply Company Incorporated

P.O. Box 61 · Joyce Kilmer Avenue at 12th Street · North Brunswick, N.J. 08902 · (908) 545-1018
FAX (908) 545-9879
Showroom (908) 247-5026

KEVIN LYONS, SENIOR BUYER   JULY 06, 1992
RUTGERS UNIVERSITY
PROCUREMENT AND CONTRACTING DIVISION
P.O. BOX 6999
PISCATAWAY, NJ 08855-6999

REF: "PACKAGING AMD SHIPPING MATERIALS REUSE AND REDUCTION
      PLAN"

DEAR MR. LYONS:

WE WOULD BE HAPPY TO HELP OUT IN YOUR GOAL OF REDUCING SOLID WASTE AT RUTGERS. WE HAVE RECYCLED FOR MANY YEARS AT GRANTS, LONG BEFORE IT WAS MANDATORY, AND SHARE YOUR CONCERNS FOR THE ENVIRONMENT.

OUR PRODUCTS (PLUMBING AND HEATING SUPPLIES) ARE NORMALLY PACKED IN CARDBOARD BOXES OR PUT IN PLASTIC BAGS WHICH WE WOULD EITHER RECYCLE OR REUSE.

OUR SHIPMENTS TO RUTGERS ARE NOT NORMALLY SCHEDULED BUT ARE ON A DEMAND BASIS. WHEN YOU NEED OUR PRODUCTS, WE SHIP THEM TO THE BUILDINGS DESIGNATED OR SOMEONE MAY PICK THE MATERIAL UP. SOMETIMES THERE ARE EMERGENCY REPAIR SITUATIONS TO DEAL WITH.

SINCE OUR SHIPMENTS ARE SO RANDOM AND THE DESTINATIONS ARE SO VARIED, THE MOST EFFECTIVE WAY FOR US TO COOPERATE IN THE "REUSE" PROGRAM WOULD BE TO KEEP OUR ARRANGEMENTS INFORMAL. A RUTGERS DEPARTMENT COULD ACCUMULATE A BAG OF OUR PACKAGING MATERIALS AND GIVE IT OUR DRIVER ON THE NEXT DELIVERY; OR ONE OF YOUR PEOPLE COULD DROP A BAG OFF THE NEXT TIME THEY COME IN TO PICK UP MATERIAL AT OUR COUNTER.

WITHIN THE FRAMEWORK OF COOPERATION I OUTLINED, THERE WOULD NOT BE ANY ADDITIONAL COSTS TO RUTGERS UNIVERSITY. WE WOULD ABSORB OUR ADDITIONAL RECYCLING COSTS.

I'VE ENCLOSED A PRINTOUT INDICATING THE DEPARTMENTS WE NORMALLY PROVIDE MATERIAL TO. IF YOU HAVE ANY QUESTIONS, PLEASE GIVE ME A CALL.

YOURS TRULY,

WILLIAM R. STANBACH
GENERAL MANAGER

seasons. "By the time the product or service is delivered or performed," says Lyons, "it has been tested and the user has been sent information and samples, or has visited other departments to see how the product is working elsewhere."

Staff Investment and Training

Nurturing faculty, custodians, students and other administrators' investment in the new objectives has required perseverance. Most important, says Lyons, was convincing the administration that he "could meet and exceed compliance via contracts that are written, without compromising on quality." He has sent mailings to key administrators, describing relevant state laws and outlining proposed responses, and has followed up with telephone calls and presentations. The Recycling and Source Reduction Committee, which Lyons chairs, assists with this outreach.

Custodian involvement is crucial. Lyons works closely with the Custodial Staff Director Al Lewis to identify alternative products and train staff. Explains Lyons, "I try to write the contracts so they will have little or no effect on the custodial staff, [but] if there is a projected change I will meet with them first, discuss the changes, and ask for their feedback."

When the switch from virgin to recycled-plastic garbage and recycling bags required a new sizing system, for example, custodian involvement sent purchasing staff back into negotiations with the vendor. Previously, bag sizes had corresponded to their color, but all the new bags were clear. The new vendor was simply asked to label the boxes with the size of bag, and all custodians were introduced to the new system before the contract began.

It was worth the effort. The change in this single contract from a vendor who supplied virgin petroleum-based bags to one offering recycled bags resulted in a savings of $18,000 a year for Rutgers. Lyons attributes the price difference to the fluctuating market for petroleum, which made the average cost of virgin bags higher.

Lyons and Lewis have begun round table discussions with cleaning-supply vendors to identify more natural alternatives to other products currently in use. Rutgers, like many campuses, has already moved from aerosols to pump sprays mixed on site in order to reduce volume, waste and cost. (See Chapter 7, Hazardous Waste Minimization.)

Student Roles

Lyons and Lewis depend on student assistance with outreach and research. Throughout the 1993–1994 academic year, students conducted a campus-wide waste audit—an in-depth analysis of what entered the university waste stream.

Lyons purchases a wide variety of recycled items, including recycled ceiling tiles, wall boards, insulation, plastic lumber, roofing products, snow fences, decks, and parking bumpers.

They then devised creative ways to communicate the results to the departments and dorms they evaluated. Students also helped develop a procurement and recycling survey for department chairs, and are investigating how Rutgers might establish a closed-loop cooperative purchasing system for recycled paper. Under the arrangement, Rutgers and collaborating institutions would purchase recycled paper manufactured, in part, from their own used office paper.

Room to Grow

The New Jersey State Department of Environmental Protection and Energy (DEPE) consulted with Lyons when developing the New Jersey State Executive Order 91, which encourages state institutions and businesses to buy recycled products. Rutgers' purchasing efforts are cited by the DEPE as a model for other state institutions. Lyons, however, insists the Rutgers programs are only in their infancy. He hopes to broaden the university's efforts in ways that will further promote local economic development, and envisions a thriving instate market for recycled commodities. In March of 1993, Lyons held a forum on the role that recycled products and environmental services can play in New Jersey's economic development, and he has since been building upon the contact base and ideas established there. Attended by Rutgers administrators and faculty, New Jersey State officials, and local business leaders, the forum has inspired Lyons to continue his pursuit of "economic development initiatives that will benefit Rutgers University and New Jersey businesses."

The switch to recycled bags saved Rutgers University $18,000 a year.

☙ LAB PURCHASING AT MINNESOTA

Campuses with hundreds of science laboratories face particular challenges when pursuing environmentally responsible purchasing. At the University of Minnesota, with more than 2,000 labs, lab purchasers and campus waste managers are working closely to identify new recycling markets and ways to reduce waste. Coordinated purchasing and innovative communication structures help the university chart what may well be a new course for lab industries.

Coordinated Purchasing

Dee McManus' position as Lab Services Coordinator was created in the fall of 1992 to consolidate lab-supplies and equipment purchasing and information. The result: facilitated waste reduction, enhanced safety, and reduced costs.

Before lab purchasing was consolidated, the University of Minnesota bought chemicals from 35 different companies, spending an average of $80–$90 each on thousands of transactions annually. "We're talking about a $4–$4.5 million market of chemical purchases on campus, each department ordering independently," says McManus, "so you can see the volume is just incredible." Decentralization also decreased safety. McManus says moving to a one-vendor contract will make it possible to provide the environmental health and safety office with an annual record of campus chemical procurement.

Centralization also allows for bundling and reducing the size of purchases. "In the *1994 University Stores Catalog*," says McManus, "we encouraged laboratories not to buy for the longer term, but to consider short-term purchases, so that they are not storing an excessive amount of hazardous chemicals." Now that purchases are bundled by Lab Services, labs can requisition smaller quantities of materials and pay less than was possible when they bought directly from vendors.

Dr. Dewayne Townsend explains a genetics experiment to Dee McManus. By learning more about lab applications, she can better anticipate the need for new products for the University of Minnesota's thousands of labs.

A Structure that Works

At the University of Minnesota, a Products Review Committee representing hundreds of labs and a campus-wide Waste Abatement Committee covering campus-wide environmental issues work jointly on waste reduction efforts. McManus brings laboratory issues to the Waste Abatement Committee meetings chaired by Recycling Coordinator Dana Donatucci and, in turn, informs the Laboratory Products Review Committee of campus-wide environmental initiatives. "It was through these groups," says McManus, "that we initially became extremely interested in ecology and in seeing what role the laboratories might play."

The committees ensure coordinated efforts. Before paths of communications were well-established, for example, the Bioprocessing Technical Institute (BTI) persuaded one prime vendor with a $2 million-a-year contract to substitute water-soluble packing peanuts for polystyrene ones. Around the same time, the central recycling office made provisions for recycling polystyrene peanuts. Only when the water-soluble peanuts gummed up the polystyrene recycling machinery did central recycling discover that the BTI had switched materials. Such miscommunications are now avoided.

Lab Waste Reduction

Glassware and Rockets

Part of the labs' challenge is to recycle materials for which there are not yet markets. Two ongoing efforts focus on borosilicate glassware and on rockets, the polypropylene casings around syringes. With the help of student researchers, the lab staff are seeking avenues for recycling borosilicate, which is fired under extremely high temperatures and thus cannot be recycled with normal glass. Because the university spends close to $1 million a year on glassware alone and a large percentage of it breaks, staff are especially hopeful that they can locate a recycling market or create their own. Syringe rockets are another offbeat item the laboratories use in bulk and would like to recycle. There are precedents for recycling the noncontaminated, noninfectious polypropylene rockets, says McManus, but the challenge lies in integrating them into the university's central recycling system.

McManus is determined to begin recycling what may seem like esoteric items, since they become quite significant when their aggregate use in thousands of laboratories is considered. "It really harkens back," she says, "to three years ago when there wasn't much of a market for plastics, and now everybody is recycling plastic because we have designed products based on recycled plastic. The laboratory industry end of recycling is still very new."

Catalogs

A simpler campaign addresses lab-product and equipment catalogs. Each department receives dozens of these three-inch-thick, hard-bound catalogs from outside vendors each year. McManus initially collaborated with the central recycling staff, who removed the hard covers and recycled the rest. Limited staffing and a limited recycling budget made this too resource-intensive. McManus got one of her primary lab-supply vendors to agree to ship catalogs with return-to-sender labels, but only a few departments have participated in the mail-back because they have to pay the return postage. Ultimately, these catalogs should be recyclable in standard university recycling systems, says McManus, who has taken advantage of industry-sponsored forums to spread this message. "One of the things you could do to be a forerunner in the industry," she tells vendors, "is to substitute hard-bound catalogs with soft-bound, recyclable ones."

Polystyrene

One of Lab Services' more cost-effective initiatives is the recycling of polystyrene insulation used to pack restriction enzymes. "Laboratories today are using a great deal of restriction enzymes doing molecular biology work," says McManus, "and because restriction enzymes have to be frozen and sent out in styrofoam containers, there is just an incredible amount of styrofoam" on campus. The containers are now recycled by central recycling or stored in the central stores warehouse for reuse.

University of Minnesota labs now purchase smaller quantities of materials and pay less than was possible when they bought directly from vendors.

Thermometers

A more recent laboratory initiative focused on removing mercury thermometers from inventory. Laboratories now substitute alcohol thermometers for the mercury ones, which McManus says were "one of the biggest causes of mercury spills on campus."

Students Assist Labs

Students have been vital to environmental initiatives in lab services. The University Student Environmental Audit Research Program (USEARCH), launched by Karen Linner while she was a graduate student in the Department of Urban and Regional Planning, teamed students with administrators interested in reducing waste in their departments. USEARCH was formally a one-year program (1993–94), but it provided a model for the Waste Abatement Committee, which continues to broadcast environmental research opportunities. Students "can spend the time doing the footwork, making the phone calls, trying to establish the markets out there, and then bring the information back to us," says McManus. "It's a very good marrying of resources."

Though the University of Minnesota Lab Services program is very new, McManus anticipates that environmental goals and objectives will be integrated into an annual planning process with all university staff. This, in addition to their strong communications structure, she hopes, will ensure that the source-reduction programs they are currently researching and implementing are sustained.

🍂 UNIVERSITY BOOKSTORES

Front and center in many students' experience as consumers, college bookstores present a superb opportunity for environmentally smart buying and merchandising. With the support of the Environmental Concerns Committee of the National Association of College Stores, many bookstores across the U.S. and Canada now stock earth-friendly wares. And managing stores with the environment in mind, while attractive to many customers and often good for the bottom line, runs deeper for many staff. For Jim Williams at the University of Oregon and Douglas Carlsen at Whitman College in Walla Walla, Washington, efforts to green their bookstores and industries have gone hand in hand with their local efforts to protect wilderness areas.

Williams is an avid fly angler and one of the founders of Oregon Trout, a conservation group working to preserve the genetic diversity of wild fish. He traces his personal empowerment back to a successful effort to block a dam project in the free-flowing "North Fork" (the North Fork of the Middle Fork of

> *Students can spend the time doing the footwork, making the phone calls, trying to establish the markets out there, and then bring the information back to us. It is a very good marrying of resources.*
>
> *—Dee McManus, University of Minnesota*

the Willamette River, which flows out of Waldo Lake, to be exact). He and four fly fishing buddies took up song writer and performer Mason Williams' challenge to organize a concert to save the river. Despite their inexperience organizing such events, they held three sold-out performances and achieved scenic waterway status for the river and Waldo Lake. The concert has since toured the country. Says Williams: "This was the greatest example—and I am 47—of finding out that you can really make a difference."

Carlsen traces his involvement in bookstore ecology to coordinating "Earth Day 1970" events at Inglemore High School in Kenmore, Washington, and to his current role in the Umatilla Forest Resource Council, for which he helped draft exhaustive forest management plans. Working to protect the forest has meant bringing "the disparate voices together to discuss the issues," says Carlsen, who for seven years has worked with ranchers and timber workers, environmentalists, fruit-growers, fishermen, and Native American tribal leaders.

Jim Williams fly fishes on the McKenzie River just a few miles downstream from the University of Oregon Bookstore.

National Stores Networking

Their environmental organizing experience made Williams and Carlsen natural candidates for leadership in the Environmental Concerns Committee of one of their industry's primary trade organizations, the National Association of College Stores (NACS). Since Williams held office as the committee's first chair (and, fittingly, was the first to take a NACS committee camping), NACS has become one of the most environmentally active associations in higher education. This has been a labor-intensive transformation.

"We began a couple of years ago," says Carlsen, "thinking why don't we do a booklet on buying and merchandising environmentally, but we realized how overwhelming that would be for a volunteer group to manage." Instead of publishing one exhaustive guide to purchasing, NACS decided to segment the task; their bimonthly *College Store Journal* now features a regular "EnviroNews" section. This forum allows for regular surveying of members, whose responses on environmental concerns have ranged from "Could you produce a list of environmentally conscious suppliers and their products?" to "I believe there are more important things than the environment right now." One "EnviroNews" section carried the punchy "Environmental Responsibility Scorecard" (from the June 1992 issue of *Catolog Age*), which sets high environmental standards for mailing practices, vendor criteria, internal practices, and outbound packaging.

With committee help, NACS has begun to audit its own internal procedures, seeking out soy inks and recycled paper for its publications and encouraging waste reduction initiatives such as the use of reusable mugs at NACS conferences and seminars. NACS estimated that if participants brought their own mugs to one annual meeting, they would divert four to six cups per person (about 100,000 cups in all) from landfills *during the trip to and from the meeting alone.* Carlsen says that when he pops out a reusable mug on airplanes or in takeout places, he finds "more and more now that people say, 'That is a neat idea,' as opposed to 'Are you crazy?'" Ultimately, though, says Carlsen, the mission of the Environmental Concerns Committee is to "get stores' managers and buyers to see that this is an issue that is of vital importance to us all."

Smart Buying

Dozens of stores have taken the initiative to reduce waste, offer healthier products, and promote recycling, and many of them entered NACS 1994 "Environmental Merchandising That Works Contest." Examples include:

🍂 Concordia University Bookstore in Montreal, Canada, offers a 10 percent discount coupon towards the purchase of new batteries for every battery returned for recycling;

🍂 McNeese State Bookstore in Lake Charles, Louisiana, offers tree-free filler paper, note pads, and notebooks;

🍂 Ned's Bookstore at Michigan State University recycles all parts, including wire binding, of used notebooks and offers 10 percent discounts on new notebooks when old ones are returned;

🍂 Whitman College, instead of using plastic or paper bags, gives each customer a free unbleached cotton bag (with soy ink logo) at the beginning of the year; and

🍂 University of Oregon Bookstore staff ask customers if they need a bag only when they are obviously struggling with numerous items and have no backpack or bag of their own.

Recycled and earth-friendly products, says Williams, are "the fastest-growing area of our school supply." But Carlsen seeks to apply environmental principles to the key product sold in campus stores: books. How books are bought is crucial, argues Carlsen, because unlike most other stock, books can be returned. "It should be troubling when we consider that mass market books, unlike trade and text titles, are typically not resold upon return," he writes in the January

Carlsen has worked since the mid-1980s with ranchers, timber workers, environmentalists, fruit-growers, fishermen, and Native American tribal leaders to save the Umatilla Forest.

1994 issue of *The College Store* (p. 94). As many as half the mass market books published are returned to the publisher for credit with their covers removed, says Carlsen, who tries to buy only what he can sell, and returns books with their covers intact, with the hope that the publisher will resell them. He also encourages stores to buy titles in smaller quantities and to purchase trade editions (which can generally be returned to the marketplace and resold) instead of mass market editions. "We must look to purchasing with realistic sales in mind, rather than be taken in by the excitement of the moment," writes Carlsen.

On its side, the book publishing industry has been relatively slow to change. In addition to flooding mass markets with books, it generally lags behind consumer demand for recycled and chlorine-free paper, less toxic inks and alternative photo processing methods. Luckily, college stores are finding a powerful, collective voice for encouraging more sustainable publishing practices. (Campus publishing practices are examined in Chapter 6.)

Making the Tough Decisions

Both Carlsen and Williams view campus bookstores as vital for educating and encouraging new markets, but their approaches to buying differ slightly. Carlsen prefers to decide himself what will be carried in the store, especially when recycled products are at issue. "My particular philosophy," explains Carlsen, "is that we will offer only the recycled [product], whenever possible, because it is not a significant enough savings for the customer to make the choice." At the University of Oregon, Williams prefers to "take a lower margin" on recycled or nontoxic products when they are slightly higher in price, thus "taking away price as a reason you wouldn't buy the product." Except in the case of toxic art supplies, which he and staff have removed from inventory, Williams lets the customer choose.

Making environmentally sound selections is a challenge for any buyer. On campuses, students, environmental publications, and nonprofit organizations can help but, ultimately, the purchaser is left with many of the tough decisions. "There are many issues that come into play when determining whether a particular product is more environmentally safe than another," admits Carlsen, "but I encourage managers and staff to make a choice to think environmentally and to bring into their store those products that they believe are best." Because it takes time to solicit, collect, and evaluate the claims of various manufacturers, more often than not, suggests Carlsen, it is not incorrect decisions, but failure to make a decision at all, that impedes the greening of campus stores.

Recycled and earth-friendly products are the fastest growing area of our school supply.

—Jim Williams,
University of Oregon

Building Markets

Williams and Carlsen use a variety of techniques to cultivate support from vendors. Williams thinks that by letting vendors know he is giving a price preference to recycled and easy-to-recycle products he is sending one of the strongest signals he can. Stores can increase the availability and lower the price of earth-friendly products by encouraging regional buying cooperatives to use new bidding criteria, such as specific minimum percentages of post-consumer waste. This is one reason, according to Williams, for the resurgence of membership in buying groups such as the Western College Bookstore Association, which is rebounding from financial struggles. Carlsen says he and other ECC members use trade shows around the NACS annual meetings as opportunities to request data on post-consumer content, use of soy inks, recycling, minimal packaging, and other environmental initiatives. "[This] lets vendors know that there is a demand for a particular product," explains Carlsen, "and I believe that is one of the major reasons we are seeing more products out there—whether correctly or not—claiming to be environmentally sound."

Successful Merchandising and Promotion

Manufacturers sometimes receive mixed signals from the stores, admits Williams. Bar codes, for example, are popular because they foster expedient, point-of-sale inventory, but they may require more packaging than do individual price stickers. Another challenge is to solicit vendor support in marketing environmental products—without ending up burdened with cardboard and plastic displays that can only be landfilled or incinerated, bags of sample products laden with advertising, or book inserts that litter the campus. Both Williams and Carlsen have dispensed with inserts and most displays, instead encouraging staff creativity in promoting products.

Ultimately, it is the customer who generates and sustains the demand for smart practices and products. "Faculty and students who are concerned," suggests Carlsen, "should be encouraged to work with their bookstore to promote environmental products." Indeed, some stores that do not make the choice for the customer or offer price preferences claim they have struggled to sell earth-friendly wares. Yet suggestion boxes and surveys indicate great interest in these products and in waste reduction efforts. "Part of our dilemma in the committee," says Carlsen, "is to encourage stores to purchase these things, but to help them sell them as well." Students and faculty who have helped identify new products and develop product standards must then follow through by purchasing the new products once they are on the shelves.

> Faculty and students who are concerned should be encouraged to work with their bookstore to promote environmental products.
>
> —Douglas Carlsen, Whitman College

MAKE YOUR VENDORS WORK WITH YOU

Ask tough questions. Smart purchasing is good for the environment *and* good for business. The following questions were developed by National Wildlife Federation purchasing staff to guide their selection of vendors for some 300–400 orders each month of supplies, merchandise, printing, and services:

1. Is it possible to make the product from post-consumer recycled materials? What is the difference between the two manufacturing processes? What by-products does each produce? What is the difference in cost and quality? What is the percentage of post-consumer content?

2. How is the product packaged? Is post-consumer, recycled-content, or less wasteful packaging available? Are the product and packaging recyclable? What can they be recycled into? What market is available for the recycled product? Do you reclaim packaging?

3. Do you know of, or currently have, a recycling program for the product and/or packaging?

4. Does the Material Safety Data Sheet (MSDS) for the product contain hazardous chemicals that must be reported under the Superfund Amendments and Reauthorization Act (SARA), commonly known as the Community Right-to-Know Act? Does the MSDS contain such hazardous chemical key words as: CORROSIVE, IGNITABLE (FLAMMABLE), REACTIVE, TOXIC, ACUTE, CHRONIC, INHALATION HAZARD, EXPLOSIVE, LETHAL, MUTAGEN, POISON, or CARCINOGEN? If so, consider an alternative product.

5. Does the product contain VOCs (volatile organic compounds), CFCs (chlorofluorocarbons), or chlorinated substances? (VOCs contribute to ground level ozone problems and add to air emission levels. CFCs deplete the stratospheric ozone layer. Chlorinated substances are toxic and some are also ozone-depleting.)

6. What is the energy efficiency of the product? Is there a more energy-efficient product available?

7. Are there new products or ways of using products that will decrease the environmental impact?

Vendors who demonstrate satisfactory commitment to addressing these issues may qualify for NWF Vendor Certification. NWF also gives top consideration to products certified by Green Seal and continually strives to conform to the CERES Principles for environmentally responsible business practices (reprinted in Chapter 9). For more information, contact NWF's purchasing department. (See networking section for contact information.)

CUTTING BACK ON CHLORINE-BLEACHED PAPER

With the support of the director of purchasing, students in the campus environmental organization ENACT helped the University of Michigan become one of the first campuses to address the issue of chlorine-bleached paper products. They circulated the following memorandum, which may serve as a model for other institutions, in order to educate and involve departments and groups throughout their university.

Resolution for University-Wide, Environmentally Sound Paper Procurement Policy

WHEREAS, the use of chlorine-based chemicals in pulp and paper making processes are widely recognized as forming persistent toxic by-products which pose a hazard to the environment and a threat to public health, and

WHEREAS, technology exists to provide all of society's legitimate paper needs without the use of any chlorine-based compounds, and

WHEREAS, the recent implementation of recycling programs is an important step in the conservation of our natural resources, a strong market for these recyclable goods needs to exist, and

WHEREAS, the stimulation of growth in the post-consumer (recycled) paper products industry is vital to the success of the recycling programs currently in operation, and

WHEREAS, we realize that recycling programs will fail unless there is active purchasing of the post-consumer products created from these programs, and

WHEREAS, it is presently recognized that our excessive current levels of paper consumption are having a negative effect on the overall health and biodiversity of our planet's forests, and

WHEREAS, the _____ has a long-standing tradition of leadership in all
(YOUR COLLEGE/UNIV. HERE)
aspects of academic, scientific, and social responsibility;

Be it resolved that _____ believes that the _____ should
(YOUR GROUP OR DEPARTMENT HERE)   (YOUR COLLEGE/UNIV. HERE)
implement a policy that favors the procurement of non-chlorine bleached paper products, including high post-consumer content recycled papers. In addition, the University should seek to reduce substantially the overall consumption of paper throughout the campus.

Signed,

_____,_____   _____
NAME   TITLE   DATE

BIBLIOGRAPHY

Campus Green Buying Guide, Green Seal, Inc., 1994, 1730 Rhode Island Ave., N.W., Ste. 1050, Washington, D.C. 20036-3101.

"Campus Recycling and Procurement Survey," 1992, U.S. Environmental Protection Agency, Region 5, Solid Waste Section, 77 West Jackson Boulevard, Chicago, IL 60604.

"Consultation for Environmentally Sensitive Contract Writing," Kevin Lyons, Rutgers University, Procurement and Contracting, P.O. Box 6999, Piscataway, NJ 08854.

"Closing the Loop: Recycled Paper Purchasing and Office Paper Recycling at the University of Wisconsin-Madison," Anderson, Casserly, Michaud, et al., Institute for Environmental Studies, University of Wisconsin-Madison, 1992. (608) 263-5492.

"Institute an Environmentally Responsible Purchasing Policy," Campus Earth Summit, *Blueprint for a Green Campus*, Heinz Family Foundation, 1995. (202) 939-3316 or shadow@igc.apc.org.

Environmental Standard for Household Cleaners, Green Seal, Inc., 1993. (Contact for standards in other product categories.)

"EPA Guidelines for Purchasing Cement and Concrete Containing Fly Ash," Environmental Fact Sheet, U.S. Environmental Protection Agency, January, 1992. (See also for guidelines on paper, office equipment, re-refined oil, retread tires and building insulation.)

"Making Every Day Earth Day," College Store Journal, J/A, 1994, p. 78–79. (216) 775-7777.

"NAEB Recycling Seminar," National Association of Educational Buyers, 1990, 450 Wireless Blvd., Hauppauge, NY 11788. (516) 273-2600.

"General Tradebooks and the Environment," Douglas Carlsen, *The College Store*, J/F, 1995, p. 94. (216) 775-7777.

"Procurement," Ellen Harrison and Richard Angell, *Waste Prevention Tool Kit for Local Governments*, Cornell Waste Management Institute, 1992, pp. 83-107, The Cornell University Resource Center, 8 Business and Technology Park, Cornell University, Ithaca, NY 14850.

Recycled Products Guide, Recycling Data Management, 1995. (800) 267-0707.

"We Use And Throw Away an Estimated 2.5 Billion Batteries a Year," *The College Store*, N/D, 1993, p. 66. (216) 775-7777.

NETWORKING

Campus

Bethel College
Attn: Robert Kistler
Biology Department
3900 Bethel Drive
St. Paul, MN 55112
(612) 638-6313
Post-consumer recycled paper, nontoxic cleaning products.

Birmingham-Southern College
Attn: Roald Hazelhoff
900 Arkadelphia Road/Box A-43
Birmingham, AL 35254
(205) 226-4954
Buy Recycled program.

Black Hawk College Bookstore
Attn: Betsy Hall
6600 34th Ave.
Moline, IL 61265
(309) 796-1311
A winner of the 1994 "Environmental Merchandising That Works Contest" sponsored by the National Association of College Stores.

Cabrillo College
Attn: Sue Jacobs, Purchasing
6500 Soquel Drive
Aptos, CA 95003
(408) 479-6100
Cabrillo is a community college that purchases post-consumer recycled paper, hand towels, and tissues.

If you find that an organization listed here has moved or a contact has been replaced, let the Campus Ecology Program staff know. We'll help match you with the latest source for the information you need.

Concordia University Bookstore
Attn: Lina Lipscombe
Montreal, Quebec
CANADA
(514) 848-2424
Offers 10% discount coupon towards the purchase of new batteries for every battery -returned; sends out old batteries for recycling.

Erie Community College
Attn: Sister Ruth Marie Penska, GNS
121 Ellicott Street
Buffalo, NY 14203
(716) 851-1016
Recycled computer and copy paper, nontoxic cleaning products, local foods and goods, strong recycling program.

Georgetown University
Attn: Jon Miller, Recycling
Washington, D.C. 20057
(202) 687-2033
Purchasing and recycling departments jointly held Earth Day 1994 recycled products vending fair, substantially increased procurement of recycled-content paper products this year.

Humboldt State University Bookstore
Attn: Ron Durham
Arcata, CA 95521
(707) 826-3741
"Making Earth Day everyday" in the stores.

Indiana University Bookstore
Attn: Steve Pierce
Bloomington, IN 47405
(812) 855-6823
Earth Day merchandising, activities and education.

McNeese State Bookstore
Lake Charles, Louisiana 70609-2495
(318) 475-5000
Offers tree-free filler paper, note pads, and notebooks; free copies of the Louisiana Environmentalist; reusable bags, etc.

Michigan State University
Ned's Bookstore
East Lansing, Michigan
Recycles all parts, including wire binding, of used notebooks and offers 10% discount on new notebooks when old ones are brought in.

Paul Smiths College
Attn: Purchasing
Paul Smiths, NY 12970
(518) 327-6255
Exploring citrus-based cleaning products, unbleached papers and tissues, and source reduction.

Rutgers University
Attn: Kevin Lyons
Procurement and Contracting
P.O. Box 6999
Piscataway, NJ 08854
(615) 322-7311
Offers consulting services and resource materials; specifications for recycled-content building and construction material; recycled paper and tissues; green cleaning supplies; sample letters to vendors; packaging take back program.

Southwest Missouri State University
Attn: Student Government Association
901 South National
Springfield, MO 65804
(417) 836-5500
SGA established "Paper Mandate," encouraging a shift to 100% recycled-content paper and envelopes as supplies are exhausted; implemented surcharge on color paper that cannot be recycled; by limiting the use of water-marked heavy bond paper is helping to finance procurement of recycled paper.

Tulane University
Attn: Steven Regan, Director
Purchasing Department
New Orleans, LA 70118
(504) 865-5000
Coordinates printer cartridge take back program and other green programs with assistance of Dean Oliver Houk of the Law School and students.

University of Michigan
Attn: Purchasing Department
Ann Arbor, MI 48104
(313) 764-2330
Supported students in development and circulation of memorandum encouraging purchase of non-chlorine bleached, post-consumer paper products.

University of Minnesota
Attn: Dee McManus
Lab Services, University Stores
2901 Talmadge Ave., S.E.
Minneapolis, MN 55414-2794
Source reduction and recycling in lab products procurement, vehicle for centralized vending, innovative communication structure, lab products and materials catalog reduction program.

University of Oregon Bookstore
Attn: Jim Williams
P.O. Box 3176
895 E. 13th Ave.
Eugene, OR 97403
(503) 346-4331
Source reduction, environmental merchandising; also contact the print shop for information on use of tree-free papers and vegetable-based inks.

University of Wisconsin-
Madison
Attn: Rex Owens
UW Stores
Madison, WI 53706
(608) 262-2415
Developed recycled paper and products sample folder and distributed to all potential purchasers; actively participates in Administrative Recycling Committee to coordinate purchasing with recycling and to pinpoint opportunities for closed-loop recycling; conducted telephone interviews with administrative and office services personnel to determine their awareness of and criteria for purchasing available recycled products.

Vanderbilt University
Attn: Marilyn Edwards
General Services
Nashville, TN 37235
Post-consumer recycled paper, unbleached papers and tissues, nontoxic cleaning products.

Whitman College Bookstore
Attn: Douglas Carlsen
Walla Walla, WA 99362
(509) 527-5111
Environmental merchandising, self-designed reusable bags, waste reduction programs.

Regional and National

National Association of College
Stores (NACS)
500 East Lorain Street
Oberlin, OH 44074-1294
Their bimonthly College Store
Journal *includes "EnviroNews" and environmental articles tailored to the unique needs of purchasers and store managers. NACS also offers a brochure on purchasing recycled products and lists of state and regional associations and schedules for meetings and seminars, including their annual Campus Market Expo (CAMEX)—a strong venue for eco-friendly goods and service providers. They also have an active National Environmental Concerns Committee.*

National Association of
Education Buyers (NAEB)
450 Wireless Boulevard
Hauppauge, NY 11788
(516) 273-2305
FAX: (516) 273-2305
An electronic mail service for members covers environmental topics periodically; they held a recycling and recycled products purchasing conference in 1992.

U.S. Environmental Protection
Agency
Region 5
77 West Jackson Boulevard
Chicago, IL 60604-3590
Contact Paul Reusch for midwest region recycling and procurement surveys and consultation.

National Wildlife Federation
Campus Ecology Program
1400 16th St., N.W.
Washington, D.C. 20036-2266
(202) 797-5435 (for general information)
(313) 769-9970 or
midwest@nwf.org (M.W.)
(202) 797-5468 or
noreast@nwf.org (N.E.)
(404) 876-2608 or
soeast@nwf.org (S.E.)
(503) 222-1429 or
western@nwf.org (West)
Write or call for Campus Purchasing Information Packet or Chlorine Action Kit, $5 each, one free per membership.

Green Seal
1730 Rhode Island Ave., N.W.,
Ste. 1050,
Washington, D.C. 20036-3101.
(202) 331-7337
Offers a Campus Green Buying Guide *as well as information packets on standards developed for over 22 product categories that can be incorporated into bid requests and contracts; also call for updated lists of certified products.*

Institute of Scrap Recycling
Industries
Paper Stock Institute
1627 K St., N.W. Ste. 700
Washington, D.C. 20006
(202) 466-4050

The United States Conference of
Mayors
Attn: Richard Kochan
1620 Eye St., N.W.
Washington, D.C. 20006
(202) 293-7330
For information on how your city can join the "Buy Recycled" Challenge and a list of participants, and the "National Office Paper Recycling Project."

CHAPTER 2

Landscaping and Grounds

Maintaining campus grounds which fit centuries-old aesthetic norms typically requires considerable quantities of fertilizer, pesticides, and water. The result, unfortunately, is often an environment which is inhospitable to songbirds and other wildlife, and in which soil and water quality are reduced. In mirroring qualities of another time and place, moreover, such landscapes become mute. They tell us little about where we reside or what makes this setting, in which we invest years of our lives, unique.

The grounds managers featured in this chapter have chosen to let campus landscapes grow in ways that reflect local biodiversity and protect natural resources, thus enhancing a sense of community and place. From Twyla Hansen, landscaping director at Nebraska Wesleyan, who plants native grasses and shrubs throughout the landscape, to Ciscoe Morris, director of grounds at Seattle University, who replaced heavy pesticide use with more natural methods of pest control, these innovators are helping to define the campus landscape of the future.

🌿 GOING NATIVE

Twyla Hansen begins her story about the evolving landscape at Nebraska Wesleyan University, a 50-acre campus in Lincoln, Nebraska, with a primer on the bioregion. "Over the millennia, what was here before people settled this region was grass," she says. The grasslands, or prairie, covered most of the region from Canada to Texas and from the Rocky Mountains to Illinois. Nebraska straddles the transition between the cool, humid eastern portion of the United States and the dry, arid west. It is a land of extreme weather—bitter winters, hot summers, and violent thunderstorms created as dry, mountain air collides with moist air from the gulf. In eastern Nebraska, where Nebraska Wesleyan is located, rainfall averages 24 inches a year, but the evapotranspiration rate is very high, so much of the water quickly returns to the atmosphere. It is a congenial environment for the grasslands, which rank among the most biologically diverse ecosystems in the country.

Twyla Hansen is reintroducing native species to the campus of Nebraska Wesleyan.

Over time, dozens of grasses with such names as big and little bluestem, Indian grass and buffalo grass (all warm season grasses, going dormant with the first frost and turning green again in May) evolved with roots as deep as 15 feet. They withstood thousands of years of drought but succumbed in short order to settlers, whose specially designed plows cut easily through long, sturdy roots. The soil below the tallgrass prairie of much of Nebraska was especially rich in nutrients and retained moisture better than the sandy, shortgrass prairie in the northwestern part of the state, which gave way mostly to ranching. Prairie soils are also virtually free of rocks. "There was an old saying," recounts Hansen, "that they could put a plow down at the Missouri River, go west, and not hit a tree root or a rock for 500 miles." Now that agriculture ranks as the primary source of income in the state, the tall grasslands have dwindled down to inadvertently preserved parcels.

The Native Advantage

As part of her undergraduate program in horticulture at the University of Nebraska in the late 1970s, Hansen studied with faculty who were researching the appropriateness of buffalo and other native grasses for use in lawns. They compared the maintenance needs of the cool-season grasses favored by local institutions and homeowners with the requirements of warm-season native grasses. Their findings drove home the point, says Hansen, that "cool-season grasses like fescue and bluegrass need a lot of input; we need to add water, fertilizer, pesticides, and so forth, to keep them green like they are supposed to look." In her landscape design courses she also became familiar with native perennials and learned how to propagate native grass seeds. Incorporating these plants, she began to create more natural, less resource-intensive landscapes, starting with her own one-acre yard.

David Drylie's native nursery provides species which require less maintenance to flourish.

Replanting a Campus

After a two-year stint with the grounds department at her alma mater, Hansen was hired as grounds manager by Nebraska Wesleyan. This position has offered her the creative space in which to experiment further with native grasses and perennials. She has collected seeds from surviving prairie patches and grown many of the grasses herself—using them, along with wildflowers and native plants, wherever possible. "Obviously, I couldn't come in and just tear out what was here and start over," laughs Hansen. The best time to replant, she finds, is after construction or when the landscape has been otherwise disturbed. Plants she has not been able to grow herself, for lack of either greenhouse space or time, she buys from a nursery that offers native and well-adapted perennials. "We are really lucky," exclaims Hansen. "A nursery about 100 miles from here in Clarkston, Nebraska, Bluebird Nursery, supplies this region with all kinds of natives and perennials . . . so we have been able to actually *buy* them, which is ironic." (See networking section for additional native plant sources.)

Elements of the campus landscape have evolved considerably during Hansen's 12-year residence at Nebraska Wesleyan. She and staff have converted more than a dozen flower beds from annuals to perennials and native plants. In fact, no annual beds remain. "It's not that I don't like annuals," muses Hansen, "it is just that they are quite a bit of work to keep watered and maintained." Annuals are also expensive to purchase and replant every year. Perennial beds now also substitute for turf in places where mowing or weeding is difficult—along the sides of buildings or in the oddly placed, separated plantings common to parking lots.

Hansen is gradually reducing turf, especially in the highest-maintenance areas. "One of our goals here is to eliminate all trim mowing," explains Hansen. "We are trying to get away from that intensive input, which requires man-hours and mowers." Displaced turf is composted on campus along with other landscape debris. (Lincoln, like many cities nationwide, has banned landscape trimmings—leaves, grasses, and twigs—from their landfills.) Staff now leave clippings in place when they mow the remaining turf. "You can reduce your fertilizer needs by about a quarter," says Hansen, "if you return the clippings."

Hansen hopes to feature native grasses in a 1,000-square-foot parcel adjacent to a new health and fitness center. Irrigation funds have run low, and the plot is sufficiently large for a mini-prairie. Hansen and the architect proposed that the area be planted in little bluestem, a two-foot tall grass which turns red in winter, perhaps with buffalo grass around the edge to contain the little bluestem.

Unexpected Returns

Native landscaping has yielded unexpected benefits. For one, staff at Nebraska Wesleyan have planted perennials for sufficient time that they can now avoid the cost of nursery-bought natives and the effort inherent in propagating from seed by dividing perennials for replanting in other areas. The day may come soon, says Hansen, when the university will be able to share some of its native plants with the community.

With the increase in native flora, moreover, has come an increase in fauna. "There is no doubt that our bird population has increased since we have planted

Once established, native grasses don't require *any* water because they are deeply rooted.

—Twyla Hansen,
Nebraska Wesleyan
University

more trees, shrubs, and other seed-bearing plants," says Hansen, who has sighted flickers, warblers, wrens, blue jays, cardinals, white-breasted nuthatches, downy woodpeckers, and many other bird species. The campus now offers a crucial urban refuge for birds stopping to nest or continuing their migration along the central flyway.

Changing a Mind-Set

Hansen occasionally meets opposition to the use of native plants in her home landscape, but reads this less as a strong preference for carpet-like landscapes than as a need for some education. When her yard, which she developed with much care, was cited for local weed-ordinance violations, Hansen convinced the city to back off. With education, she believes, comes appreciation for the native landscape—and the ability to differentiate between weeds (the water-intensive plants which thrive in high-input settings) and native grasses and wildflowers (the low-input plants which thrive under natural conditions):

> I don't understand the resistance to native grasses. To me the little bluestem, and even the big bluestem, have wonderful seed heads. And in my own yard, chickadees and other birds feed on those all winter. You can't measure that in terms of money. You are saving money by doing it, but it has other benefits that go beyond the human.

Water scarcity may be persuasion enough. Because local water is highly saline, Lincoln pipes in water from the Platt River, 25 miles away. Lincolnians, like Americans all over the country, saturate their Kentucky bluegrass lawns all summer with scarce drinking water. The city has aired infomercials on how to water more efficiently, but Hansen hopes they will go a step further, encouraging residents to "plant native grasses that, once established, don't require *any* watering because they are deeply rooted."

Native grasses at Nebraska Wesleyan provide a habitat for butterflies and songbirds.

Student Participation

Although Hansen warmly welcomes students' interest in the landscape at Nebraska Wesleyan, so far their environmental priorities have lain elsewhere. Across the country, however, students have played vital roles in ecological restoration projects and have helped to create the National Wildlife Federation's Campus Wildlife Habitat Program, launched in spring 1995 (see page 38).

An Enthusiastic Public

Interest in low-input, more natural landscapes grows daily. The Ecological Restoration Society, the Society for Sustainable Landscape Architecture, and the National Wildlife Federation's Backyard Wildlife Habitat Program provide information to the burgeoning number of homeowners and landscaping professionals eager for more sustainable and cost-effective techniques.

Beyond campus boundaries, Hansen lends a hand wherever she can. She has worked with Bud Dasenbrock, director of landscaping services at the University of Nebraska's East Campus, to restore a five-acre prairie. The area is big enough to allow annual, managed burning which reinvigorates growth, and to fairly nearly replicate native biodiversity. She has also led tours of her own and other homes that feature native landscapes that attract wildlife.

One of the most promising recent developments in the field of landscape management involves adapting prairie grasses for use on golf courses (notorious for their appetite for pesticides and water). Through an initiative led by Ben Crenshaw, a former golf pro, the golfing industry has signed a multi-million-dollar deal with the University of Nebraska for research and development of buffalo grass varieties. The program aims to reduce the use of petrochemicals, lower maintenance costs, and provide wildlife refuge on the nation's golf courses.

For Hansen, who says restoring native habitat is "not just how I make my living, but how I want to live, too," the excitement over native landscaping marks a fundamental shift in human perception of our place in the natural world.

> There is no doubt that our bird population has increased since we have planted more trees, shrubs, and other seed-bearing plants.
>
> —Twyla Hansen, Nebraska Wesleyan University

❧ INTEGRATED PEST MANAGEMENT

For years, the landscaping crew at Seattle University carried out a mission to kill every bug and weed on campus. Using the same spraying equipment with which he painted buildings, the campus painter drove around with open 55-gallon drums, blanketing many of the campus's 58 acres with diazinon. By the time Ciscoe Morris took charge of the grounds in 1978, the environment looked lovely—but lady beetles and other harmless insects had virtually ceased to exist, and very few birds remained. When Morris did stumble upon a bird, it was often a dead one. "The first thing I noticed was that it was endangering people's safety to spray indiscriminately," reminisces Morris, and "it made me feel bad to find dead birds." Appalled by the idea of student workers pruning the very shrubs the crew had sprayed a few days earlier, or people walking innocently under sprayed trees with open cups of coffee, Morris launched a dramatically different kind of landscape management.

As a master gardener certified through the Washington State Cooperative Extension Service, Morris had learned an alternative approach known as Integrated Pest Management (IPM). In its simplest form, IPM means spraying only as a last resort. Small farmers practicing IPM spray only when they reach the "economic threshold," explains Morris, the point at which alternative strategies have failed and insects threaten to do considerable crop damage.

Mechanical Controls

Following these farmers' lead, Morris dispensed with the paint sprayer, bought one for spot spraying, and began honing IPM strategies on campus. The first approach he and the staff employed was mechanical: they squashed bugs by hand, laid sticky traps to catch them, and blasted them with water. Slugs were cut in half or thrown in soapy water. "Those are all basically mechanical controls, and there are a whole bunch of them we use," says Morris, but mechanical controls alone are not effective in preventing brown rot fungus on flowering fruit trees, controlling adelgids on the blue firs, or removing aphids from the birches.

Cultural Remedies: Well-Planned Planting

For many of these problems, IPM calls for cultural solutions. As a diagnostician for the master gardener program, Morris has found that more than 80 percent of the sick plants he sees suffer from cultural (or environmental) factors. "Most of the time it means somebody planted a plant in the sun when it should go in the shade, or put it in the wrong soil," says Morris. "You have to put the plant in the right place with the right drainage, and to plant a plant that is not going to get too big, so that you don't have to hack it down year after year, which weakens the tree."

The essence of cultural control lies in selecting plants that will resist the predominant pests and diseases of the area and adapt well to their surroundings. Cultural methods can do little to help existing trees if they are poorly suited to their spot in the landscape. Rather, cultural methods inform the planning stage, when managers decide which plants to introduce into the landscape. Morris generally selects plants from the lists of native and well-adapted plants

If you employ a lot of pesticides in pursuit of a weed-free campus, you are going to end up killing butterflies, earthworms, birds, and on up the chain. We would rather overseed and hand weed, accept some weeds, and put some work in.

—Bill Hochstin,
Dartmouth Recycles

developed by his State Cooperative Extension. Quite often, but not always, he chooses native plants. Morris has had great luck with the *Cornis kusa* from Korea. But less well-adapted exotics—or overly successful ones like the kudzu strangling the South, the maleleuca rampant in Florida, or the purple loosetrife taking over shallow wetlands in many parts of the country—pose their own cultural problems. The Japanese pines on campus, while popular with local birds, have not weathered the summers as well as the native lodgepole pines have. Imported bamboo, in contrast, thrived and ran amok, out-competing other plants on campus and requiring days to remove.

Biological Approaches

Staff at Seattle University also employ biological controls in their IPM program. One approach calls for the use of deterrents specific to one insect or disease that pose little threat to human beings, wildlife, and beneficial insects. Among the first such controls developed was an isolated bacterium, *Bacillus thuringiensis* or B.T., which causes disease and death of insects in the Order Lepidoptera (butterflies and moths). Farmers and gardeners, discovering that diseased caterpillars could infect and kill others, were the first to employ this technique. "Old time gardeners," explains Morris, "used to go out and actually get caterpillars, put them in a blender or somehow grind them up, add water, put it through a cheesecloth, spray it on trees, and the insects would get the disease and die."

The subsequent isolation and application of B.T. occurred as scientists searched for an alternative to ground-up caterpillars, which were discovered to carry diseases that could infect humans. A whole host of biological controls have since been designed to work in multifarious ways, from causing disease to affecting reproductive systems in specific insects. But such controls are not a panacea. "Just like anything else, if we use just this strategy without alternatives," cautions Morris, "we are going to build up resistance in the caterpillars, and already researchers are trying to find strains that caterpillars are not resistant to."

Fighting Insects with Insects

Introducing beneficial insects which feast on or parasitize detrimental ones is a second approach to biological control. "It is a really effective method," says Morris, "and we were one of the first places ever to do it around here." Years of spraying had decimated lady beetles, lacewings, assassin bugs, parasitic wasps, praying mantises, predacious stink bugs, and other beneficial insects. When Morris stopped spraying, the aphid population, enjoying a predator-free environment, rapidly grew into the millions. "The birch trees were covered from top to bottom with crawling aphids," to the point at which birch trunks appeared green instead

Now our lady beetle population is probably the best anywhere in Washington state. They migrate, but they come back every year. We have whole buildings covered with their pupae cases.

— Ciscoe Morris, Seattle University

of white, remembers Morris. "They were so thick that honeydew, which is the fruit of these guys, was raining down from the trees and students were getting free dippidydew treatments." Students went to class covered with aphids.

Morris took some heat. Abandoning pesticide sprays, one of his first decisions as grounds director, did not appear to be working. He promised his supervisors that the aphids would disappear as leaves dropped from trees in late fall, and that sprays at this moment would come too late. He planned instead, he explained, to introduce predators to control the aphid population as it reemerged in the spring. The administration thought he had lost his mind. "I convinced them that I could do it and it would work," recalls Morris, "but they said that if it didn't, I would be looking for a job."

First, Morris decided to try lady beetles (a popular beneficial insect), but after calling other gardeners and entomologists, he realized the abundant ants in the landscape would probably prompt the lady beetles to flee. "There were hundreds and hundreds of ants in all the trees to fight off the few lady beetles that we had," Morris observed. Rather than spray to control the ant population before introducing lady beetles, as some suggested, he searched for another beneficial insect—and discovered lacewings, which have "little tricks they use to get by the ants." At the time, lacewings were hard to find, but Morris finally obtained thousands of lacewing eggs to spread around campus. Staff put up signs: "If you see a green mosquito, don't swat it, it's a lacewing," and the school paper ran a story on the new residents.

The students excitedly backed the experiment, despite its rocky start. "The lacewings bit us because there were a few more hatching than there were supposed to be," recollects Morris, "and for the first week, I thought we had failed because I waited a little longer than I should have to put them out. But then the second week, I started seeing the little lacewing larvae crawling around and grabbing aphids. After the third week, no doubt about it, we had won—the aphid population just crashed."

At this point, Morris began collecting lady beetle larvae in film containers at every opportunity and bringing them back to campus. As the aphid and ant populations declined, the lady beetles began to thrive, maturing to adulthood on campus and laying their eggs there.

"Now, our lady beetle population is probably the best anywhere in Washington state," says Morris. "They migrate, but they come back every year. We have whole buildings covered with the pupae cases."

BENEFICIAL INSECTS

Assassin bug

Trichogramma wasp

Damsel bug

Green lacewing

Predacious stink bug

Hospitable Sites

Campuses make ideal environments for beneficial insects, believes Morris, especially where there is enough space to protect them from spraying elsewhere. After more than a decade without pesticide sprays, the beneficial insect population at Seattle University has blossomed and diversified. One example of this presented itself as Morris conducted a tour of the landscape for students in the forestry and entomology programs at the University of Washington. A couple of the students brought some strange looking aphids to his attention. "I looked at them with my magnifying glass and the wasps that had parasitized them were emerging right then," relates Morris. "I am seeing this all the time now. The better my IPM program works—it has been over 13 years and every year it gets better—I find more and more beneficial insects. They know this is the place to live."

Sprays as a Last Resort

Morris may resort to spraying when alternatives fail. More often than not, he says, the need to spray results from cultural problems. "We shouldn't use Colorado blue spruces here because we know that they are very susceptible to aphid attack," admits Morris, "but we have got really old ones that are famous and add a lot to the landscape here." When Morris does spray (when he finds, after monitoring, at least 12 aphids per needle, for example), he uses three criteria for deciding when and how to spray and which sprays to use.

Safety is his primary consideration. "If I have to use a spray," Morris explains, "I must use one that is safe for the environment, humans, other animals, and other insects." Second, the spray selected and the timing of its application must meet the specific need. This necessitates identifying the pest and the affected plant, then selecting a control appropriate for both. It also means destroying the pest at the correct point in its life cycle. The third criterion is that whatever method he selects must prove effective. Myths such as combatting moles with chewing gum (which was quickly dismissed by the Cooperative Extension Service), says Morris, discredit the IPM methods which are effective. "One of the things that I stress when I give talks about this is that it has got to work, so do some research and do your own tests," suggests Morris. "You have really got to monitor, then you have to go back and see if it worked."

Sprays which meet Morris's criteria frequently come in the form of horticultural soaps or oils. The horticultural soaps, while effective for many uses, can harm annuals and burn Japanese maples, but they tend not to harm lady beetles, unless they contain pyrethrin—in which case, says Morris, they are not a true

For the first week, I thought we had failed, but then the second week, I started seeing the little lacewing larvae crawling around and grabbing aphids. After the third week, no doubt about it, we had won—the aphid population just crashed.

—Ciscoe Morris,
Seattle University

soap. Morris has found that horticultural soaps are effective for his Colorado blue spruces, but he uses them in moderation and never sprays when birds are nesting.

A Contented Campus

By selecting pest-resistant plants, Morris not only saves money, but also sees an increase in worker satisfaction:

> Don't let anybody fool you, spraying takes a long time. You have to come in before 5:00 a.m., put on safety gear (even with soap), drive around, pull hoses way out, mix, spray, triple rinse, fill up again, spray out again. It takes forever. Then you have to put up signs. Our staff hated spraying! We are all becoming much more expert at the IPM approach. It has turned what was a drudgery into one of the most exciting types of work I have ever done.

IPM has also brought a marked increase in wildlife. Morris and staff began monitoring bird activity in the early 1980s, keeping lists of birds they sighted. They have put up birdhouses and planted perennials that feed birds in the winter. "We have hawks now that live here all winter long—I never saw those before; there weren't any birds for them to eat here. We have got nuthatches, finches, sapsuckers, flickers . . . . The list is a long one; all sorts of birds have moved back in. We have even sighted a bald eagle."

Ron Jerido's initiatives at Texas Southern University encourage faculty, students, and nearby residents to shape their local landscape.

COMMUNITY LANDSCAPING

One university gears its landscaping program to encourage one particular species: humans. At Texas Southern University in Houston, the 131-acre landscape builds community in a way rare among inner-city, nonresidential campuses. For Ron Jerido, who is as much a volunteer coordinator and trainer as he is a traditional grounds manager, the inclusion of students, faculty and staff is motivated by more than a constrained budget. Jerido, who studied horticulture at Tuskeegee University, sees the campus landscape as a pedagogy and a classroom unto itself. "When you come to an environment that is considered 'inner-city,' you are constantly trying to positively influence young people," says Jerido. "If you also change the environment, it seems to make a difference."

A Plot of Their Own

To this end, Jerido has developed a lecture series on horticulture, as well as a variety of hands-on programs to engage students and staff. One of the most popular programs is "Adopt-a-Plot." Rather than design the entire landscape himself, Jerido engages students and faculty by providing them with assistance and tools for developing their own sites. Participants provide the funds and the maintenance, while Jerido keeps their work to a manageable level by steering them towards native and other well-adapted plants. "Low maintenance is everything," he emphasizes. "Once you get the students out there, you want them to be happy and productive . . . . Instead of putting out blooming annuals, we incorporate foundation plants like evergreens and some deciduous plants that bloom in spring so that participants see different things going on at different times."

Newly planted trees will serve as a noise buffer at TSU.

His training on maintenance of adopted plots includes an introduction to drip irrigation and to the university's "Don't Bag It" campaign. Jerido is slowly expanding drip irrigation capacity—auguring under sidewalks and around buildings as new plots are adopted. He touts this watering method as more specific and efficient than sprinkler systems, which often water sidewalks, buildings, and everything but their intended sites. "Don't Bag It" encourages mulching in place, composting, and recycling (TSU both recycles and composts paper). Students use campus-generated compost on their plots instead of fertilizers and, in turn, contribute any prunings, leaves, or other organic debris to the compost pile. It is effectively a closed-loop, waste-free system.

To generate interest each year in "Adopt-a-Plot," Jerido seeks coverage in the campus paper, posts flyers, and makes presentations to various campus organizations. "I have a network on campus that is getting stronger," says Jerido, who now counts on the student government association, as well as several campus fraternities and sororities, to support the program. This year, the faculty provided funds for a work-study student and donated many hours of their own labor to create an indoor garden in the law school atrium. Alumni, too, support Jerido's efforts through volunteer gardening and, in some cases, earmarking a portion of their donations for campus beautification.

The Urban Forest

Trees are Jerido's pet issue, and the tree plantings he coordinates at Texas Southern have proven popular. In the spring of 1993, more than 200 volunteers helped plant 200 30-gallon live oak trees along the campus perimeter and an additional 400 native trees of diverse types and sizes. Local organizations and businesses provided the trees, helped coordinate matching grants from the Forest Service, and provided food, tools, and gloves.

Jerido gives presentations on tree protection and planting ("urban forestry" as he calls it) throughout the city of Houston. He finds receptive audiences wherever he emphasizes the connection between trees and increased property values. "I talk to them about the natural characteristics of the trees . . . how they reduce pollution, conserve water, and save energy by shading buildings, but what strikes home," says Jerido, "is reducing noise pollution and increasing property values."

Shaping community tree ordinances, says Jerido, is an important method of protecting healthy trees and urban forests. "We are concerned," he says, "that people have been removing native landscape, building concrete parking lots and buildings, and leaving few trees and little wildlife habitat." But ordinances alone are seldom sufficient; many communities are dealt poor hands when landscape plantings and funds for parks and other green spaces are allocated. Jerido finds it particularly troubling when areas with lower tax bases receive insufficient funds for beautifying elementary schools, parks, and other places where children play. To help ameliorate this, Jerido volunteers with Houston's SPARK Program. Founded by Council member Eleanor Tinsley, the SPARK program coordinates the creation of "parklike learning environments" in elementary schools throughout the Houston area.

A Full Array of Flora

By coordinating native wildflower plantings and growing native plants in campus greenhouses, Jerido hopes to further protect native biodiversity. Students helped raise more than $1,000 to purchase 80 pounds of diverse native North American wildflower seeds for planting on campus and on local utility easements. "The utility company is receptive," says Jerido, "because they otherwise have to mow those areas. You put in wildflowers to keep down competing weeds, reducing their labor costs, and they'll work with you in terms of equipment." Jerido assesses drainage, soil type, and other factors before selecting wildflowers for each new site because, though the wildflowers are native, he says the plants can be finicky about their placement.

Reclaiming native plants is another facet of Jerido's effort to protect biodiversity. "As people replant their trees and shrubs," Jerido notices, "they generally plant what the nurseries have available, so what you have is a monoculture." He and students have germinated native Texas saybal palm seeds and propagated diverse native cuttings in campus greenhouses for use in the campus landscape and distribution to SPARK and other community programs.

In the future, Jerido hopes to strengthen networks among inner-city campus horticulturists and landscapers in other parts of the country. Few of the many

I talk to local residents about the natural characteristics of trees . . . how they reduce pollution, conserve water, and save energy by shading buildings. But what strikes home is reducing noise pollution and increasing property values.

—Ron Jerido, Texas Southern University

creative models for solving urban problems, he says, fully address landscaping. "Restoring plant health and biodiversity should be on the front burner, not the back burner, of community development, and with some coordination," he believes, "more universities may play a leadership role."

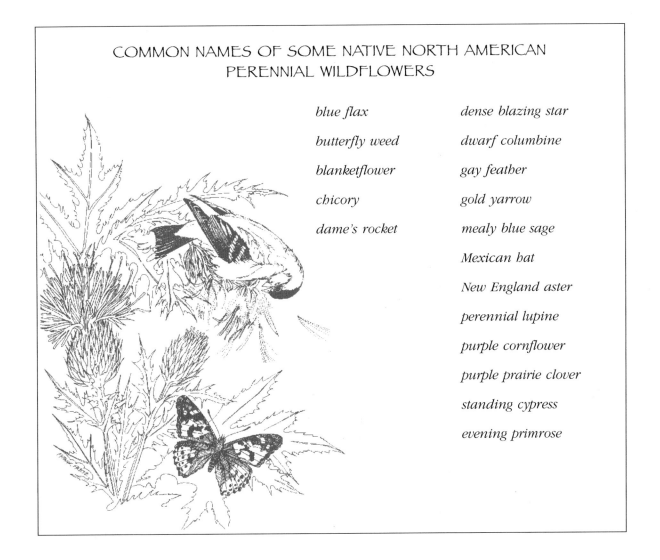

COMMON NAMES OF SOME NATIVE NORTH AMERICAN PERENNIAL WILDFLOWERS

blue flax	dense blazing star
butterfly weed	dwarf columbine
blanketflower	gay feather
chicory	gold yarrow
dame's rocket	mealy blue sage
	Mexican hat
	New England aster
	perennial lupine
	purple cornflower
	purple prairie clover
	standing cypress
	evening primrose

CAMPUS WILDLIFE HABITAT: Preserving Native Biodiversity

Colleges and universities in every region of the United States have started projects to restore native plant and wildlife ecosystems. Through a variety of means—such as reducing pesticide use, substituting turf with native plants, restoring soil nutrient levels through mulching and composting, and providing seed-bearing plants and water—campuses are seeing the return of songbirds, butterflies, earthworms, and other wildlife common to healthy landscapes.

The National Wildlife Federation has developed a resource packet for university administrators, staff, faculty, and students interested in campus ecological restoration projects. The packet provides background articles on landscaping for wildlife, campus urban forestry, habitat preservation, and protection of endangered species, as well as guidelines for project development, contacts and resources, and several campus case studies, highlights of which include:

- A St. John's University prairie, oak savannah, and wetland restoration project at St. John's Abbey in Collegeville, Minnesota;

- A large xeriscape and native species garden at Mesa Community College in Mesa, Arizona;

- The "Campus Keepers" exotic species removal program at the University of Wisconsin at Madison;

- The restoration of a natural oak-hickory forest at Central College in Pella, Iowa;

- A 185-acre wildlife habitat preservation project at Troy State University at Dothan/Fort Rucker, Alabama;

- Native plant arboreta at the University of Idaho in Moscow, Idaho; Gustavus-Adolphus College in St. Peters, Minnesota; and the College of the Desert in Palm Desert, California.

This project is an offshoot of NWF's Backyard Wildlife Habitat program, which in its 20-year history has helped more than 10,000 citizens protect biodiversity by gardening and landscaping for wildlife. The Campus Wildlife Habitat packet may be ordered through NWF's Endangered Species or Campus Ecology programs (see networking section). Campuses may apply for certification of their habitats and receive organizing assistance through either program.

BIBLIOGRAPHY

A Project on Alternative Landscaping in Response to the University of Waterloo's Watgreen Initiative, Cento, McLaughlin, Proud, Rehder, and Smith, University of Waterloo, Environmental Studies Program, 1991. (519) 885-1211.

Backyard Wildlife Habitat, Craig Tufts, National Wildlife Federation, 1992. (202) 797-6800.

Complete Book of Composting, Rodale Press, 1978.

Growing Greener Cities: The Global ReLeaf Tree Planting Handbook, Living Planet Press, 1992.

Gray Water Use in the Landscape, Robert Kourik, Metamorphic Press, 1988.

Landscaping with Wildflowers and Native Plants, William H.W. Wilson, Ortho Books, 1984.

"Making a Habit of Habitat," Leah Barash, *National Wildlife*, A/M, 1994, 10–17.

National Wildflower Research Center's Wildflower Handbook, Voyageur Press, 1992.

Out of Place: Restoring Identity to the Regional Landscape, Michael Hough, Yale University Press, 1990.

Pesticides in Schools: Reducing the Risks, G. Oliver Koppell, New York State Department of Law, 1994.

Redesigning the American Lawn: A Search for Environmental Harmony, Balmore, Bormann, and Geballe, Yale University Press, 1993.

"Singing the Blues for Songbirds," Bill Lawren, *National Wildlife*, A/S, 1988, 18–24.

"The IPM Process," *Common Sense Pest Control*, Summer, 1988, Box 7414, Berkeley, CA, 94707.

Worms Eat My Garden, Mary Appelhoff, Flowerfield Enterprises, 10332 Shaver Rd., Kalamazoo, MI 49002. (616) 327-0108.

Xeriscape Gardening: Water Conservation for the American Landscape, Ellefson, Stephens, and Welsh, Macmillan Publishing Company, 1992.

Xeriscape Training Manual, Dr. Ron Dinchak, Mesa Community College, Spring 1991.

NETWORKING

Campus

Campus Center for Appropriate Technology (CCAT)
Humboldt State University
Buck House #97
Arcata, CA 95521
Graywater recycling.

Connecticut College
Attn: James Luce
Landscaping and Grounds
New London, CT 06320
(203) 439-2259
IPM

Cornell University
Attn: Professor Tom Richard
Ithaca, NY 14853
(607) 255-2488
Composting.

Dartmouth Recycles
Attn: Bill Hochstin
Dartmouth College
Hanover, NH 03755
Large-scale composting (see Solid Waste Chapter for details), organic vegetable gardening on campus, IPM.

Davidson College
Attn: George Morris
Landscaping and Grounds
Davidson, NC 28036
(704) 892-2000
IPM.

Florida International University
Attn: Jack Parker
Environmental Studies Program
College of Arts and Sciences
Miami, FL 33199
Ecological restoration

Fond du Lac Community College
Attn: Joe Hudsputh
2101 14th St.
Cloquet, MN 55720
e-mail: jhud@mail. spl.pc.mn.us
(218) 879-5377
1,800-acre native landscaping, research and education program.

Gustavus-Adolphus College
Attn: Dr. Charles Mason
Biology Department
St. Peters, MN 56082
Conversion of soybean field to native plant arboretum.

Mesa Community College
Attn: Professor Ron Dinchak
Mesa, AZ 85202
Xeriscaping.

If you find that an organization listed here has moved or a contact has been replaced, let the Campus Ecology Program staff know. We'll help match you with the latest source for the information you need.

Mohave Community College
Attn: Haul Reddick
1971 Jagerson Ave.
Kingman, AZ 86401
(602) 757-0879
Xeriscaping.

MSU Natural Areas Committee
Attn: Dr. Glen Duderar
Michigan State University
East Lansing, MI 48823
(517) 353-1990
Wetland restoration.

Nebraska Wesleyan University
Attn: Twyla Hansen
5000 St. Paul
Lincoln, NE 68504
*Use of native grasses in
landscape, prairie restoration.*

Seattle University
Attn: Ciscoe Morris
Grounds Department
564 12th Ave.
Seattle, WA 98122
IPM, landscaping for wildlife.

St. John's Abbey
Attn: Father Paul Schweitz
Collegeville, MN 56321
(612) 363-3163
Native plant arboretum.

Texas Southern University
Attn: Ron Jerido, Horticulturalist
Houston, TX 77004
*Urban forestry, Adopt-A-Plot,
mulching, and paper-waste
composting.*

Troy State University at Dothan
Attn: Bob Willis
Student Support Services
Dothan, AL 36304
(205) 983-6556
*185-acre wildlife habitat
preservation/management
project.*

University of Guelph
Attn: Michael Bladdon
Grounds Division
Guelph, Ontario
Canada N1G 2WI
*Premier natural landscaping
program in Canadian higher
education, turf reduction,
landscaping for wildlife,
slideshow, guest lectures.*

University of Iowa
Attn: Dave Jackson
Hawkeye Physical Plant
Iowa City, IA
(319) 335-5062 or
djackson@uiowa.edu
*IPM; coordinates national IPM
mailing list on Internet, see
below.*

University of Nevada at Las Vegas
Attn: Dr. James Deacon
Environmental Studies
4505 Maryland Parkway
Las Vegas, NV 89154
(702) 895-4440
Project Desert Landscape.

University of Wisconsin at
Madison
Attn: David Eagan
Institute for Environmental
Studies
70 Science Hall
University of Wisconsin
Madison, WI 53706
(608) 263-3985 or
djeagan@students.wisc.edu
*"Campus Keepers" exotic species
removal program.*

Wofford College
Attn: Chuck Doster
Physical Plant
Spartanburg, SC 29303-3663
(803) 597-4380
Sustainable landscaping.

Regional and National

American Association of
Botanical Gardens and Arboreta
786 Church Rd.
Wayne, PA 19087
(610) 688-1120

American Forests
Global ReLeaf Program
1516 P St., N.W.
Washington, D.C. 20005
(202) 667-3300

Hortus Northwest
P.O. Box 955
Canby, OR 97013
*Distributes annually updated
directories of native plant
nurseries and mail order
sources ($9).*

National Wildflower Research
Center
2600 FM 973 North
Austin, TX 78725-4201
(512) 929-3600
*Provides lists of native species
recommended for each state
and dozens of fact sheets.*

National Wildlife Federation
1400 16th St., N.W.
Washington, D.C. 20036-2266
(202) 797-5435 (general
information)
(313) 769-6960 or
lyee@igc.apc.org (Campus
Habitat Certification)
(313) 769-9970 or
midwest@nwf.org (M.W.)
(202) 797-5468 or
noreast@nwf.org (N.E.)
(404) 876-2608 or
soeast@nwf.org (S.E.)
(503) 222-1429 or
western@nwf.org (West)
*Campus Wildlife Habitat
Resource Packet and
Certification Program;
Composting, Ecological
Landscaping and Tree
Planting Issue Packets; and
consultations.*

National Pesticide Telecommuni-
cations Network
Dept. Preventative Medicine
Texas Technical University
Health Science Center
Lubbock, TX 79430
(800) 858-7378

Plant Materials Program
Soil Conservation Service
U.S. Department of Agriculture
(202) 205-0026
*Call U.S.D.A.'s Soil Conservation
Service or see Campus Wildlife
Habitat Resource Packet for
state and regional listings of
Plant Materials Specialists who
can assist with identification
and selection of native plants.*

"PESTCON" *Integrated Pest
Management at Colleges and
Universities*
Dave Jackson, Listowner
Physical Plant,
University of Iowa
Iowa City, IA 52242
(319) 335-5062
*"PESTCON" is a "listserv" or
electronic correspondence group
on the Internet. It was established for campus pest control
contract administrators, facilities
directors and others concerned
about the application of
pesticides and herbicides. To
subscribe to the list, send the
following message to
LISTSERV@UIOWA.EDU: subscribe
PESTCON "your name" QUIT.*

U.S. Fish and Wildlife Service
Publications Unit-Mail Stop 130
Washington, D.C. 20240
(703) 358-1711
*Call or write for updated lists of
endangered and threatened
flora and fauna.*

CHAPTER 3

Transportation, Parking, and Fleet Maintenance

Walking, bicycling and mass transit may be the cleanest, healthiest ways to get around, but growth and development decisions in this country are still driven by the automobile. Our car-centered transportation system is the largest fossil fuel dependent sector in the U.S. economy, burning more oil each year than residential, commercial, industrial and electric utility uses combined.[1] Over-reliance on inefficient, gasoline-fueled vehicles not only pollutes air and water, but is a primary reason why the U.S. is among the largest per capita contributors of carbon dioxide (the predominate greenhouse gas) to the Earth's atmosphere.[2]

Colleges and universities often contribute to the problems associated with automobiles. Until recently, the thrust of most campus transportation plans has been building more parking lots and garages, widening roads, and otherwise placating commuters. A running joke in campus transportation circles suggests the car conundrum: "What is a university?" "A group of administrators, faculty and students held together by a common grievance over parking."

Recently, several factors have propelled campuses into leadership roles on issues of sustainable transportation: the prohibitive cost of building parking structures, constraints on growth, new resources for the research and development of transportation alternatives, and student and staff concern for safety and environmental quality. In anticipation of new demands and opportunities, campus transportation professionals nationwide have begun to think beyond unlimited accommodation of single-occupant vehicles. Their creative efforts to limit the

JEFF MILLER

Lori Kay employs a variety of creative strategies to reduce the need for new parking at UW-Madison.

---

[1]*Steering a New Course*, 1991, p. 34. See bibliography.
[2]"Charting Development Paths," 1994, p. 16.

demand for parking and to promote alternatives to cars are collectively known in the trade as transportation demand management (TDM). Creating bicycle- and pedestrian-friendly campuses, increasing transit ridership, and addressing the needs of those commuters with longer trips or irregular hours are key TDM strategies.

Many campuses also employ a number of measures—such as recycling fluids and testing alternative fuels—to reduce the environmental impact of their fleet operations. To conclude this chapter, Gaylen Liska, assistant director of fleet maintenance, imparts what a greener fleet entails at the University of Kansas and what it may mean soon for other colleges and universities.

MANAGING CAMPUS TRANSPORTATION DEMAND

When Lori Kay began her job as director of transportation at the University of Wisconsin at Madison in April 1992, the campus had only 11,000 parking spots for a population of nearly 60,000 people. The number of single-occupant drivers had doubled in eight years, and the Madison area had recently seen its first Clean Air Act non-attainment days.

Despite pressure from many students, staff, and even the state government to build more parking lots, Kay and other UW-Madison administrators chose to explore alternatives. "We have a window of opportunity," says Kay, to "do something before we actually reach non-attainment status and have government regulations imposed upon us." With effort, she hopes, the university will change people's behavior, promoting environmental conservation through new transportation habits.

With support and guidance from a broad-based committee appointed by the chancellor, Kay has begun implementing a transportation demand management program. Because the University of Wisconsin already has one of the highest per-capita campus rates of bicycle use in the country (boasting as many as 26,000 riders when weather permits), the TDM strategy at UW will focus over the next five years primarily on automobile-dependent commuters. The idea, says Kay, is "to do some other things financially with our infrastructure—to catch up, frankly, with our strong bicycle and pedestrian programs."

Novel Approaches

Twelve years worth of annual transportation surveys provide UW-Madison with a strong base for developing nontraditional transportation solutions. Changes in the "workday/workplace" routine are high on the list, including such strategies as: increasing telecommuting opportunities (whereby an employee may work at home one or more days a week); instituting flex-time, which would not

> We have a window of opportunity to do something before we actually reach non-attainment status.
>
> —Lori Kay, UW-Madison

reduce automobile use but could thin out rush hour congestion; and, where appropriate, replacing five eight-hour days with four ten-hour days.

Parking management, especially the concept of part-time (or "flex") parking, is another novel approach. "We will not likely be adding much parking earmarked for staff, and we have virtually none for students, anyway," says Kay, who is currently designing a part-time parking pilot program, which she hopes to expand over the next two years. By coordinating parking schedules and offering passes for limited days of the week, UW can designate shared parking spaces and minimize need for new spaces. Kay expects part-time parking to encourage carpooling; it may also reduce the total number of cars on campus, especially if combined with perks such as free or discounted bus passes.

The challenge will be to enforce the part-time parking system, without spending more money than new lots would have cost. The University of Washington at Seattle, an oft-cited TDM model, spent $18 million over three years (1991–1994) on incentives, personnel, vanpools, and buybacks of unused bus tickets. Options for enforcement include attended booths, automated gates which stamp tickets or read barcoded passes, and coded stickers.

Ridesharing and Transit

Ridesharing and subsidized transit are more traditional components of TDM. UW-Madison, like many campuses, has had an under-used carpooling program in place for years and is now exploring ways to boost participation. Kay favors inducements—providing alternative ways to get around, such as point-to-point shuttles, bicycle rentals or storage, and guaranteed rides home. Improved car and vanpool marketing and updated rideshare lists, anticipates Kay, should also improve the program.

The University of North Carolina at Chapel Hill operates a relatively active rideshare program. In 1989, the Transportation and Parking Department hired Randy Young as marketing specialist to coordinate the program and assist with other aspects of TDM. Young adapted an Excel database matching program to maintain van and carpool lists. The unwieldy number and the large size of departments makes personalized marketing at UNC a challenge.

The solution: volunteer parking coordinators. Two hundred seventy "communications specialists," drawn from every department in the university, make publicity friendly and efficient. They post announcements throughout their departments, talk with new employees, and provide transportation-related information. Some of the more enthusiastic coordinators work as hard at promoting carpooling and other TDM programs, reports Young, as they do at tasks in their formal job descriptions.

Two hundred seventy "communications specialists," drawn from every department in the university, make TDM publicity at UNC-Chapel Hill friendly and efficient.

Measuring actual program use is difficult. Young usually hears of carpools only when cars or vans are filled to capacity and drivers ask to be deleted from UNC's rideshare roster. Nevertheless, he has seen steady growth in the list from a handful of people when he started to more than 200 participants a year later, and he thinks participation will continue to rise with increased awareness of incentives. By allowing multiple licenses on a parking permit, UNC enables carpool participants to rotate vehicles and share permit costs. A point-to-point shuttle operating around the clock and a student-run escort program allow carpoolers and others to move around campus safely without their own vehicles. A motorist assistance program jump-starts vehicles, retrieves locked keys, and fixes flats—giving drivers more confidence in the reliability of their cars for ridesharing. Guaranteeing emergency rides home and offering free or discounted bus passes provide additional incentives. (UW-Madison's Emergency Ride Home Program, for which 500 staff are eligible, is used twice a month on average.)

Incentives such as free or discounted parking spaces and preferential parking, however, may again pose the problem of enforcement. As with part-time parking, car and vanpool programs may require stickers, signs, gates, attendants, cameras, or other enforcement mechanisms where "honor systems" have been abused. When more than one rideshare participant at UNC collected free bus passes, purchased discounted tickets, and parked in preferential lots, all while continuing to drive to and from the campus alone, Young was forced to suspend some incentives until the university can finance sufficient enforcement.

Many colleges and universities reduce automobile traffic on campuses by providing transit between campus and surrounding communities. The Transportation and Parking Department at UNC-Chapel Hill has worked closely with the Chapel Hill Transit and the Triangle Transit Authority to extend vanpool and bus service to the campus, broaden transit routes, and increase the frequency of service. The university subsidizes up to 46 percent of the Chapel Hill Transit's total operating budget, and students receive heavily discounted passes. Federal subsidies, student fees, parking permit fees, bus pass sales, and even vehicle impoundments help fund the program. Transportation Director Kay is investigating a similar program for UW-Madison that would offer inducements geared to separate constituencies—students, faculty and staff.

> In the long run, the vision here might be that we would have few or no gas cars on campus.
>
> —Lori Kay,
> UW-Madison

Auto-free Zones

A few campuses—the University of California at Davis, Colorado State University, Agnes Scott College in Georgia, and the University of Illinois—have closed their main campuses to all but emergency and service vehicles. Reasons cited include safety and noise concerns and, at the University of Illinois Urbana-Champaign (UIUC), providing safe pedestrian and bike crossings.

Jim Trail, a dedicated TDM advocate who has worked as university traffic engineer and supervisor of the garage and carpool at the University of Illinois for 33 years, says there is talk of once again closing main streets adjacent to the campus and other thoroughfares which had been closed in 1981 and reopened shortly thereafter. When asked if the closings were due to cost, aesthetics, or environmental quality, "It is all three without a doubt.... Vehicles detract from our mission of teaching, research and service," Trail replies. "We need maintenance vehicles and spoke access to deliver things, but," he asks, "do we really need automobiles adjacent to academic buildings?"

Closing roads may be a realistic option. Even if the university does not own the streets in question, Trail has found, staff can negotiate with government officials and residents for a transfer of the title. Where turning streets over to campuses means lower municipal maintenance costs, officials have sometimes been receptive. If there is resistance, Trail admits, it is usually from local business owners who think that "cars driving by allow advertising.... We try to point out to them that it is pedestrians who buy, not cars."

Traffic Engineer Jim Trail nurtures bike riders and pedestrians at the University of Illinois.

Bicycles and Pedestrians

The University of Illinois' TDM program has a long and exceptional history of encouraging bicycles and pedestrians. Administrations and their official priorities have come and gone, but Trail has stood steadfast in his commitment to TDM. The result: seven (soon to be eight) miles of Class I bike lanes, custom-designed bike racks, and bicycle accommodation in most parking structures. The university master plan has included integrated transportation alternatives for decades. According to Trail, UIUC has a policy, "that goes back over 20 years in major street plan studies, that we would like to favor the pedestrian/bicyclist over the motorized vehicle operator." The campus consists of superblocks entered primarily by pedestrians, and circumnavigated by bicyclists on inner rings and vehicles in outer ones.

Bike Lanes

Bike lanes and bike racks of the highest quality visibly demonstrate the University of Illinois' commitment to cyclists. All UIUC bike lanes are set off from the street and are therefore designated Class I. (Class II lanes consist of partially protected zones on existing streets, and Class III lanes are delineated by painted lines.) White edge lines and yellow center lines, exposed aggregate concrete, or crushed stone separate two-way bicycle traffic and distinguish bike lanes from

Making alternatives to cars easy at UIUC involves attention to details such as these: a bike path adjacent to a bike parking lot (left) and a bike path separated from both the street and the sidewalk (right).

sidewalks. Because of its durability and smoothness, Trail favors concrete over asphalt bike lanes. Lanes range in width from three to eight feet, with six feet the standard. Subsurface layers of crushed stone provide the support necessary for maintenance vehicles to clear the lanes of snow and debris without damaging the surface.

Bike Racks

Designing functional bike racks and placing them wisely are crucial components of bike-focused TDM. Ray Magyar, planner in the Department of Transportation and Parking at UNC-Chapel Hill, talked extensively with students, the primary users of bike racks on campus. He surveyed all users and spent hours observing and videotaping bicycle and bike rack use. He also counted rack space, evaluated rates of ingress and egress, and monitored bike traffic in various weather conditions and at various times of day, studying bike use with a seriousness usually reserved for cars. Both UNC's Magyar and UIUC's Trail have had bike racks and lots custom-designed in response to their research and contact with riders.

Cyclists with the popular quick-release wheels, as well as riders with larger mountain- and road-bike frames and tires, often want to lock both tires to the frame and need ample room to do so. After testing and modifying numerous designs over the years, Trail has found that a customized "circle" rack best accommodates both wheels and the frame. This rack consists of pairs of one-inch diameter pipes, forming one-foot-wide circles attached to a long, two-inch diameter pipe. The University of North Carolina at Chapel Hill, which has tripled the number of bicycle racks on campus in the last three years, chose a wavelock design they found more affordable and aesthetically pleasing than pipe rails. Space-saving wall racks and "inverted-U" racks are also popular.

TDM experts research the number and placement of bike racks with care. Trail, who periodically surveys cyclists to find out how far they are willing to walk from bike racks to various destinations, has found them typically unwilling to walk more than half a block. If racks are conveniently located, he says, staff and students are most likely to cycle between home and their initial destination (usually classrooms or libraries), using the bus system to get around once on campus. (Student fees finance a very successful unlimited-use transit program on the UIUC campus and within the Urbana-Champaign metropolitan areas.)

So providing sufficient rack space close to classrooms and libraries has been a priority for Trail, who in addition to creating separate bike lots, integrates bicycle parking into vehicle lots and garages. End lots and center aisles go to bike racks, along with anywhere else cars cannot easily fit, including corners and the spaces between supporting beams. "We do whatever necessary to accommodate bicycles in a cost-effective manner—even passing some of the costs on to the car operator when necessary," asserts Trail.

Measuring Bicycle Use

Campuses with strong commitments to bicycling tend to evaluate bike use and safety as carefully as automobile use and safety. Techniques developed to monitor the automobile, says Trail, can enhance bicycle programs as well. Trail placed an induction loop in the concrete pavement at a busy point along UIUC's bikepath network. Crossings are tallied and provide a record of ridership across the seasons and of changes in usage patterns over the years. Other techniques to measure bicycle use include pneumatic tubes attached to counters, as well as photographic, video, and visual surveys. As a result of its monitoring, says Trail, the University of Illinois boasts bike lanes that "are amongst the densest in use that we know about in the country."

Keeping ridership high during winter months is a challenge on campuses with severe winters. Because cyclists are more reluctant to ride with automobile traffic in winter than in other seasons, Class II and III bike lanes maintain ridership less effectively than separate, Class I lanes. But Class I lanes are useless in winter unless they are snowplowed. "We find that our bicycle usage never goes below about one-third of what it would be in the heaviest use months," claims Trail, who attributes this low drop off rate to snowplowing, separate Class I lanes, and mixed-use parking that provides some shelter for bicycles.

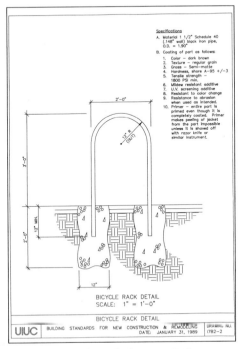

Bicycle rack design, UIUC.

Bicycle Safety Measures

Creating bicycle-friendly campuses increases safety in general. The UIUC, for example, reported 15 bicycle-related and 150 automobile-related accidents on campus in 1993–94, which Trail says accurately reflects an average of 10 car accidents for every bicycle accident. Automobile accident and fatality rates are serious enough on campuses that some, such as Colorado State University, have closed especially dangerous intersections and roads to bicycles. Because on many campuses they share paths with pedestrians and can be locked almost anywhere, bicycles are frequently the subject of pedestrians' complaints; however, "based on the record," says Trail, " bicycles are by far the safest method—after walking— of getting around on campuses."

Bicycle safety, though, can be complex, requiring that campuses balance pedestrian welfare with measures to promote bicycle use. The campuses that best accommodate bicyclists, in fact, also enforce some of the most stringent bicycle regulations. The University of Illinois allows bikes on sidewalks and streets only where there is no nearby bike lane, and Trail feels that pedestrian safety is enhanced by the clear separation of bike lanes from footpaths. UIUC frequently tickets cyclists for violating yield and stop signs and for failing to halt at red lights. Riders who lock their bikes to trees or in wheelchair and other access-ways frequently find them impounded and sold at auction.

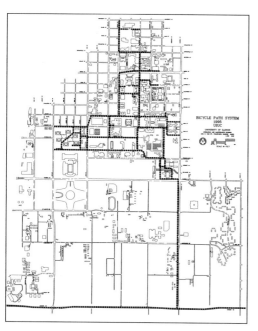

Map of the network of bike paths at UIUC.

Cyclists who balk at such measures may not realize that on many campuses assuring safety goes in tandem with getting funding for new racks, lanes, and other bicycle amenities. Both Trail and Young, in fact, suggest that cyclists can best enhance bicycle provisions on campuses by learning the rules and riding carefully through pedestrian zones. To put a positive spin on bicycle safety, Young and Magyar at UNC-Chapel Hill distributed 50 free helmets in "Carolina-blue" to those who registered their bikes earliest in the 1994–95 academic year.

Point-to-point shuttles offering 24-hour or late night service, escort programs with pairs of student volunteers who accompany pedestrians to their destinations, and energy-efficient motion-sensor lighting also make campuses friendlier to pedestrians and cyclists. (UW-Madison's SAFE Program keeps three teams of two student escorts on duty every night—serving some 3,000 people per month—and provides shuttle backup only when escorts are not available.)

Funding and Networking

Trail views the Intermodal Surface Transportation Efficiency Act (ISTEA), enacted by Congress in 1991, as one of the most promising measures to have come along in his tenure at the University of Illinois. ISTEA requires public involvement in transportation decisions and encourages the allocation of funds for bike lanes, public transit, ridesharing and other non-highway projects. Granted through the Department of Transportation, ISTEA monies have funded new bike racks and motion-triggered parking lot lights at UNC-Chapel Hill, as well as the $230,000 one-mile bike lane extension under construction in 1995 at the UIUC. To qualify for federal funding, campus transportation planners often must work closely with regional planners to develop the long-range plans and environmental impact studies required of municipalities with 50,000 residents or more, says Trail, who was instrumental in the creation of the Champaign Urbana Urbanized Area Transportation Study (CUAATS).

Trail now receives several calls a month from campus transportation coordinators interested in TDM. To facilitate national networking, he has established an electronic mail group on the Internet, and in 1994, UIUC hosted the 16th annual Big Ten and Midwestern Transportation and Parking Conference, at which interest in campus TDM, he says, marked an all-time high (see networking section).

Student Roles

The University of Wisconsin at Madison involves students in TDM and other environmental research projects through such innovative programs as the Environmental Studies Capstone "IES 600" seminars lead by doctoral candidate David Eagan and the Campus Ecology Research Project facilitated by Environmental Management Coordinator Daniel Einstein. The programs work hand in hand, often using a client-server model to provide both environmental and non-environmental studies majors with the opportunity to hone their research and problem-solving skills by working on real-life campus environmental projects for administrators and staff.

As director of transportation services, Lori Kay was among the programs' first clients. Involving students, she says, "has certainly added a research element which might not otherwise have been accomplished." Students have surveyed campus TDM and fleet management programs, producing such reports as "TDM Programs: Profiles of Selected Universities" written by Tabitha Graves in 1993 when she was a student in "IES 600." After graduating, Graves was hired to continue working on TDM projects for the university.

The prospects for students seeking to influence campus transportation policies are not always so promising. Though he has lobbied the Board of Trustees for fee-based services, surveyed students, and attended Parking Fee Committee meetings for several years, Rich Nielsen has yet to see much tangible evidence of his efforts. As a transportation representative to the student senate and a

Based on the record, bicycles are by far the safest method—after walking—of getting around on campuses.

—Jim Trail, University of Illinois

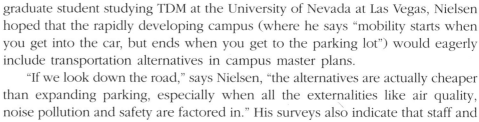

graduate student studying TDM at the University of Nevada at Las Vegas, Nielsen hoped that the rapidly developing campus (where he says "mobility starts when you get into the car, but ends when you get to the parking lot") would eagerly include transportation alternatives in campus master plans.

"If we look down the road," says Nielsen, "the alternatives are actually cheaper than expanding parking, especially when all the externalities like air quality, noise pollution and safety are factored in." His surveys also indicate that staff and students largely favor paying fees to support a transit system and other transportation services. Still, says Nielsen, the prevalent opinion is that shifting the emphasis away from cars would be unpopular with staff and students. Administrators themselves admit that grappling with the psychology of parking is one of the more difficult challenges they face in implementing campus TDM alternatives.

Marketing

UNC-Chapel Hill recognized the need to change perceptions about transportation when it hired Young to boost carpooling, public transit, and other alternatives. "I have been termed the bravest man on campus," says Young, adding, "you are certainly ready to market just about anything after [marketing] transportation and parking alternatives." In addition to general enmity towards any effort to curtail parking, drivers frequently fail to support the measures they indicate they will, says Young, who calls it "psychological dissonance" when people show theoretical support on surveys, but fail to actually change their behavior. "Although everybody does not necessarily want to be the one to carpool," he notices, "everybody likes to think of themselves as the kind of person who would." In such an atmosphere, "making alternatives easier and safer, and providing inducement packages," Young believes, "help build the educational foundation and consensus that will ultimately decrease the demand for parking."

Institutionalization

Campus TDM coordinators emphasize the need to ease into transitions and, where possible, to integrate TDM into building design and construction, so that expensive and controversial changes can be avoided. Integrated planning, says Young, can incorporate an array of alternatives. Examples include not only bike lots and bike lanes but, where parking lots must be built, recycled-content construction materials (in use at the University of Illinois and at Rutgers University in New Jersey) and efficient, motion-sensor lighting (UNC-Chapel Hill). Building design modifications such as permeable paving, ground water recharge trenches, and other storm water management techniques can also enhance transportation while protecting the environment.

Daniel Einstein and Tabitha Graves assist with research and development of transportation demand management at UW-Madison.

Such integration is often termed "total quality management" (TQM)—a longer-range and more inclusive approach to policy and planning on campuses and at other institutions. TQM has positive environmental implications, fostering the institutionalization and acceptance of initiatives such as energy efficiency, recycling, and TDM. Besides marketing TDM, Young also consults on Total Quality Management for departments throughout UNC. The TQM brochure he created at the behest of the vice chancellor for facilities management states: "We are stewards of the environment. We recognize that our facilities and services affect the natural surroundings and as such, we will conserve and protect these resources through responsible management, sound technical judgment, conscientious work methods, and individual efforts."

TQM encapsulates the approach to transportation demand management at UW-Madison, as well, where it is embodied in the Transportation Demand Management Committee. Co-ordinated by Transportation Director Kay, the committee cuts across disciplines and involves students, faculty, and staff in long-range planning—reflecting the inclusiveness, team-building and vision which are TQM benchmarks.

Ray Magyar and Randy Young at UNC-Chapel Hill study bike use with a seriousness usually reserved for cars, surveying students, videotaping bicycle and bike rack use, and monitoring bike traffic.

Looking Forward

When asked about the future, TDM staff tend to have short-range goals—"improving bicycle safety," or "increasing participation in rideshare programs." But some longer-term explorations are underway. Experiments with propane and other alternative fuels have begun at Dartmouth and at several universities in California, including UCLA, where 2 percent of all newly registered vehicles must be emission-free by 1995. Dartmouth College, Cal State LA, Purdue University, Marquette University, and the University of Michigan rank among the universities developing solar cars, and the University of South Florida runs a fleet of solar-powered electric vehicles (see Chapter 4, Energy and Utilities).

"I think ultimately that is a TDM program goal," says UW-Madison's Lori Kay. She and faculty who are researching and developing electric cars are now discussing possibilities for a campus fleet pilot project. Kay also monitors developments in light rail, which she says the university would be well suited for. In the long run, says Kay, the "vision here might be that we would have few or no gas cars on campus."

GREENING FLEET MAINTENANCE

Maintenance of conventional automobiles on campus presents several opportunities for reuse and recycling. At the University of Kansas, Gaylen Liska, the assistant director of vehicle maintenance, and staff have been at the forefront of such changes.

One of their first initiatives was to procure a $5,000 machine for capturing chlorofluorocarbons (CFCs)—before such recycling was required by the federal Clean Air Act. Until recently, most maintenance shops when servicing vehicle air-conditioning units simply opened valves, releasing freon (a CFC-based coolant) into the atmosphere. This caused fairly significant emissions, since cars, vans, and trucks carry between two and six pounds of freon, and large universities often maintain hundreds of vehicles.

The university's freon-capturing machine draws out CFC-12 to be filtered, pressurized and reused as needed for their 700-vehicle fleet. The process conserves about a third of the freon, resulting in savings of more than $10,000 for the university. Although their resulting product is perfectly usable, the vehicle maintenance department must continue to purchase new bottles of freon, since vehicles invariably leak some of the gas. Preventive maintenance helps, explains Liska, but there is no way to control completely the loose connections, leaky seals in compressors, and blown hoses. Until manufacturers develop non-CFC-based coolants, Liska will continue to phase in, and eventually recycle, 134-A (a less ozone-depleting alternative) systems as new vehicles are purchased.[3]

In addition to recycling 20 to 30 car batteries a month, Liska and staff recycle motor oil, transmission fluids, elevator oil and compressor oils. Oil and fluids are collected in 20-gallon containers as vehicles and other equipment are serviced. Oil is then stored in a 500-gallon underground tank for transport to Kansas City, where it is recycled and sold as recycled oil and lower-grade fuel oil. (The vehicle maintenance staff at UIUC has found that recycled oils perform better than premium brands, do not affect vehicle warranties, and cost less than virgin oil.)

To assure immediate detection of any underground storage leaks, the University of Kansas invested $18,000 in a monitor which records tank temperature and volume on computer printouts. In case they order more

---

[3] The "Montreal Protocol" ratified by the United Nations Environmental Program in 1988, called for a freeze in production of ozone-depleting CFCs to 1986 levels and a 50 percent reduction in production by 1999.

gas than they can use, they have overfill protection; when fuel levels rise beyond a certain point, "buzzers and bells and red lights and everything else come on," says Liska, "to make me shut that thing down before it spills over and gets out on the drive." Liska touts the system as essential for safety and cost control, explaining:

> If you have a tank that doesn't have a monitoring system on it, you have had it in the ground for 20 or 25 years and there has been a leak for six or seven years, then it is not a matter of just digging up the tank and disposing of it; the tank has to be disposed of as a hazardous material, and there are only certain places where you can do that . . . . you also have to dig out all that contaminated dirt, and you have to dispose of it as a hazardous waste or contaminated dirt and that costs you too.

Liska has also requisitioned a machine to recycle glycol-based antifreezes, which are too hazardous for disposal down drains or sewers. The department currently pays $25 per 55-gallon drum to have the antifreeze hauled away and recycled, but Liska hopes to procure the unique recycling machine (dubbed "Bad Ethel") to heat and distill it for reuse. "Clean water goes into the drain and the antifreeze comes out like you buy it in the store," says Liska, who compares the machine to "your old whiskey distiller."

Staff have set up a similar system for recycling solvents. At $250 per 55-gallon drum for disposal, they have financial incentive. But, Liska cautions, when collecting materials and operating this machine in particular, mixing the input will compromise the final product. "What you get out of the machine depends on what you put into it," he says:

> If you put a high-grade enamel reducer for automotive finishes into it, that is what you are going to get out, but if you mix that with a lacquer thinner and mix that with a turpentine-type solvent and mix cleaning solvent with that . . . You are going to come out with a low-grade mixture which you are going to use mainly for cleaning.

Liska credits the university's Environmental Ombudsman program, staffed and funded by the chancellor, for supporting and documenting many of his department's endeavors. He hopes the program will encourage student research on alternative vehicles and fuels. "There is interest in less-polluting vehicles," he says. "We have done a bit of experimenting with this in the state, and it will be interesting to see where it all goes."

BIBLIOGRAPHY

Bicycle Blueprint: A Plan to Bring Bicycling Into the Mainstream in New York City, Transportation Alternatives, 92 St. Marks Place, New York, NY 10009. (212) 475-4600.

"Charting Development Paths: A Multicountry Comparison of Carbon Dioxide Emission," William R. Moomaw and D. Mark Tullis, G-DAE Discussion Paper #2, Tufts University, 1994.

Citizen Advocacy: Working for Sustainable Transportation Alternatives in Your Community, Advocacy Institute, 1730 Rhode Island Ave., N.W., Ste. 600, Washington, D.C. 20036. (202) 659-8474.

Citizens Guide to Mass Transit: How to Use the Intermodal Surface Transportation Efficiency Act (ISTEA), Campaign for New Transportation Priorities. (202) 408-8362.

The Greenhouse Debate, Curtis Moore, National Wildlife Federation, 1989, 8925 Leesburg Pike, Vienna, VA 22184.

Steering a New Course: Transportation, Energy and Environment, Deborah Gordon, Island Press, 1991.

Surface Transportation Policy Project Resource Guide and Bulletin, Surface Transportation Policy Project. (202) 939-3470.

"Reinventing Transport," Marcia D. Lowe, in *State of the World: 1994*, Lester Brown et al., New York: Norton.

"TDM Programs: Profiles of Selected Universities," Tabitha Graves, *Campus Ecology Research Program Report No. 5*, University of Wisconsin-Madison, 1993.

Transportation Action Guide: Fair and Sustainable Mobility in the 1990's, Environmental Defense Fund, 257 Park Ave. South, New York, NY 10010. (212) 505-2375.

Transportation Resource Book, A Chesapeake Bay Foundation Resource Series, I(6), 1994, 162 Prince George St., Annapolis, MD 21401. (410) 268-8816.

Transportation Programs and Provisions of the Clean Air Act Amendments of 1990: A Summary, Federal Highway Administration, U.S. Department of Transportation, 400 7th St., SW, Washington, D.C. 20590. (202) 366-0660.

NETWORKING

Campus

If you find that an organization listed here has moved or a contact has been replaced, let the Campus Ecology Program staff know. We'll help match you with the latest source for the information you need.

Cornell University
Attn: William Wendt
Transportation Services
Ithaca, NY 14853
(607) 255-5592
Reports on a variety of TDM strategies.

University of Colorado at Boulder
Transportation Center
Boulder, CO 80309-0030
(303) 492-7152
Extensive Class I bike trails.

University of Illinois at Urbana-Champaign
Attn: Jim Trail, Transportation Safety
Facilities Management
Urbana, IL 61801
(217) 333-4122
e-mail: jimt@msmail.o&m.uiuc.edu
Comprehensive bicycle/ pedestrian planning documents; transit subsidies and incentives; community planning; ISTEA; closed-loop recycling in fleet maintenance.

University of Kansas at Lawrence
Environmental Ombudsman Program
Lawrence, KS 66045
(913) 864-4665
Recycling and pollution prevention in fleet maintenance.

University of North Carolina at Chapel Hill
Chapel Hill, NC 27514
(919) 962-7145
Fax: (919) 962-2572
Bicycle/pedestrian incentives, rideshare program.

University of Washington at
Seattle
Transportation Systems
Seattle, WA 98195
(206) 543-3535
*Comprehensive transportation
demand management program.*

University of Wisconsin at
Madison
Rm. 120 WARF Bldg.
610 Walnut St.
Madison, WI 53705
(608) 265-3417
*Will provide copies of 1993
comprehensive transportation
demand management survey,
and related reports.*

Regional and National

Bicycle Federation of America
1818 R St., N.W.
Washington, D.C. 20009
(202) 332-6986

Big 10 & Midwestern
Universities Transportation and
Parking Conference
Attn: Jim Trail, Transportation
Safety
University of Illinois
Urbana, IL 61801
e-mail:
jimt@msmail.o&m.uiuc.edu
*Copies of newsletter on
sustainable transportation issues
available to campus
transportation professionals.*

Clean Air Washington
6502 106th Ave., NE
Kirkland, WA 98033
(206) 827-8908

National Bike to Work Day
c/o Washington Area Bicycle
Association
1819 H St., NW, Ste. 640
Washington, D.C. 20006-3603
(202) 723-5625

National Wildlife Federation
Campus Ecology Program
1400 16th St., N.W.
Washington, D.C. 20036-2266
(202) 797-5435, N.E.
(404) 876-2608, S.E.
(313) 769-9970, M.W.
(503) 222-1429, W.
*Offers Campus Transportation
Resource Packet including
campus case studies on
transportation demand
management, bicycle/pedestrian
incentive programs, alternative
fuel vehicles, mass transit, using
ISTEA, and "critical mass ride"
organizing materials.*

CHAPTER 4

Energy and Utilities

Oil spills, strip mining, air pollution, accelerated climate change, acid rain . . . the health and environmental problems resulting from our heavy reliance on energy from fossil fuels are many. By using oil and coal to meet more than 80 percent of our energy needs, we have unnecessarily pitted energy against our environment.

Alternatives to our current patterns of consumption become more inviting with each decade of research and innovation. Renewable energy technology, which harnesses solar, geothermal or wind power, has now achieved efficiency levels comparable to those of fossil fuels and has become remarkably cost-competitive for many applications. It is estimated that every dollar invested in efficiency and renewables produces about twice as many jobs as a dollar invested in fossil or nuclear power.[1]

Cleaner fuels such as natural gas are gaining popularity for transportation and many other applications, and the nation is using fossil fuels and other nonrenewable energy sources more efficiently. Thanks largely to Amory Lovins of the Rocky Mountain Institute, who introduced energy professionals worldwide to the concept of the "negawatt" (a measure of energy conserved), many utilities in the U.S. now recognize that it is less expensive to reduce consumer demand for energy than to build new power plants. Thousands of institutions and households have received free or discounted energy-efficient products, rebates and other conservation incentives from farsighted utilities.

Although only a few campuses are at the forefront of the sustainable energy revolution, institutions of higher learning are anything but complacent about their energy use. Where campus concern for global stability and a healthy environment fails to overcome institutional inertia, the prospect of serious dollar savings often adds the necessary kick. If any campus pollution-prevention effort can be considered "money in the bank," the experience of the State University of New

Mary Jane Kosel displays some of the energy-efficient, money-saving lights now used at R.I.T.

1. *Energy for Employment*, 1992, p. 9. See bibliography.

York at Buffalo, Brevard Community College, the Rochester Institute of Technology and other campuses highlighted here demonstrates that the energy conservation and efficiency drive is that program.

Institutions of higher education have played a central role in researching and developing solar and other forms of renewable energy. Solar cars are just one campus application of this research. Austin College and Georgetown University use early incarnations of applied solar hot-water heating and photovoltaic technologies, while the Georgia Institute of Technology, University of South Florida, and Humboldt State University showcase a few of the more modern adaptations.

BUILDING AN ENERGY-EFFICIENT BASE

Whether or not campuses are ready for solar or other forms of renewable energy, most institutions are ripe for energy conservation and vast improvements in efficiency. While renewable energy technologies can be incorporated throughout an institution's energy infrastructure, the cost-effectiveness of some applications—such as photovoltaic-powered buildings—improves in proportion to energy efficiency. Leveraging such a shift in energy use, though, requires institutional will, often coupled with the know-how and dedication of a key individual. Campuses with progressive energy programs usually have progressive managers skilled at encouraging creative employees. The Rochester Institute of Technology (R.I.T.) is a case in point.

When Mary Jane Kosel secured a receptionist position in R.I.T.'s physical plant, she did not realize she had just launched her career in energy conservation. "I was always very inquisitive," says Kosel, "about how the computerized energy management system [EMCS] was used to change the temperature in response to requests."

It wasn't long before Kosel began operating the EMCS and plugging in equipment data for new buildings as well. From there, Lou Boyon, R.I.T.'s Director of Energy, encouraged her to develop expertise in lighting efficiency, to meet with lighting product manufacturers, and to help identify lighting upgrades. Eventually, Kosel began to assist Boyon in securing grants and rebates and in identifying new conservation projects. Although R.I.T. had a history of energy conservation and efficiency efforts stretching back to 1977, Kosel helped the university achieve its first decrease in electricity consumption in 21 years. In 1993, consumption plummeted by one million kilowatts—to 2 percent below 1992 levels. Boyon largely credits Kosel's success to her "contagious enthusiasm . . . . If you look at this as a straight job, you aren't going to go anywhere," he explains. "Whoever deals with energy or [the] environment has to be a super salesperson."

Whoever deals with energy or [the] environment has to be a super salesperson.

—Lou Boyon, R.I.T

Kosel is a harbinger of growing receptivity among campus administrators to the notion that it pays to provide innovative, driven staff with the support necessary for them to concentrate on conservation—preferably by creating a full-time position for a deserving candidate. After persistent student and faculty lobbying, Brown University created such a position in 1990 for a recent graduate and environmental activist, James Corless, whose results prompted Brown to retain the position when he moved on.

Now led by Kurt Teichert, the Brown is Green program facilitates a wide range of energy and other conservation projects and manages a corps of work-study students and volunteers. Similarly, in the early 1990s, the Tufts University facilities department financed a resource coordinator position for recent graduate Karen White, as the University of Rochester did for graduate student Morris Pierce. As Pierce writes in his chapter, "Campus Energy Management Programs," in *The Campus and Environmental Responsibility*:

> Although I came to the University of Rochester to work on a doctorate in history, the facilities director, William Daigneau, did not hesitate to employ my engineering skills to reduce his energy costs. After complaining for several months about the lack of a coherent energy program, I was hired (on a part-time basis) as the university energy manager, largely on my assurance that, at the very least, I would save the university in energy costs several times the amount of my salary.[2]

R.I.T.'s Kosel and Boyon note that providing staff for conservation programs is an approach that Walter Simpson, the energy officer at SUNY-Buffalo (UB), has advocated for years.

Simpson was hired in 1982 to spearhead Conserve UB, a comprehensive energy efficiency and conservation program that has resulted in considerable savings. Approximately 300 conservation projects between 1982 and 1993, says Simpson, shaved more than $3 million off the university's projected energy bill. Instead of spending an anticipated $22.5 million to provide power to 80 buildings and 8 million gross square feet, UB now spends less than $20 million per year. After spending $17–18 million on additional conservation projects, Simpson expects to see UB's annual energy bill reduced by another $2–3 million by mid-1996.

It was not simply the prospect of saving the university lots of money, however, that drew Simpson to UB. Prior to his arrival at UB, Simpson spent several years as a volunteer with the Western New York Peace Center, eventually serving as its director. By the late 1980s, the links Simpson perceived between peace and energy led him to pursue a second masters degree in environmental studies with a concentration on energy policy and technology. He explains, "I felt that if I

After spending $17–18 million on additional conservation projects, Simpson expects to see UB's annual energy bill reduced by another $2–3 million by mid-1996.

2. Eagan, Orr, eds., 1992, p. 32.

wanted to work for peace (and that was my primary motivation), I needed to learn something about energy and environmental issues . . . . I saw [for example] when the Soviets invaded Afghanistan, there was concern in the Carter Administration that they might go into Saudi Arabia for oil . . . that unless we address the energy issue, we might end up stumbling into nuclear war."

"Future wars like that in the Persian Gulf were almost inevitable," says Simpson, who in becoming energy officer at UB began what is now a 13-year effort to change the status quo on the institutional and state level.

The conservation guidelines Simpson has formulated might be reduced to the single principle that technical skills must be balanced with people skills. "The technical [work] is only part of it," he asserts; "a lot of what I do is really teaching and community organizing." Simpson divides his time among all three: "I have, in a sense, created a niche here that allows me to be interdisciplinary . . . to cross staff, faculty and student lines, get involved in different activities, and create new programs. Most all the activities that I have gotten involved in, whether helping to start an environmental task force, doing educational activities, or serving as an adjunct teacher . . . have been appreciated on some level, so I haven't had to continually defend myself."

Providing staff such as Simpson with the time, resources, and creative license to manage the demand for energy has made it possible for UB, R.I.T., and other campuses to tap a variety of rewards and incentives often ignored in more supply-driven atmospheres.

> The conservation guidelines Simpson has formulated, if reduced to a single principle, might be that technical skills must be balanced with people skills.

Finding Financial and Other Resources

Since 1977—with a marked acceleration in the mid-90s—more than $2 million-worth of energy efficiency programs at R.I.T. have been financed by the fines levied against major oil companies when they over-charge consumers. Funds resulting from these fines are distributed by the U.S. Department of Energy (DOE) to state energy offices, which in turn allocate them (usually in the form of 50/50 matching grants) on a competitive basis to public and private institutions. In 1993–94, such grants at R.I.T. helped finance occupancy sensors in five buildings, installation of more energy-efficient fluorescent T-8 lamps and electronic ballasts, a switch from incandescent exit lights to the new light-emitting diode (LED) exit fixtures, controls on stand-alone cooling units in one building, and heat-reflective glazing on two buildings. Even without the grants, the projects would have paid for themselves in an average of 3.5 years.

Utility rebates and incentive funds are financing $4.3 million of UB's $17–18 million demand side management (DSM) project, which Simpson describes in "Recharging Campus Energy Conservation" in the Winter 1994 issue of *Facilities*

WHEN ENERGY AND DOLLAR SAVINGS DON'T COINCIDE

by Walter Simpson, Energy Officer, SUNY Buffalo

JAMES ULRICH

Motivation for campus energy conservation may be environmental on the part of many campus energy coordinators, but higher level college and university administrators tend to concentrate on dollar savings. While these two motivations often overlap, this could change with electric utility deregulation. Many electric utilities are scrambling to develop new electric rates to keep their larger customers from building cogeneration plants or buying power from third party generators. Depending on how these new rates are structured, they can save the customer money while discouraging energy conservation.

For example, Niagara Mohawk recently offered UB a new two-tiered energy rate with low marginal electric rates for all electricity consumed after consumption exceeds a pre-established baseline. This rate would undermine financial incentives for conservation because conservation is evaluated at the margin. Lower marginal rates significantly lengthen the payback of contemplated energy measures, possibly putting them out of reach.

I have protested this rate structure to the utility and the New York State Public Service Commission and asked UB to insist that NiMo develop a more socially responsible marginal rate proposal which maintains the full savings potential of energy conservation measures. While this resistance has not won me any friends, I am fighting the Niagara Mohawk proposal because it could destroy our campus energy conservation effort.

In my opinion, addressing this issue is crucial because it goes to the heart of the national debate over the future of the electric industry. It has taken years for state public service commissions to encourage or compel electric utilities to promote energy conservation and demand side management. We can't stand by and let all this progress evaporate as utilities do anything in their power to hold on to large customers whose only interest is the lowest possible electric rate.

> Depending on how new rates are structured, they can save the customer money while discouraging energy conservation.
>
> — Walter Simpson, SUNY Buffalo

Manager magazine. When UB's DSM project was being developed, their local utility, Niagara Mohawk Power Corporation (NiMo), was providing subsidies of more than $1,000 per kilowatt of reduced demand to customers working with CES/Way International, a Houston-based energy services company (ESCO) now under contract with NiMo to reduce the power company's demand by eight megawatts. CES/Way's contract requires the company to guarantee the persistence of savings for 15 years and to implement customer-oriented comprehensive energy conservation projects which combine long and short payback measures, conditions that Simpson found not only acceptable but desirable.

With the help of physical plant staff and Professors Sandra Gilchrest and Kenneth Tucker, students at the New College in Sarasota, Florida, estimated financial costs, resource savings and paybacks for water and energy-efficiency projects in the Pei Dorms.

SAVINGS FROM ENERGY INNOVATIONS AT ONE CAMPUS
Conservation at New College in 1990

Change	Cost	Annual Resource Savings	Annual Dollar Savings	Estimated Payback
Shower heads	$462	902,400 gal (20 pools)	$4,512	1 month
Toilets	$2115	532,980 gal (12 pools)	$2679	10 months
Faucets	$4,653	2,538,000 gal (55 pools)	$12,690	4 months
Lighting	$42,307	246,693 kWh (411 oil barrels)	$17,898	2.4 years
Fans	$13,395	104,678 kWh (174 oil barrels)	$6,804	2 years
Window Film Passive Heat	$5,456 $45,000	not determinable 260,147 kWh	$764 $18,210	7.1 years 2.5 years
Dehumidification Chiller	$97,500	(435 oil barrels) 354,000 kWh	$27,000	3.6 years
Air Handlers	$163,560	(590 oil barrels) 303,206 kWh	$21,224	7.7 years
Totals	$374,448	3,973,380 gal (87 pools) 1,268,724 kWh (2115 oil barrels)	$111,781	

The most common approach to energy conservation projects is to do the less expensive, quick payback measures first. There is, however, a danger in this approach, says Simpson, since it may make it difficult to impossible to ever financially justify the measures which take longer to pay for themselves. When quick payback projects are completed, the savings these projects generate rarely are made available to help finance longer payback measures; typically, the savings are used for other, more immediate purposes. That leaves the longer payback projects "standing alone," and on that basis they may never seem attractive enough to be addressed.

UB, with the help of CES/Way, solved that problem by developing a large, comprehensive project which includes both long and short payback measures, in effect using the latter to leverage or help finance the former. "By doing it all at once," Simpson explains, "it all gets done!"

In addition to identifying financing for projects, campus energy coordinators must expose and overcome the financial disincentives to conserve energy. This is especially true at most state educational institutions. Simpson, for example, has lobbied to stop the SUNY central office's practice of siphoning off energy savings produced at individual SUNY campuses. "Energy conservation will never take hold," he argued, "if those who produce the savings can't benefit by them." Another approach to overcoming disincentives, Simpson has found, is to use life-cycle cost analysis when evaluating proposed energy measures. (See *Life-Cycle Costing* by the National Technical Information Service and the DOE's *Life-Cycle Costing Manual*, listed in the bibliography at the end of this chapter.) Success in this area will require some re-engineering, notes Simpson, at the many schools which still make decisions based on simple payback and other short-term principles.

Although the federal government has abandoned many of its tax and financial incentives for renewable energy, some state governments and utilities have begun new programs. A survey conducted by the North Carolina Solar Center (NCSC) identified 24 states that offer one or more incentive programs for solar applications. Seven states, they report, have income tax credits, 16 offer property tax exemptions, four offer industry recruitment incentives, and six states have sales tax exemptions. Perhaps of greater interest to universities, eight states have loan programs for solar technology and other energy-conserving technology, and eight states have special grant programs which cover solar applications. Progressive utility companies offer a variety of incentives, including equipment leasing options, customer rebates, grant programs, and loan programs.[3]

Lou Boyon and Mary Jane Kosel pose with the fuel cell that powers their microelectronics building. The fuel cell strips hydrogen from natural gas in a chemical reformer to generate electrochemical power. First used on NASA missions and adapted for commercial use, the fuel cell saves R.I.T. more than $40,000 annually.

3. "State and Utility Financial Incentives," 1993, pp. 11–14.

Although organizations which provide information and consultation seldom finance projects directly, they often help campuses save money in the long run. Campus energy conservation coordinators tout the benefits of such programs as the U.S. Environmental Protection Agency's Green Lights campaign: "The updated materials they send us with new energy-efficient technologies every six months or so is an advantage," says R.I.T.'s Kosel, "and their newsletter keeps us informed on what colleges, universities, hospitals and businesses have done to upgrade their facilit[ies]."

An array of information and technical assistance for energy efficiency and renewable energy projects is available through the programs listed in the networking section of this chapter.

Least-Cost Opportunities

Of the five major sectors in which energy can be conserved and provided more efficiently on campuses—insulation, ventilation, lighting, office equipment, and heating and cooling—lighting usually has been the easiest and least expensive to transform. And that transformation has been a significant one. After surveying R.I.T. facilities, Boyon and Kosel concluded that about 30 percent of the energy used on campus is for lighting; 40 percent for heating, air conditioning and ventilation; 10–15 percent for processing equipment, such as printing presses and other major teaching aids; and the remaining 15–20 percent for office equipment, computers and other appliances used by students and staff.

Low-tech lighting initiatives on campuses fall into two categories—conservation and efficiency. Conservation, on the one hand, encompasses those energy-saving measures which eliminate waste without overhauling technology, focusing instead on people and habits: shutting off lights, using only the light, water or heat necessary, etc. Energy efficiency, on the other hand, employs relatively new technology to provide comparable lighting, cooling, heating, etc., while expending less energy.

Conservation-oriented lighting changes are some of the simplest and most affordable. They include reducing light levels, delamping (eliminating some lights), adding light switches, installing devices such as photocells and occupancy sensors, and other measures to eliminate wasteful light usage. In 1992–94, Boyon and Kosel installed in 12 R.I.T. buildings a total of 600 occupancy sensors, which automatically turn lights off after several minutes in which they detect no motion. Occupancy sensors generate significant savings in common areas such as class and meeting rooms, where lights are frequently left on. Boyon and Kosel estimate that their 600 sensors reduce electricity use by 325,938 kilowatts annually, for a savings of $24,461 per year.

The switch from incandescent lights to long-life, compact fluorescents saves energy, labor, and dollars.

Identifying areas on campuses where lights are not needed or where light levels can safely be reduced has also proved fruitful. "We found we could delamp— i.e. disconnect—50 percent of the corridor lights in most of our campus buildings and still have adequate illumination levels," writes UB's Walter Simpson in his "Recipe for an Effective Campus Energy Conservation Program."[4] Disconnecting unnecessary entrance lamps in just two R.I.T. buildings saved an estimated $432 annually.

The bulk of energy-efficiency projects on campuses also involve lighting. 1993–94 saw a frenzy of exit sign replacement and other improvements in lighting efficiency at R.I.T. By replacing the 40-watt incandescent exit signs with 5-watt light-emitting diodes (LEDs) in 25 buildings, R.I.T. achieved an estimated $36,000 (220,000 kilowatts) annual energy cost reduction. Because LEDs are replaced only every 25 years, the virtual elimination of maintenance and disposal costs is a key benefit. "Perhaps the greatest advantage is the safety factor," adds Boyon, since LEDs are less vulnerable to the power surges, vibrations, and other conditions which damage incandescent exit lights.

Campuses began switching from incandescents to compact-fluorescent bulbs and ballasts in the late 1980s and, by the mid-1990s, had begun substituting T-8 fixtures (ultra-efficient 32-watt fluorescent lamps and electronic ballasts) for less efficient fluorescent fixtures. By replacing 800 incandescent bulbs with compact-fluorescent bulbs and ballasts between 1992 and 1994, R.I.T. saved approximately $27,000 a year—with an average payback of three months! "These lights are on 18 hours per day," explains Kosel, adding, "We have many opportunities like this and are replacing incandescent lamps almost continuously." R.I.T. has saved an additional half a million kilowatts and $23,461 annually by replacing older T-12 fluorescent lamps and magnetic ballasts with T-8 lamps and electronic ballasts in four buildings. A similar conversion at UB is underway for 50,000 light fixtures.

In addition to lighting projects, campuses have implemented a variety of other measures to promote energy conservation and improve efficiency. On the conservation side, they have insulated buildings; instituted heating, ventilating, and air-conditioning (HVAC) policies; and, more recently, encouraged conservation-minded computer and office equipment habits (see Chapter 6, Communication Service, which covers this burgeoning sector of campus resource use).

On the efficiency side, campuses have reduced water use and water heating costs by retrofitting toilets and installing energy-efficient faucets and showerheads. Residence halls are obvious candidates for such overhauls. After testing a number of models, Bob Francisco, the director of student life at the Colorado School

Boyon and Kosel estimate that their 600 sensors reduce electricity use by 325,938 kilowatts annually, for a savings to R.I.T. of $24,461 per year.

4. 1991, p. 8.

of Mines, chose a non-aerated, low-flow showerhead that uses 2.5 gallons of water per minute for installation in the 56 showers in campus residence halls. "I would venture to say we were putting out 15 gallons per minute, because we had those old nozzle showerheads that put out some serious water," admits Francisco. UB's Simpson tested various showerheads and also decided to use a non-aerated, low-flow design because "they give a better shower and don't cool off the water as much." By installing 200 energy-saving showerheads, UB saved an estimated $28,000 a year in seven of its residence halls. Brown University, which retrofitted 750 showers with low-flow heads, expected to recoup its cost of $11,368 in less than six months, saving an anticipated $26,066 per year.

These are only the first in a flurry of improvements in energy efficiency expected on campuses by the turn of the century. New developments in efficient lighting, according to the Rocky Mountain Institute, include ultra-thin fluorescent tubes, "pocket-sized" compact fluorescent lamps, and "smart" lights with built-in controls.

Thinking Big

Even budget-strapped state institutions of higher education, with their often complex decision-making structures, are finding ways to finance comprehensive energy conservation programs with long-range goals in mind. Such projects have involved capturing waste heat, improving the efficiency of motors in water pumps and air fans, cogeneration, and in several instances, the use of renewable energy technologies. The initial investments of time and money exceed that required for the simpler retrofits described above, but the financial and resource savings over time can be considerable.

SUNY Buffalo

Energy Officer Simpson has identified building heating and air-conditioning systems and lab ventilation as two of the largest remaining energy-saving opportunities at UB. CES/Way International, UB's energy services company, has identified 200 areas where the use of motors can be made more efficient. Many buildings, especially those designed 10 years ago

INDOOR AIR QUALITY AND SOLID WASTE

When weatherizing buildings and upgrading lighting, collaborating with campus purchasing and recycling staff can be helpful. Why? Because the better-insulated a building, the more important indoor air quality becomes, and purchasers can help identify non-toxic paints, finishes, carpets, and cleaning products that will enhance environmental health and safety. The switch to ultra-efficient lighting may also entail dealing with considerable solid and hazardous waste. Campus recyclers and purchasers can help arrange for recycling and hazardous-waste recovery from old lamps and ballasts. Kevin Lyons, the senior buyer at Rutgers University has assisted staff with both issues. See Chapter 1, Procurement, for details and contact information.

or earlier, explains Simpson, have fan systems that were designed to run at a constant volume to meet the temperature control demands of 100 percent occupancy on the worst-case day—90 degrees at 90 percent humidity. However, "you are at the worst case less than 2 percent of the year," says Simpson, "and you rarely have full occupancy." By retrofitting constant-volume fan systems with variable-speed drives, Simpson anticipates UB can "satisfy comfort and indoor air quality issues by operating at 70–90 percent of full volume for much of the year." By cutting the air flow even 10 percent in these systems, he says, fan horsepower is reduced by nearly 30 percent—in proportion to the cube of fan speed reduction.

Lab buildings represent a magnification of typical ventilation problems, notes Simpson, who has made UB lab buildings his top priority for conservation: "With 100 percent ventilation . . . because you have fumes and toxic materials in laboratory fume hoods, you not only have all the fan horsepower moving perhaps more air than you need, but you have all that air that has to be heated during the winter or air-conditioned during the summer."

By reducing air flow, switching fuel, and recovering heat via an underground chilled-water loop and glycol "run-around" loops, Simpson expects to reduce the $1.8-million electric bill for two connected lab buildings by $500,000 a year. Installation of a variable air-volume hood control system in the College of Science at R.I.T. has saved an estimated $27,521 and 433,733 kilowatts each year, and paid for itself in just over five years.

Brevard Community College

With five campuses and centers, Brevard Community College (BCC) in Cocoa Beach, Florida, is one of the largest community colleges in the nation. In the early 1980s, BCC initiated a comprehensive energy-conservation and management program, which included installing motion sensors and computer-managed air conditioning and lighting control systems; installing lower-wattage fluorescent lights; and using waste heat generated by high-efficiency chillers to heat an Olympic-size swimming pool during the winter months.

As a result of these and many other ongoing efficiency improvements, BCC's total electric bill between 1982 and 1989 rose by only $1—despite inflation of 25 percent and a 25 percent increase in campus square-footage in that period. According to a college BCC press release, the college saved close to 50 million kilowatts in the first seven years of the program and $6 million in the first decade. Harold Creel, the associate vice president of plant maintenance and operations, was instrumental in instituting these changes. BCC President Maxwell King, its board of trustees, the college's business office, and the public relations staff play crucial

Brevard Community College's total electric bill between 1982 and 1989 rose by only $1—despite inflation of 25 percent and a 25 percent increase in campus square-footage in that period.

roles in the program's financing, publicity, and continuity.

Brevard Community College's Cocoa Campus, shared with the University of Central Florida, will soon house the Florida Solar Energy Center's state-of-the-art New Energy Center. The building is anticipated to use 30 percent of the energy and one-third the peak demand of its 70,000-square-foot counterparts elsewhere in the state. Proper siting and the use of lighting sensors to automatically adjust wattage relative to the amount of natural light available together optimize "day-lighting," the use of natural light indoors. Spectrally selective windows will transmit visible light but greatly reduce the amount of heat lost or gained.

Carleton University

In the fall of 1993, Carleton University in Ottawa, Canada, launched a $20-million energy conservation program. Highlights of their program include replacing 60,000 fluorescent fixtures with more energy-efficient tubes and electronic ballasts, installing a new cogeneration facility, and using geothermal storage to heat buildings in winter. The geothermal system stores water 100 meters below the more extreme temperatures of the earth's surface, saving on both air conditioning in the summer and heating in the winter. The savings from these and other energy efficiency projects are anticipated to total $2 million a year; the projects will pay for themselves within ten years.[5] Bryan Beazer, the physical plant director who instituted these changes, was an enthusiastic player in the energy roundtable which helped produce the *Blueprint for a Green Campus*, a series of recommendations for improving higher education curricula and operations, drafted at the Campus Earth Summit held at Yale University in February 1994.

Public Participation

Launching energy conservation programs on campuses clearly entails more than pasting "a penny saved is a penny earned" or "turn it off" stickers over light switches. Indeed, campaigns like these, though moderately effective, are viewed with skepticism by many energy management professionals, who often forego student and staff involvement in favor of technology that will compensate for human neglect. By applying some creativity, however, campus energy coordinators have elevated the role of public participation beyond mere gimmicks and rhetoric. Where these programs have not become an integral, sustained component of energy conservation, they have at least made more than a marginal difference during their duration.

Carleton University's geothermal system stores water 100 meters below the more extreme temperatures of the earth's surface, reducing air conditioning costs in the summer and heating costs in the winter.

5. "Saving Energy: Prosperity at No Cost," 1993, p. 30.

Building Conservation Contacts

With the help of UB's recycling coordinator and student assistants, Simpson coordinates a team of volunteer "building conservation contacts." Much like the program at UNC-Chapel Hill promoting transportation alternatives (see transportation chapter), the building contacts program at UB relies on volunteer monitors to disseminate information about university environmental policies, monitor participation levels, and act as liaisons to UB's conservation programs and its environmental task force.

Contacts receive an "environmental checklist"—which, in addition to energy, covers solid waste, hazardous waste, water, purchasing, and transportation. Contacts are asked to turn off unused lights and office equipment, including computers; maintain a heating-season temperature of 68 degrees and a cooling-season temperature of 76 degrees; and report overheated and undercooled areas. They are also asked to identify conservation opportunities, such as areas where lower-wattage equipment could be used.

Simpson also raises energy awareness by posting annual building energy costs in the entry vestibule of all campus buildings. The primary obstacle to the use of this tactic on many other campuses, however, is the absence or unreliability of building utility meters. In 1990, James Halligan, president of New Mexico State University, authorized the physical plant to allocate $35,000 for the installation of electric meters "to better monitor the timing and magnitude of electrical demand" as part of a campus-wide energy conservation and efficiency initiative.

Student Research

Students have provided valuable research assistance to campus energy managers. Morris Pierce's evaluation of potential savings at the University of Rochester led to the creation of his job as university energy manager. He, in turn, has involved students in research and other energy conservation projects. Student interns at Stetson University researched opportunities for reducing energy use through improved building and classroom scheduling. Graduate students in the natural resources program at the University of Waterloo have conducted research on the applicability of solar hot water heating and photovoltaic-power for a wide variety of specific buildings and needs.

Mary Jane Kosel and Lou Boyon at R.I.T. have trained students to conduct energy audits and have assisted them with class research projects ranging from the feasibility of wind turbine use on campus to opportunities for the use of LED exit signs. The students who conducted the LED study mapped out dozens of areas on campus where exit signs could be switched, greatly assisting Kosel and Boyon with this enormous project. Says Kosel of student involvement, "We can

> The building contacts program at UB relies on volunteer monitors to disseminate information about university energy and environmental policies, monitor participation levels, and act as liaisons to UB's environmental task force.

teach students what to look for in a building. As a matter of fact, most of the field work is performed by students. They enjoy working with us; it takes them behind the scenes on campus and they learn what effect energy use has on their lives."

Inter-dormitory Energy Conservation Contests

Known as Green Cup competitions and often based on the contest begun at Harvard University in 1990–91, inter-dorm energy- and resource-conservation contests have yielded impressive results on several campuses. In spring of 1990, core members of Harvard's Environmental Action Committee mentioned to Michael Lichten, director of facilities for the Faculty of Arts and Sciences, the possibility of creating some kind of conservation competition. That fall, Lichten called the group members into his office to pursue the idea further. Not only had Lichten delineated a pattern of increased resource consumption at Harvard (a 15 percent increase over five years), but oil prices were rising as a result of the crisis in the Persian Gulf.

> Lichten offered students a budget of $5,000 for coordination of Harvard's Green Cup Campaign.

Lichten offered students a budget of $5,000 for coordination of the campaign, which consisted of four elements: (1) data processing, (2) dorm coordinating, (3) a media campaign, and (4) prizes. The plant managers of the houses and the house superintendents, to whom organizers sent letters enlisting their participation, proved integral to the campaign. In the six months from October to March, the competition saved the university approximately half a million dollars and energy consumption decreased by 25 percent.

George Washington University, the University of Wisconsin at Madison, Tufts University, and others have subsequently held their own Green Cups. While each campus experienced decreases in resource use, especially in the areas of water use and water heating costs, none of the campuses mentioned above sustained their programs beyond the first or second year. Although a relatively effective program educationally and environmentally for some campuses, the Green Cup effort can be difficult to sustain.

But given sufficient support, campus energy officers can involve students and other staff in myriad projects designed to prevent pollution and save money. These projects—whether research programs, building conservation contact networks, or a Green Cup competition—have helped to channel student and staff enthusiasm for a clean energy future in ways that are cost-effective for the campuses and compatible with their educational missions.

❧ LOOKING FORWARD: RENEWABLE ENERGY

At first glance, it appears that sustainable energy technology is still on the sidelines in the campus energy game. Throughout the years when oil enjoyed heavy subsidies and artificially low prices, solar and other renewable energy competed, at best, on an uneven playing field. Many of the matching grants and incentives which in the late 1970s and early 1980s helped campuses launch alternative energy projects had disappeared by the mid-1980s. Given the odds, one might expect to find just a few dilapidated solar panels at a handful of campuses—but the reality shines a little brighter.

On dozens of campuses, prize-winning solar cars are the most headline-grabbing (if not the most replicable) applications of renewable energy. According to Daniel Cuoghi, Technical Specialist at the Energy Efficiency and Renewable Energy Clearinghouse, in the first American Solar Cup, held in September 1988 in Visalia, California, the only car to finish the race was one built by MIT students. The racecourse covered 160 miles and the winning car was clocked at 85 mph. Thirty-two universities competed in the first Sunrayce USA sponsored in 1990 by the U.S. Department of Energy (DOE), General Motors and others. The University of Michigan team, made up of 100 students, won both the 1990 race and the subsequent one in 1993.

In addition to the Sunrayce, the federal government has helped finance dozens of solar research and development programs and a number of showcase solar energy applications at colleges and universities. Although federal funding for renewable energy research and development pales in comparison to that for non-renewable energy, academic funding remains a priority for the DOE's solar program. "We look at the universities and colleges for innovative research," says Jim Rannels, director of the DOE's Photovoltaic Technology Division. "They have excellent ideas that can help us push the envelope of technical performance to meet our long-term goals."

The DOE's National Renewable Energy Laboratory (NREL) awarded more than 150 research

CAMPUSES SUPPORT SUN DAY

Sun Day is to energy conservation and renewable energy what Earth Day is to broader issues of environmental awareness. Sun Day, usually held on April 24, offers a forum for campus renewable-energy enthusiasts, schools, businesses, non-profits and others. On Sun Day, campuses nationwide schedule conferences and hearings on sustainable energy policies, conduct energy audits, and survey available library books on energy issues. For ideas on how your campus can support Sun Day, call the Campus Ecology Program.

Sun by day, light by night: The Meadowcreek Environmental Retreat and Education Center in Fox, Arkansas, uses solar hot-water heating and PV-powered electricity.

contracts totaling more than $47 million to 54 colleges in 25 states between 1980 and 1989. Universities receiving more than five contracts since 1980 include Colorado State, Harvard, North Carolina State, Stanford, the University of Colorado, and the University of Delaware. More than 80 university students from 35 institutions have received advanced degrees since 1985 under full or partial support of NREL. According to NREL, most of these graduates go on to develop renewable energy technology in high-tech industry, in government, or as postdoctoral researchers and professors. Their research topics cover a wide range of solar cell materials and devices, including amorphous silicon, polycrystalline thin films, high-efficiency concepts, and crystalline silicon—all meant to move more photovoltaic technology out of the laboratories and into the marketplace.

Research Becomes Practice

Through their own purchases of applied solar and other clean-energy technology, campuses can help stimulate the domestic market. Solar hot-water heating and electrical applications on campuses, while less mediagenic than solar cars, compete more effectively against fossil-fuel technology.

The cost, performance, and ability to store and distribute solar energy have improved dramatically. Despite the market impediments, photovoltaic (PV) paneling (which converts sunlight to electricity) is one-tenth as expensive in the mid-1990s as it was in the early 1980s. Electricity from large-scale solar power generating stations, such as the Solar One demonstration system in California and the Solar Total Energy Project in Shenandoah, Georgia, costs less than 10 cents a kilowatt (only 2 cents a kilowatt above the national average) in a number of applications.[6]

The performance of renewable technologies, according to Rannels of DOE, has risen steadily—to levels comparable to fossil fuels and nuclear power. The efficiency with which fossil fuels or nuclear energy is converted to electricity is approximately 35 percent; photovoltaic laboratory cells have converted sunlight at about the same rate and, with the development of new cell materials, are expected to become even more efficient.[7]

Researchers have developed increasingly effective batteries and other devices for storing and transporting solar energy. Solar hydrogen technology may be the most promising development yet. The Schatz Solar Hydrogen Project at Humboldt State University's Telonicher Marine Laboratory is one campus application. Making use of the natural solar hydrogen cycle, solar electricity is harnessed to split water into hydrogen and oxygen. The clean-burning hydrogen fuel can be stored indefinitely and transported by pipeline. In Humboldt State's case, the solar-generated fuel powers an air compressor used to aerate fish tanks.[8]

Solar Hot Water Systems

Campus solar projects implemented in the late 1970s and early 1980s have often involved more trial and error and have proved less cost-effective and higher-maintenance than the applications of today.

A solar hot water heating (SWH) system at Austin College, a small liberal arts college in Sherman, Texas, and a large photovoltaic array on the student center at Georgetown University, in Washington, D.C., illustrate campuses' early experience with solar technology. While no longer state-of-the-art and never a central source of campus energy, both systems generate a good deal of positive P.R. and prompt many inquiries from businesses, local homeowners, and other campuses.

Financed via a matching grant from the federal government in 1977, Austin College's SWH system is an impressive one, with more than 150 panels stretching across a parking lot next to the gymnasium. The initial goal was to heat the gymnasium's pool and showers. For a variety of reasons, however, the system was disconnected and lay dormant until the arrival of Roy Griffin, a retiree from Texas Instruments. Throughout his 26 years at Texas Instruments, Griffin liked to tinker with systems to save energy—designing a set of coils, for example, that

Photovoltaic paneling, which converts sunlight to electricity, is one-tenth as expensive in the mid-1990s as it was in the early 1980s.

6 *Renewable Energy Fact Sheets*, 1993, p. 5

7. *The NIRS Energy Audit Manual*, 1992, p. 57.

8. *Solar Today*, Sept/Oct., 1994, p. 21.

With what we have right now, I am convinced that we can heat half this campus off those solar panels.

—Roy Griffin, Austin College

went around the stacks off the boiler, heating the air for a five-story warehouse, or, with a colleague, diverting water used to cool compressors for a second use washing the filters in air-handling units. Austin College's solar hot water heater, with its mystifying problems, was a natural for Griffin.

After initial inspections, it was clear that the SWH system had not been designed for high pressure, says Griffin. "They put normal line valves just like the ones for a normal city water system in there, and the water got so hot that it distorted the teflon fitting on the ball valves to where you can't open or close them."

To remedy this, he plans to install high-pressure steam hoses between the panels so that if they expand or rupture, they will not explode. He will also add reliefs with automatic valves, "so that if somebody closes a valve or otherwise creates pressure downstream, diaphragms will rupture and dump water onto the concrete near a drain."

There are other problems. The panels were placed so close together that when the sun strikes at the optimum angle for heating, only about a fourth of the panels in the interior section are exposed. "They are made on racks where they can be tilted to the sun, but they are so close together that you can't," Griffin explains. There are also many more panels than needed to heat the pool. Griffin plans to use only a third of the panels, space them out so they can be rotated, and redesign the system to heat the pool and showers. He has also removed the plants and trees that had grown between panels.

Griffin has plans for the extra panels, as well. "With what we have right now, I am convinced," he says, "that we can heat half this campus off those solar panels." To do so, he will have to build storage for the hot water. "With thermal storage we could probably cut our boiler use in half," he explains, by pre-heating water to 85 or 90 degrees with the solar panels before it enters the heat exchanger on the boiler, and then using less energy to heat water to the desired temperature. Solar pre-heating can be used to reduce air-heating costs, as well.

Austin College's experience with their solar water heating system—which will require modifications before reaching satisfactory efficiency—is mirrored in numerous solar applications in the Florida public school system. 1982 Florida legislation required all new schools that would use 1,000 gallons or more of hot water a day to investigate SHW. Site inspections and surveys conducted by the Florida Solar Energy Center (FSEC) between 1983 and 1993 revealed that, of the approximately 80 SHW systems in the public school system, 50 percent were not working at all. Even where systems operated satisfactorily, subsequent technical inspections by the FSEC showed that relatively few systems performed optimally.

But FSEC technicians were able to restore and improve the operation of 40 percent of the systems within one visit; another 25 percent of the systems had correctable problems but required more attention.[9]

FSEC Director Dr. David Block encourages campuses to give solar technology a second—and better-informed—try. "Over 20 years of applied experience and technical improvements," he says, "make SWH systems an excellent energy investment for colleges, particularly those with swimming pools, food services, dormitories or other areas which require a lot of hot water." Tufts University in Medford, Massachusetts, which conducted a feasibility study for SWH on their campus, concluded that SWH would be appropriate for their dining service, where large quantities of hot water are used to wash dishes. Patricia Lee, Tufts dining service director, is evaluating SHW systems for inclusion in upcoming renovations. With proper freeze protection and well-constructed storage, SWH systems can be cost-effective in particular applications, even for campuses in northern climates.

Photovoltaic Systems

Photovoltaic (PV) systems, which generate electricity from sunlight, are another solar energy application for campuses. Larger-scale projects include the photovoltaic array at Georgetown University, a PV-powered natatorium at Georgia Tech, and a PV-powered electric-car recharging station at the University of South Florida.

Photovolatic panels grace the roofline of Georgetown University's Intercultural Center.

Georgetown University

The Georgetown PV system, although dated, is large and striking. The slanted roof of the 214,000-square-foot Intercultural Center was specially designed in 1981 for the PV array installed in 1984. The panels provide approximately 300,000 kilowatts annually, 50 percent of the building's average electricity requirements. There is no storage system, so on the rare days when the array generates more electricity than the building needs, the power is sent to other buildings. Energy savings are estimated at $30,000 annually, but the system cost $5 million (as much as 10 times what it might cost in the mid-1990s)

9. "Technical Inspections . . ." 1989, pp. 1–8.

A solar recharging station powers a fleet of electric vehicles at the University of South Florida.

and, while it has been virtually maintenance-free, the panels require a $15,000 cleaning every few years. Georgetown's PV system is rated at eight percent efficiency (significantly lower than modern PV technology), but even so, says Jon Miller, Georgetown's environmental coordinator, the staff appreciates the system: "We had a problem a few months back on the converter and had to have a part made, so there was some downtime there, but overall, it has been a very effective and successful system for augmenting our energy usage."

University of South Florida

The solar recharging station for electrical vehicles at the University of South Florida was installed as part of a state-wide effort to encourage the use of clean cars. Four vehicles in the campus fleet of six are continuously charged by the 20-kilowatt PV-array until they are needed. It takes about eight hours to fully charge the vehicles, which have an average range of 90 miles. "Better batteries and lighter chassis," anticipates Howard Lamb, one of the project's researchers, "will quadruple this range within as few as 10 years." Any excess power generated is sold to the local utility. System designers are conducting a series of engineering tests, including monitoring the power produced by PV panels installed in different orientations to the sun. "I can foresee a day in the near future," says Lamb, "when stores will attract customers by allowing them to plug their vehicles into the utility grid for free while looking around—and, hopefully, the utility, like SMUD [the Sacramento Municipal Utility District], will be solar- or wind-powered."

Georgia Institute of Technology

With support from the Sandia National Laboratory, the DOE, and the Olympic Committee, the Facilities Department at the Georgia Institute of Technology is constructing a largely PV-powered natatorium. PV panels incorporated into the roof structure will power water pumps for the swimming pool, as well as lights in the natatorium. Rannels of DOE expects this project not only to introduce PV technology to the 1 billion people who watch the Olympic Games, but also to demonstrate "how American technology is at the forefront of these applications."

According to Rannels, "over 70 percent of the equipment that is produced in the United States is exported."

Bridges to Renewable Energy

Until buildings are designed to be more energy efficient, PV paneling will continue to seem expensive for many applications. "In general, prices still favor fossil fuels," admits Rannels, "but that is changing. When you look at niche or specific applications, there are a lot of places where the market is rapidly growing and a lot of applications where PVs are not only environmentally attractive but have solid cost benefits."

Two such PV applications are not yet common in campus settings, but are nevertheless highly practical for campuses concerned about safety. Almost all new emergency call boxes on U.S. highways, for example, are PV-powered, says Rannels. These and PV-powered, motion-sensor actuated lights are especially cost-effective where campuses would otherwise have to extend power lines. "The Sacramento Utility District in California," relates Rannels, "wanted to install lights in an alley—this is an urban environment thoroughly served by their grid—but they found it would be less expensive and far quicker to simply bolt PV-powered lights to the sides of buildings than to extend electrical service to the point of use."

If solar and other forms of renewable energy are to become the cornerstone of the nation's energy infrastructure, more campuses will need to help make this gradual transition. Using solar emergency call boxes and motion-sensor lights and involving students in the identification of other applications where renewable energy technologies would be cost-effective are good first steps. By retrofitting older buildings to be more efficient and designing ultra-efficient new buildings, meanwhile, staff and students are helping to bring the U.S. closer to the possibilities of renewable energy and a clean energy future.

When you look at niche applications, there are a lot of applications where PVs not only are environmentally attractive but have solid cost benefits.

— Jim Rannels
Photovoltaic
Technology Division,
DOE

BIBLIOGRAPHY

"1993 State Survey-Solar in the USA," *Solar Industry Journal*, First Quarter, 1993, pp. 21–28.

Apartment Energy Audit, Allen Cook, David Lindsay, and Jason Kennedy, Rochester Institute of Technology, Spring Quarter, 1993. (Student report; see Campus Ecology for more information.)

"Barriers to Energy Efficiency and Renewable Energy," Hal Harvey and Bill Keepin, *Energy From Crisis to Solution*, The Energy Foundation, 1991, pp. 28–32. (415) 546-7400.

Brown is Green: Program Summary Year Two, Brown University, 1992.

"Building Conservation Contact Network: A Program of the University's Task Force," Walter Simpson, SUNY Buffalo, April 11, 1994. (716) 645-3636. (Includes environmental checklist.)

"Campus Energy Management Programs," Morris A. Pierce, *The Campus and Environmental Responsibility*, David Eagan and David Orr, Eds., Jossey-Bass Publishers, No. 77, Spring, 1992, pp. 31–44.

"Campus Utility Use and Impacts at Tufts University," Margaret McClennen, and Sarah Hammond Creighton, Center for Environmental Management, August, 1992. (617) 381-3486.

"Can Brown Be Green?" James Corless and Harold Ward, *The Campus and Environmental Responsibility*, David Eagan and David Orr, Eds., Jossey-Bass Publishers, No. 77, Spring, 1992, pp. 45–54.

"Clemson University Energy Conservation Program," *South Carolina Wildlife Federation College Conservation Award*, Spring, 1994. (803) 703-8626.

"Creative Funding of Energy Conservation Projects," *Critical Issues in Facilities Management: 6 Energy Management*, Association of Physical Plant Administrators of Universities and Colleges, 1992. (703) 684-1446.

"Developing an Economically Efficient Energy Conservation Program: An Analysis of Conservation Programs Which Decrease Energy Use and Budgetary Expenditures in the Memorial Union at the University of Wisconsin-Madison as well as at Other State Owned Facilities," Neil Michaud, Campus Ecology Research Project, University of Wisconsin-Madison, May, 1993. (608) 265-3417.

"EC343 Energy Efficiency Assignment," Eban Ebstein, Skidmore College, 1992. (Contact Campus Ecology Program for details.)

Ecolink: Where Energy and Education Meet, Florida Solar Energy Center, 300 SR 401, Cape Canaveral, FL 32920.

Energy Conservation, Kevin O'Brien and David Korn, Center for Study of Responsive Law, 1981. (Colleges and universities respond to energy price increases in the late 1970s early 1980s; numerous case studies.)

"Energy Conservation Due Renewed Efforts," *Florida Today*, Sec. A-8, October, 1990. (Brevard Community College's total electric bill rises only one dollar between 1982 and 1989.)

"Energy Conservation Log 1977-1994," Physical Plant Energy Department, Rochester Institute of Technology, 1994. (716) 475-5885.

Energy Efficiency Issue Packet, Campus Ecology Program, National Wildlife Federation.

Energy For Employment: How to Heat Up the Economy, Not the Planet, Tom Lent, Greenpeace Atmosphere and Energy Campaign, July, 1992. (415) 512-9025.

"Environmental Studies 101: Final Research and Writing Assignment," Reed Zars, Williams College, November 30, 1990. (Outline of energy efficiency and carbon dioxide emissions reduction undergraduate-level class assignment.)

"Exit Sign Replacement Plan," Nick Abbatiello, Doug Patterson, Bruno Albano, Rochester Institute of Technology, Spring, 1993. (Student report available through Campus Ecology or R.I.T.)

"From Nader to Nordstrom," *Rocky Mountain Institute Newsletter*, Fall/Winter, 1993, p.9.

The Fuel Cell, Rochester Gas and Electric Corporation, September, 1993. (Describes fuel cell technology and application at Rochester Institute of Technology; contact R.I.T. listed below for more information.)

"Green Cup: A Program at the University of Washington-Seattle," Alicia Jellison, Environmental Awareness Committee of the Residence Hall Students Association, April 2, 1993. (206) 545-0584.

Green Cup Issue Packet, Campus Ecology Program, National Wildlife Federation. (See contact information below.)

"Hydrogen Fuel From the Sun," Peter Lehman and Christine Parra, *Solar Today*, September/October, 1994, pp. 20–22.

"Indoor Air Quality," *Annual Report*, Florida Solar Energy Center, 1994.

Life Cycle Costing: A Guide for Selecting Energy Conservation Measures for Public Buildings, National Technical Information Service, Springfield, VA 22161. (800) 553-6847.

Life-Cycle Costing Manual, Federal Energy Management Program, CE-44, US Department of Energy, 1000 Independence Avenue, SW, Washington, D.C. 20784. (202) 586-5772.

"Measured Energy Savings of an Energy-Efficient Office Computer System," P.B. Lapujade and D.S. Parker, *Proceedings of the 1994 Summer Study on Energy Efficiency in Buildings*, American Council for an Energy-Efficient Economy, Vol. 9, p. 213.

"Memorandum to ABCD Distribution Regarding Campus Wide Project on Energy Conservation and Recycling" James E. Halligan, New Mexico State University, March 27, 1990, Box 30001, Dept. 3Z, Las Cruces, NM 88003-0001. (505) 646-2035.

Recipe For An Effective Campus Energy Conservation Program, Walter Simpson, January, 1991, Union of Concerned Scientists, 26 Church St., Cambridge, MA 02238. (617) 547-5552.

"New Energy Center Gets Grant," *Solar Collector*, Vol. 17, No. 1, 1992, Florida Solar Energy Center, 300 State Road 401, Cape Canaveral, FL 32920-4099.

The NIRS Energy Audit Manual: How to Audit Campus, City and Other Buildings, Andrea Carlson, Nuclear Information and Resource Service, 1992. (202) 328-0002. (Includes audit forms, background information, and technical assistance contacts.)

"Piedmont Technical College Energy/Safety Committee," *South Carolina Wildlife Federation College Conservation Award*, Spring, 1994. (803) 782-8626.

"Prophets of an Energy Revolution," James R. Udal, *National Wildlife*, Dec/Jan, 1992, pp. 10–13.

"Queen Anne Goes Green," *Oxford Today*, Vol. 7, No. 1, Michaelmas Issue, 1994, p.40. (Describes new bio-conscious buildings at Linacre College, Oxford University.)

"Racing Solar Panel Design: Part 4," Michael Hackleman, *Home Power, No. 37*, Oct/ Nov 1993, pp. 52–56. (916) 475-0830.

"Recharging Campus Energy Conservation: The View From SUNY Buffalo," Walter Simpson, *Facilities Manager*, Winter, 1993, pp. 30–35.

Renewable Energy Fact Sheets, American Wind Energy Association, 777 N. Capitol St., N.E., Suite 805, Washington, D.C. 20002. (202) 408-8988.

"Saving Energy: Prosperity At No Cost," Edwin Smith, *National Round Table Review*, Fall, 1993. (Carleton University in Ottawa has launched a $20 million dollar program to conserve energy across its campus.)

"Securing Our Future: The SERI Photovoltaic Energy Program Invests in Higher Education," National Renewable Energy Laboratory (formally SERI), April, 1990.

"State and Utility Financial Incentives for Solar Applications," Larry Shirley and Jodie Sholar, *Solar Today*, September, October, 1994.

"SERF: A Landmark in Energy Efficiency," *NREL In Review*, December, 1993, pp. 2–5.

"Solstice: Your Link To Renewable Energy Information," Andrew Waegel and Eric Woods, *ReSource*, Second Quarter, 1994, pp. 6–7.

"Some Ideas for Sun Day 1994 Events and Ongoing Activities," SUN DAY: A Campaign For A Sustainable Energy Future, 315 Circle Avenue, #2, Takoma Park, MD 20912-4836. (301) 270-2258.

"The States Seize Power," Thomas A. Lewis, *National Wildlife*, Dec/Jan, 1993, pp. 16–19.

"Sunrayce 93," Erik Nelson and Cecile Leboeuf, *Solar Today*, Jan/Feb, 1994.

"Technical Inspections of a Large Number of Commercial Solar Water Heating Systems on Florida Schools" M. Yarosh, J. Huggins, T. Tiedemann, 1993, Florida Solar Energy Center, 300 State Rd. 401, Cape Canaveral, FL 32920.

"Thermal Solar Water Heating in the PAC: Final Report," Apr. 1992, contact University of Waterloo Waste Management Coordinator. (519) 885-1211, ext. 3245, (e-mail: qbwright@watservl.uwaterloo.ca).

"What Is The Real Cost of Energy? Putting A Price Tag On Environmental Costs of Energy Production," *Briefing Packet*, Union of Concerned Scientists, July, 1991, pp. 4–9.

NETWORKING

If you find that an organization listed here has moved or a contact has been replaced, let the Campus Ecology Program staff know. We'll help match you with the latest source for the information you need.

Campus

Austin College
Attn: Roy Griffin
Facilities Management
Sherman, TX 75090
Solar hot water heating system.

Brevard Community College
Attn: Harold Creel
Plant Maintenance and Operations
1519 Clear Lake Road
Cocoa, FL 32922
(407) 632-1111
Innovative pool heating, energy efficiency, co-host with UCF to New Energy Center of the Florida Solar Energy Society.

Brown University
Attn. Kurt Teichert
Box 1941
Providence, RI 02912
(401) 863-7837
e-mail: kurt_teichert@brown.edu

Carleton University
Attn: Bryan Beazer
Ottawa Facilities Management
Ottawa, Ontario, Canada K1S 5B6
$20-million improvements in energy efficiency.

Georgetown University
Attn: Jon Miller
B-24 Harbon Hall
37th and O Streets, N.W.
Washington, D.C. 20057
(202) 687-2033
PV-powered student center.

Harvard University
Attn: Michael Lichten
Harvard Facilities
38 Oxford Street
Cambridge, MA 02138
(617) 495-1000
One of the innovators of the inter-dorm energy conservation contest, Green Cup.

Mendocino College Community Extension
P.O. Box 3000
Ukiah, CA 95482
(707) 468-3063
Offers workshops in various renewable energy systems.

Portland Community College System
P.O. Box 19000
Portland, OR 97219-0990
(503) 244-6111
Test site for community college energy efficiency curricula and projects; contact Bill Clumpner at Integrated Energy Services for more information (503) 292-4781.

Red Rocks Community College
13300 West 6th Avenue
Lakewood, CO 80401
(303) 988-6160
Courses in active and passive solar energy systems and construction and in renewable energy electrical power generation.

Rochester Institute of Technology
Attn: Mary Jane Kosel
Physical Plant
Rochester, NY 14623
(716) 475-5885
Lighting upgrades, student training fuel cell.

Sonoma State University
Attn: Rocky Rohwedder
Energy Center
1801 East Cotati Avenue
Rohnert Park, CA 94928
(707) 664-2577
energy.center@sonoma.edu
Energy management and renewable energy education, professional training, consulting and information referral, demonstration projects and research.

SUNY Buffalo
Attn: Walter Simpson
Conserve UB University Facilities
John Beane Center
Buffalo, NY 14260
(716) 645-3528
Comprehensive energy conservation and efficiency programs, Green Computing Campaign, building conservation contacts.

Tufts University
Center for Environmental Management
Curtis Hall
474 Boston Avenue
Medford, MA 02155
(617) 381-3486
Campus energy audits and conservation program reports.

Western Wyoming Community
College
Attn: Craig Thompson
Environmental Science
2500 College Dr., Box 428
Rock Springs, WY 82901
(307) 382-1662
*Energy efficiency retrofits and
innovative educational events.*

Regional and National

American Wind Energy
Association
777 N. Capitol Street, N.E.
Suite 805
Washington, D.C. 20002
(202) 408-8988

Association of Higher Education
Facilities Officers (APPA)
1446 Duke Street
Alexandria, VA 22314-3492

Bull Frog Films
P.O. Box 149
Oley, PA 19547
*A source for renewable and
energy efficiency videos.*

Energy Efficiency and Renewable Energy Clearinghouse
(EREC)
P.O. Box 3048
Merrifield, VA 22116
(1-800-363-3732)
energyinfo@delphi.com
HTTP//WWW.EREN.DOE.GOV
*Central source of free
information and technical
assistance on energy efficiency
for renewable energy.*

Energy Efficient Building
Association, Inc. (EEBA)
1829 Portland Avenue
Minneapolis, MN 55404-1898
(612) 871-0413
*Annual building design
competitions and conferences.*

The Energy Foundation
75 Federal Street
San Francisco, CA 94107
(415) 546-7400
energyfund@igc.apc.org
*Campus energy efficiency
conservation or energy renewal
programs designed for further
replication with broad regional
or national implications may
qualify for grants; e.g., the
University of California at
Berkeley's Department of
Architecture was awarded
$238,000 in 1992 to develop a
curriculum of resource modules
and case studies on energy-
efficient and environmentally
responsible design for undergraduate and graduate students
majoring in architecture.*

Green Lights
U.S. Environmental Protection
Agency (6202J)
401 M Street, S.W.
Washington, D.C. 20460
(202) 775-6650

"Greenschools"
Kurt Teichert, Listowner
Brown is Green
Box 1941
Brown University
Providence, RI 02912
(401) 863-7837
e-mail: kurt_teichert@brown.edu
*"Greenschools" (formally
"GRNSCH-L") is a "listserv" or
electronic correspondence group
on the Internet. It has become a
dynamic forum for discussion of
energy efficiency and other
issues of environmental
responsibility in higher education. To subscribe to the list,
send the following message to
listserv@brownvm.brown.edu:
subscribe GRNSCH-L "your
name". The* Blueprint for a
Green Campus *and other
campus ecology documentation
is available via Brown's World
Wide Web site: http://
www.envstudies.brown.edu/
environ.*

National Renewable Energy
Laboratory
1617 Coal Boulevard
Golden, CO 80401-3393
(303) 231-7846
*NREL is a DOE national
laboratory.*

National Wildlife Federation
Campus Ecology Program
1400 16th Street, N.W.
Washington, D.C. 20036-2266
(202) 797-5435
(General Information)
(313) 769-9970
or midwest@NWF.org (M.W.)
(202) 797-5468
or noreast@NWF.org (N.E.)
(404) 876-2608
or soeast@nwf.org (S.E.)
(503) 222-1428
or western@nwf.org (West)
*Ask for Energy Efficiency and
Green Cup Issue Packets; NWF
Campus Ecology staff conduct
workshops, organizer trainings
and consultation on energy
related topics for students and
staff.*

Nuclear Information and
Resources Service
1424 16th Street, N.W.
No. 601
Washington, D.C. 20036
(202) 328-0002

Photovoltaic System Design
Assistance and Training Center
Florida Solar Energy Center
Attn: John Harrison
300 State Road 401
Cape Canaveral, FL 32920-4099
(407) 783-0300, x127

Portland Energy Conservation, Inc.
Attn: Lois Gordon
921 Southwest Washington
Suite 840
Portland, OR 97205
(503) 248-4636
Under contract to U.S. Department of Energy-Seattle Support Office to conduct a nationwide review of energy conservation efforts in K–12 schools.

Rocky Mountain Institute
1739 Snowmass Creek Road
Snowmass, CO 81654-9199
(303) 927-3851
Community and institutional energy efficiency and conservation technical assistance, resources.

Solar Box Cookers International
1724 11th Street
Sacramento, CA 95814
(916) 444-6616
Solar box cookers work tremendously well and are a useful renewable energy teaching aid.

Solstice Center for Renewable Energy and Sustainable Technology (CREST)
777 North Capitol Street, N.E.
Suite 805
Washington, D.C. 20002
(202) 289-0061
dja@crest.org
"Solstice" is CREST's on-line service on the Internet. It can be accessed via World Wide Web (WWW), Gopher, and Anonymous FTP Services. To reach the WWW server, use a WWW browser such as mosaic or links and direct it to "HTTP:// solstice.crest.org/". For FTP, log in to solstice.crest.org using "anonymous" for the login name and your internet mail address as your password.

SUN DAY
315 Circle Avenue, #2
Takoma Park, MD 20912-4836
(301) 270-2258
NWF Campus Ecology Program staff would be happy to assist your campus with SUN DAY organizing and follow up.

Video Project
5332 College Avenue
Suite 101
Oakland, CA 94618
A source for videos on renewable energy and energy efficiency.

Water Alliance for Voluntary Efficiency (WAVE)
Attn: John E. Flowers
U.S. Environmental Protection Agency
WH-547
401 M Street, S.W.
Washington, D.C. 20460
(202) 260-7288

CHAPTER 5

Dining Services

Campus dining services are in the business of trying to provide cost-effective, healthy and flavorful meals to anywhere from hundreds to tens of thousands of customers every day. As if this were not challenging enough, staff and students at many institutions have initiated impressive recycling and waste reduction programs and, in several cases, have begun to purchase food and other goods with environmental criteria in mind. Their inherent educational role and hefty expenditures (surpassing $100 million annually at the largest universities), position campus dining operations as national trend setters of food production, packaging, and waste management.

Food provides a natural starting point for environmental assessments of campus dining operations. Student food studies, such as those conducted at Hendrix College in Conway, Arkansas, and Carleton and St. Olaf Colleges in Northfield, Minnesota, have examined how food is grown, processed, packaged, and transported, tracing food along its journey from the field to the campus. Protecting dolphins from tuna nets, increasing the amount and variety of vegetarian menu options, and protecting farm workers from pesticides were among the most visible food-related campus environmental campaigns in the late 1980s and early 1990s. Today, dolphin-free tuna logos are ubiquitous in dining services, as are electronic databases for vegetarian and international recipes. And some campuses no longer serve those grapes grown with dangerous pesticides.

Extending their concerns about food production beyond boycotts and single-issue campaigns, students and staff on several campuses have begun to seek lasting alternatives to synthetic fertilizers, pesticides, and herbicides. Several campuses, for instance, have bolstered efforts to purchase locally grown foods—when possible, from certified organic farmers. Employing arts developed over millennia but nearly forgotten in a few decades, organic farmers make use of nature's own predation and immune systems; grow cover crops, rotate crops, and

Chef Bradford Slye has enthusiastically incorporated local, organic produce into the Bates College diet.

BLACK COW PHOTO

compost; and employ a variety of other techniques to minimize soil erosion and reduce the use of petrochemicals and other toxins.

In several cases, interest in pesticide-free foods and in purchasing locally has emanated from campus efforts to manage dining service waste. At Bates College in Lewiston, Maine; Dartmouth College in Hanover, New Hampshire; Johnson State College in Johnson, Vermont; and other campuses, purchasing or growing organic produce is an offshoot of food composting efforts. Dining services are often among the first entities on campuses to launch recycling programs and, faced with inordinate amounts of food and packaging materials, are instituting innovative waste reduction approaches such as composting, as well.

🦋 LOCAL AND ORGANIC PRODUCE

On many campuses, the desire to support local farming has prompted an occasional organic meal or the introduction of a few locally grown fruits or vegetables. Can colleges and universities support sustainable agriculture in a more substantial way? The answer, judging from efforts at Bates College, is a tentative yes. Institutions interested in increasing the variety and freshness of their produce, or concerned about the resource-intensive methods used to produce and transport much of their food, can learn from ongoing efforts at Bates and similar campus initiatives elsewhere.

Buying Local and Pesticide-Free at Bates

Student groups and pilot initiatives at other campuses have achieved shifts in purchasing comparable to those at Bates and have galvanized interest in sustainable agriculture. The Bates effort, however, is particularly promising in the degree to which it is institutionalized. Unlike several other local-purchasing efforts, the Bates initiative was not funded by grants and did not result from the efforts of students or faculty working on the fringes of the campus community. It emanated from a broad-based group of staff, students, and faculty on the Campus Environmental Issues Committee (CEIC), on which the director of dining services, Robert Volpi, is an active player.

A longtime gardener and veteran dining service professional, Volpi joined the CEIC shortly after his arrival at Bates, a college with a student population of 1,500. From day one, he says, committee members showed palpable interest in composting and the purchase of local foods. Students discussed these issues in their environmental group, the Student Environmental Coalition, and notes from those meetings were incorporated into the CEIC minutes. "It really started with composting," says Volpi. "We started talking about how we could complete a full

Here is a college in the state of Maine, and we are sending our money to California for tomatoes when there is a guy right down the road growing beautiful tomatoes.

—Chef Slye, Bates College

WHY THE INTEREST IN PESTICIDE-FREE FOODS?

Pesticide-action campaigns became visible on campuses when the United Farm Workers Union and other organizations began publicizing the acute and chronic health effects suffered by migrant and seasonal farm laborers, whose work exposes them to pesticides. As a first step, the public was asked not to buy table grapes until growers discontinue their use of carcinogenic pesticides and meet other worker and consumer safety demands. Sixteen years after the boycott was first officially announced, these demands have yet to be fully met. But growers are taking notice as a large and growing roster of higher education institutions—including Cornell, Michigan State, MIT, and Stanford—curtail their grape purchases.

More than 300,000 farm workers become seriously ill and another 800–1,000 die because of acute pesticide poisoning each year.[1] And farm workers are not the only ones at risk. Agricultural pesticides are a major source of water contamination, affecting millions of other Americans. In *Tap Water Blues*, released in October 1994, the nonprofit Environmental Working Group reported that approximately 14 million Americans, mostly within or down-stream from areas of high pesticide use, drink tap water contaminated with potentially harmful levels of commonly used herbicides.[2]

As Rachel Carson predicted in her 1962 landmark book *Silent Spring*, elevated rates of reproductive cancers and other reproductive complications in both men and women are linked with increasing certainty to chronic, low-dose exposure to organochlorine pesticides and other chemicals. Reports such as the National Wildlife Federation's *Fertility on the Brink: The Legacy of the Chemical Age,* document the current knowledge of the harmful effect which environmental toxins have on wildlife and human beings.

Even though hundreds of insect species have developed genetic resistance to the very chemicals designed to kill them, widespread reliance on pesticides continues. Since 1940, pesticide use has increased tenfold, while crops lost to insects have doubled.[3] Yet the response has been to apply greater volumes and varieties of pesticides. Success in developing herbicide-resistant hybrid crops through genetic engineering only worsens the trend.[4]

1. Rep. George Miller (D-CA), *Congressional Record*, August 1, 1990. See Bibliography.
2. *Washington Post*, October 19, 1994, A3.
3. "The IPM Process," *Common Sense Pest Control*, Berkeley, CA, IV(3), Summer, 1988.
4. *Biotechnology's Bitter Harvest*, Goldburg, Rissler, et al., Biotechnology Working Group, 1990.

Agricultural pesticides are a major source of water contamination, affecting millions of Americans.

loop and ended up discussing how we might do something positive in the community—something that would help local farmers."

Identifying Local, Organic Farmers

What happened next is a story of connections. Bates' director of publications and chair of the CEIC, Betsy Kimball, had friends in the local farming community. She put Volpi in touch with Russell Libby, who is the director of research at the State Department of Agriculture and the president of the Maine Organic Farmers and Gardeners Association (MOFGA), as well as an organic farmer. Libby in turn put Volpi in touch with local farmers, state waste reduction personnel, and cooperative extension staff. With a several-month lead on the planting season, Libby brought the Bates staff and local farmers together to formulate a plan: Wayne Ricker, a commercial composter, would pick up and compost pre-consumer food waste, charging less than Bates paid to have it landfilled. And local, certified-organic growers would form a loose cooperative, supplying Bates with as much of its produce as possible.

Following standards established by the National Organic Foods Act of 1990, these farmers grow their foods in soil on which no synthetic fertilizers or pesticides have been applied for at least three years. They do not irradiate or use preservatives, synthetic hormones, or colorings in foods they grow for Bates.

Support from the Cooks

But would the chef and the staff of cooks be willing to work with wide varieties of sometimes unusual fresh vegetables, herbs, and fruits? The experience at Hendrix College, where Gary Valen, former dean of students, conducted a five-year pilot effort, underscored the importance of cooperation from the kitchen. "I remember the day," says Valen, "when one of the older cooks looked at me and said, 'Oh, you want me to do it like we used to do it.'" Most of the cooks had grown accustomed, he says, to working with more limited varieties of produce and more processed foods than were available locally. Lack of sufficient support among the cooking staff was one of the factors that made it difficult to sustain the Hendrix effort beyond its initial five years.

The Bates experience is proceeding differently. Executive Chef Bradford Slye, who came to the college at the onset of negotiations with local farmers, has been instrumental in making the local purchasing effort successful. Not coincidentally, Volpi had chosen a chef whose training at the Culinary Institute of America and avid gardening made him a likely candidate for a local-foods project. "As soon as Bob mentioned we ought to buy locally," says Slye, "I ran with the idea as if it were my own."

The taste is so much fresher with every shipment, I don't care if it is tomatoes or basil, and the colors are more pronounced.

—Robert Volpi, Bates College

"Here is a college in the state of Maine," he thought, "and we are sending our money to California for tomatoes when there is a guy right down the road growing beautiful tomatoes." No sooner had Libby assembled the local farmers than the chef began poring through seed catalogues and creating a list of the produce he would like to see grown and delivered to the Bates kitchen. "Once the chefs say that they are interested," says Libby, "bringing the farmers along can go pretty quickly."

Reaping the Harvest

Only four months after initial discussions, the first produce—several varieties of organic basil and salad greens—arrived at the dock. The "opal basil was so rich and almost sweet in its consistency that we used it in a chocolate dessert here for our senior honors banquet," reminisces Slye.

Organic green and wax beans and heirloom purple beans arrived next. Chef Slye tossed the raw purple beans (which turn green when cooked) with sliced onions, peppers, garlic, and herbs in an oil and vinegar dressing. "People loved it," reports Slye, who served the crunchy salad at several summer luncheons.

The chef prepares local, organic cauliflower.

Organically grown summer squashes followed the beans. Slye immediately recognized the crooked-necked yellow squash as a heritage variety. "It was kind of nice," he says, "to see some of those antiques being resurrected by some of our growers." Small growers are in the best position to keep these varieties alive, says Slye, who hopes to find a local organic producer of the heirloom bluish-purple potato, which grows well in Maine.

Eagerly awaited organic tomatoes of numerous varieties arrived by mid-summer along with red Russian kale, silver-dollar sized celery, fennel, dandelions, peppers, and cilantro. The red Russian kale "is a big, broad, dark green leafy vegetable with a red tinge in the rib," the chef explains, "and is much more tender than your average kale." Bates cooks have tossed the kale into mixed green salad or wilted and tossed it with sundried tomatoes in pasta dishes.

Deliveries, Payment

Once a week, one of the six local organic providers calls the other members of the loose cooperative and tells the chef what is available. "Usually, I will just take it all," says Slye, who only turned down one shipment—100 pounds of organic basil. "I can use at most 25 pounds of basil a week," says Slye. With time, he finds that the farmers are getting a better sense of the quantities and types of produce the college can use.

The first few shipments were small—with invoices of $40 or $50—hardly enough, under normal circumstances, for trucking over to Bates. But in anticipation of larger purchases later in the growing season, one farmer agreed to drop the first diminutive shipments off on her way to work. As hoped, the college's weekly purchases of local food grew with the harvest, eventually amounting to several hundred dollars each week. "Bates has basically said they have the potential to handle a thousand dollars a week of stuff" says Libby, "and the problem this year is not that they wouldn't take it, but that the farmers didn't have as much as they wanted." But the effort is growing, as the cooperation among farmers which arose from their effort to supply Bates has encouraged them to explore similar arrangements with local restaurants, as well.

The consolidation of deliveries and invoices simplifies Bates' efforts to purchase locally. "If you were trying to deal with a dozen different people, trying to bill separately or, an even worse nightmare, trying to pay cash on the dock," says Slye, "that would be an obstacle." Bates receives one bill and issues one payment per delivery. Contributions from each farmer are subtotaled on each invoice, making it easier for them to divide payment among themselves. From the Bates end, the main logistical difference is a quicker payment schedule. "The turnaround," says Volpi, "is a lot quicker than a large company would require, but our accounting staff have been very supportive."

Bates College's weekly purchases of local food grew with the harvest, eventually amounting to several hundred dollars a week.

BLACK COW PHOTO

Overcoming Obstacles

Anticipated problems related to aesthetics, uniformity, cost, and taste make some dining services reluctant to purchase locally. The Bates experience addresses each of these. In terms of aesthetics, the college's local produce has been comparable or superior to conventional produce Chef Slye has found, in part because smaller-scale farmers can often pamper their products more. When ear worms attacked local organically grown corn (a notoriously difficult crop to grow organically), for example, the farmer cut the tips off the corn before sending it to Bates. Moreover, local produce is allowed to fully ripen on the vine before being quickly harvested and delivered to campus. And because it is handled less, there are fewer blemishes. Unlike many of their commercial counterparts, notes Slye, this local produce is not waxed, gassed, preserved, packed, shipped hundreds of miles, sized out, repacked, and otherwise jostled along its journey.

Uniformity is another issue. Diners on many campuses may have come to expect the uniformity in size and shape and the limited variety of produce available commercially, admits the chef, but there have been no such complaints at Bates. "The tomatoes are really the biggest thing I have seen that maybe don't come all sized out," admits Slye, "but the squash and the kale and the greens, the herbs, the leeks have been beautiful . . . . I got some wonderful little yellow onions," he adds. "I guess you just have to like the food as it is—not expect everything to be the size and shape of a golfball. That is not the way nature works. "

Unusual produce, such as tiny organic pumpkins, provide a venue for the chef's creativity. Slye scooped the seeds out and roasted the pumpkins, then filled them with his own vegetarian chili recipe and brown rice. For the most part, the chef incorporates local products into existing recipes or the salad bar. At least 20 percent of Bates students are vegetarian and another 10 to 20 percent eat little or no red meat, so there is a large, receptive audience for entrees created with almost any fresh vegetable.

Higher initial costs for local, organically grown foods may pose an obstacle for campuses in some regions. "It can be difficult," explains Gary Valen of the Hendrix pilot program, "for local growers to compete with commercial farming or transportation systems, where federal subsidies come into play, or with Mexico, where environmental regulations are more relaxed and the cost of living and wages are lower." At Bates, which runs its own food service, "the cost is slightly higher," admits Slye, "but we have been able to absorb it." Composting, recycling, and other waste reduction efforts help offset nominal cost increases. Many dining services and students, however, may be less flexible.

Where dining service contracts have to be won and renewed, profits often drive policy. The long-range benefits of conservation may look less attractive in such an environment. The pressure to realize quick profits, for example, may make it unrealistic to reallocate savings from one conservation program into another one, so that paybacks and savings from cardboard recycling, composting and other conservation initiatives that have saved individual dining services tens of thousands of dollars may not finance preventive maintenance or a local purchasing effort. "In a lot of places," adds Libby, ". . . there is an incentive system in place that says the lower you keep your food costs, the higher your salary." Valen concurs: "Large dining services can offer perks local farming cooperatives cannot."

Students, too, may resist price increases. Dartmouth, Tufts, and a growing number of campus dining services are replacing "all-you-can-eat" meal plans with á la carte (or diminishing balance) services at which students use the equivalent of a cash card and "dollars" are deducted with each item. Cost increases are

Higher initial costs for local, organically grown foods may pose an obstacle for campuses in some regions.

generally passed directly to the students, who will notice immediately when they go to weigh their salad, for example, if lettuce has doubled in price. This encourages waste reduction, since students are more likely to take only what they can eat when they have to pay per item or ounce, but it may complicate the incorporation of local, organic products into the menu. Campuses can conduct surveys to determine the elasticity of students' demand for organic produce (as did Harvard University in spring of 1993), but what students say they will pay and what they actually can afford are often two different things, notes Patricia Lee, director of dining services at Tufts.

As local purchasing at Bates increases, the college and the farmers may find room to negotiate on cost. "I think that if the program [the organic farmers] are running and our program grow together to the point where they are making a good living," says Slye, "then we will be able to get their prices to match some of the market prices a little more."

Plus, local farming cooperatives offer their own brand of perks. Most of the vegetables delivered to Bates in season "haven't even been off the vine 24 hours," declares Slye, "before somebody starts to consume them." Adds Volpi, "The taste is so much fresher with every shipment, I don't care if it is tomatoes or basil, and the colors are more pronounced." In the end, improvements in quality and local rapport are worth the effort. "It is not quite the same old rhythm," admits Slye, "but the produce is . . . fresher, healthier, more flavorful, and can ripen before being delivered to you."

Students and other diners, the true judges of the program's success, appear equally pleased. "I haven't heard anything but compliments so far," says Volpi, who was thrilled when members of the Student Environmental Coalition wrote a letter to the president praising the college's support of local farmers and the improved quality of the produce. Diners are informed via menu cards and signs whenever local, organic products are used. "It is not just braised kale," Volpi clarifies, "it is braised local, organic kale . . . . We have everything identified because we want people to know what we are doing."

Expanding the Program

Efforts to expand the Bates' local-purchasing effort are constrained by Maine's limited growing season. "The places that are in longer growing season areas will have an easier time than Bates," which Libby says "is facing an exceptional climate challenge here because the bulk of their meals are served at the opposite time from when most of the farming happens." Much of Bates' local produce, which begins to dwindle as the academic year commences, has been incorporated into meals prepared for camps and other summer activities.

> What students say they will pay and what they actually can afford are often two different things.
>
> —Patricia Lee, Tufts University

Russell Libby and the Bates staff are exploring ways to extend the availability of at least some local organic foods through more of the academic year. One idea is increased reliance on hoop houses, an inexpensive form of greenhouse already used by one farmer to produce much of the basil shipped to Bates in the spring of 1994. Libby also plans to broaden the existing cooperative to include farmers who can supply the college with produce later in the growing season or with products other than those the farmers closest to Bates can currently grow. Libby assisted Bates in contracting with an organic, free-range poultry farm that will supply Bates with turkeys for its harvest meal.

Processing local products for longer storage is another approach to keep business local during the off-season. This year, for example, Chef Slye preserved local basil in olive oil for use in pasta dishes throughout the winter. If stored in root cellars, potatoes, rutabagas, beets, yams, and other root vegetables can last for many months. The local potatoes Bates purchased in late spring and summer of 1994, for instance, had been harvested the previous fall.

Farming cooperatives benefit from doing some of this processing themselves. "I visited a farm that supplies a restaurant year-round—a top-notch, four-star gourmet restaurant," says Libby, "and the farmer makes his living by moving the food all the way to the point where it is ready to either cook or serve." Since very few colleges can do all their own processing, these services can be integral to a local-purchasing effort. Bates procures seven-grain cereal, an oats and barley pancake mix, bulgher, and kamut from Fiddler's Green Millers in Belfast, Maine, which grinds organic grains (some local and some grown in the Midwest) at a 100-year-old mill. Slye hopes local growers of ancho chili peppers will begin drying and stringing them for consumption year-long.

Products that cannot be preserved in oil, dried, or stored naturally can be canned or frozen. Such methods, though, come with trade-offs. A local-food purchasing study conducted by faculty and students at Carleton and St. Olaf Colleges revealed canning and freezing to be several times more resource-intensive than trucking products cross-country. If canned or frozen products are going to be used anyway, however, it is arguably preferable that these foods be grown and preserved locally. Tomato sauce, one of the biggest staples in any food service, is a good example of a product that can be locally grown and canned, allowing small farmers to intensify their harvest and earnings. Also, the energy required to can foods may be offset by recycling glass and metal containers. And since it is doubtful that campuses will move away from frozen strawberries and other such products in winter, emphasis might be placed on freezer energy-efficiency rather than on discouraging reliance on locally grown foods off-season.

The places that are in longer growing season areas will have an easier time than Bates, which is facing an exceptional climate challenge here because the bulk of their meals are served at the opposite time from when most of the farming happens.

—Russell Libby, Maine Organic Farmers and Gardeners Association

Local vs. Organic

Organic food distribution companies can provide campuses with organically grown versions of almost any food in any season. Like conventional distributors, they purchase, store, and transport impressive varieties of food, overcoming seasonal limitations by drawing from diverse global sources. Organic tomato sauce, soy beverages, and numerous cereals and pastas are just a few of their newest products.

At Bates, however, local farmers turned out to be the most affordable source of organic foods. "How can we help support our farmers and also get the organic produce at our best price?" was the question asked from the project's inception, says Volpi. Gary Valen's local-purchasing pilot project at Hendrix College in Conway, Arkansas, developed from similar concerns.

Using a video camera to document their findings, student researchers at Hendrix College traced the food served by their cafeteria to its sources, and found that 94 percent of the food for the college dining service (a $1.5-million operation) was grown outside the state. Rice, strawberries, onions, and beef were purchased elsewhere, despite the availability of local supplies. The college bought out-of-state rice, although Arkansas is the second largest rice producer in the country. And beef originated from feedlots in Texas, despite a thriving local livestock industry. A similar study conducted at Carleton and St. Olaf Colleges in Northfield, Minnesota, concluded that both colleges purchased less than 20 percent of their food from instate producers. Ironically, they found that Carleton and St. Olaf purchased rice from Arkansas.

The Hendrix local-food pilot project increased the college's instate food purchases from $45,000 (6 percent) to $212,000 (30 percent) between 1986 and 1992. Had Hendrix's purchasing catalyzed a local growing cooperative akin to the one near Bates, Valen believes Hendrix would have continued to purchase locally. As soon as Valen left his job and the college presidency changed hands, however, Hendrix reverted to large brokerage houses for its produce. Even when funding for a full-time coordinator ran out, says Valen, work-study students

---

SOME ORGANIC FOODS AVAILABLE IN BULK

unbleached white flour	kosher dill pickles
old-fashioned corn meal	spinach ravioli
white basmati rice	vegetable spiral pasta
couscous	black turtle beans
popping corn	green split peas
raisin bran cereal	chunky tomato sauce
oat bran	whole, peeled tomatoes
buttermilk pancake mix	honey
gingerbread mix	maple syrup
cocoa powder	strawberries
tortilla chips	raisins
milk powder	
apple juice	
black tea	
eggs	
cheddar cheese	
yogurt	

were able to do the research, make the calls, and line up local foods. But students could not sustain this contribution without continued institutional support and guidance.

"My impression is that the only way purchasing locally is going to succeed," Libby says from his experience with many kinds of institutions in Maine, "is if it is institutionalized in a college's policy." The active involvement of chefs, line cooks, and the dining services director is critical. If the program depends on one individual, even if that person is the food buyer, the program will be jeopardized by that person's departure. For instance, according to Libby:

> There was a food buyer for the University of Maine who was a strong supporter of local foods and went out of her way to procure them, especially for major events. They serve 10,000 people there, so it is a big institution. For special meals she would go out and solicit the ingredients for running a really nice local meal on a regular basis. But in the era of retrenchment her position was one that was considered expendable, and when that happened the University of Maine's commitment to buying local foods kind of went out the window. They went to a single-source buyer system. Once you go to that, local purveyors don't have much chance of getting in the door.

In some cases, institutional support alone may be insufficient—as at Carleton and St. Olaf. Both colleges began purchasing local apples as a result of their study, but they were hindered by a dearth of certified-organic farmers and a lack of crop diversity instate. Feed corn, soybeans, alfalfa, and wheat accounted for 87 percent of the land under cultivation in Minnesota (as reported in *The Campus and Environmental Responsibility*, see the bibliography at the end of this chapter). According to the same source, consolidated farms and decreased crop diversity are a growing trend in Minnesota, a state characterized by the loss of four farms a day between 1979 and 1987. To establish a sufficient market for foods not widely available locally, the project coordinators found they would have to form a purchasing cooperative with other colleges and institutions. Carleton's and St. Olaf's purchases combined, for example, would create only a quarter of the demand necessary for a competitive, certified-organic milk market in Minnesota. The "Campus and Biosphere" conference held by the two colleges in 1991 brought dining service staff, food industry representatives, students and faculty together as a first step toward building such a cooperative—which at this writing, is still an ongoing effort.

A Training Center and Model

Meadowcreek, an environmental retreat and education center in the Ozark Mountains of Arkansas, continues to support such cooperative models. Equipped with the lessons he learned at Hendrix College, 12 years of organic farming in Iowa, and several years coordinating sustainable agriculture projects on a na-

Hendrix College students found that 94 percent of their food was produced and packaged outside the state, despite the frequent availability of equivalent local products.

tional level, Gary Valen has assumed leadership of Meadowcreek. He is currently expanding the original "Food Project," which assisted local purchasing efforts at three colleges, to encompass more campuses and communities. "We have 1,500 acres here," says Valen, "and a working model of what I think a sustainable community ought to look like."

Professor David Orr, chair of the Environmental Studies Program at Oberlin College and cofounder of Meadowcreek, helps maintain a vital link between Meadowcreek and academia. Students, faculty, and staff from all over the world visit the center for weeks and semesters at a time to learn how to run an organic farm, set up community food brokerages, and live "off the grid" with solar energy and compost toilets.

The hands-on training students and staff receive in sustainable food production and living at Meadowcreek have been designed with communities and institutions in mind. "We recognize that a large university could literally change the economy of a whole town," says Valen, "simply by trying to buy local products." But the transition will require patience, he says, and for the time being, Meadowcreek's emphasis is more on establishing local agricultural cooperatives than on growing methods:

> Unless you are out there when the cinch beetle comes and wipes out your crop, it may be difficult to comprehend what it will take to get to true organic farming . . . . I wish we could all go to organic methods immediately, but I think developing local markets is really more important [so that the consumers] ask the farmers to grow products in as friendly a way to the environment as possible—thinking of the soil usage, . . . of what is being sprayed and carried over into the water system, and what is going into the air. I think we can get to a total organic farming system, if we just keep working at it.

Finding a Comfort Level

Meadowcreek, and other small institutions such as high schools, have shown that it is possible to rely almost completely on the surrounding community for food. In *Four-Season Harvest*, for example, Eliot Coleman writes about feeding some 50 people at the Mountain School, an alternative high school in Vermont, year-round from a garden on the campus farm. An alternative high school run by the Chewonki Foundation in Wiscasset, Maine, has taken a similar path. "When I've gone to the Mountain School in January for meetings, the food, which the students prepare, came out of their own gardens and was frozen," recalls Libby, "and that is about as cold a climate as you have in the United States, on that hilltop in northern Vermont."

But for many campuses, starting with one local, organic meal in one dining hall is ambitious enough. This was the approach taken at Tufts University, where,

We have 1,500 acres here and a working model of what I think a sustainable community ought to look like.

—Gary Valen, Meadowcreek

in spring of 1994, Dr. Molly Anderson and her students in a graduate-level nutrition class began to identify and price local organic products. For Patricia Lee, director of the Tufts dining service, student support of the research process "moved what would have been an issue on the back burner to the front burner."

Urban campuses like Tufts may have a tougher time purchasing locally. Even though small farms often thrive on the edge of cities, "the problem," says Libby, "is that most of [the farmers] have been forced into wholesale markets because they don't have the knowledge or connections to get into [institutional] markets, or the institutions have set themselves up so the farmers can't get in." For city colleges located anywhere but the most densely populated urban areas, farmers within 30 or 40 miles could supply at least some produce.

Even rural colleges start small. Colby College, also in Maine, has started its local-purchasing program with local squash, which they serve in one dining hall where they are promoting a healthier diet, Libby says. Carleton and St. Olaf initiated their efforts with local apples. Small steps are as important as big ones, suggests Libby:

> Once you get one item in the door, there is potential to show that you can [offer] other items. The word is getting around; I have a lot of people who would like to ship to Bates. One of the challenges is going to be to balance out those people who invested a lot of time and money . . . this year to get in the door with those people who say, 'Well, gee, I could grow for that market too'. . . [I]t is not very often that [a good organic buyer] comes along for small growers—in Maine, certainly, and I am sure in other states as well.

With sufficient commitment, any campus can support local farmers and introduce at least some organic foods. The important thing is that dining service staff start somewhere, using the strengths and resources they have. "Bates has taken the right approach," says Libby, "which is to work with what is available, use that as highlights for meals, round it out with the regular food service stuff, and keep building capacity."

Patricia Lee of Tufts has hosted environmental stewardship conferences for academic institutions in New England.

DINING WASTE REDUCTION AND RECYCLING

Given the high profile of the services they provide, it is not surprising that dining service professionals have often been among the first college and university staff to take decisive steps towards conservation. Staff of independently operated dining services often share tips for greening their operations through the National Association of College and University Food Services (NACUFS). NACUFS sponsors an Environmental Committee, which communicates electronically and through regional and national forums. NACUFS also supports member-initiated regional conferences on waste reduction and other environmental topics for campus dining services. Tufts Dining Service, directed by Patricia Lee, has hosted several of these.

Networking in New England

Although the committee addresses numerous topics—from energy efficiency to purchasing local foods—recycling and waste reduction drive the involvement of many participants. The urgency with which dining services in New England have had to respond to landfill closures and rising tipping fees, Lee believes, has placed these institutions slightly ahead of their counterparts elsewhere in the country. Indeed, the region boasts numerous innovations, including composting programs at several campuses and a unique Environmental Coordinator position in Dining Services at Harvard University. The position, held by Alexandra McNitt, was created by Harvard's Dining Service Director Michael Berry to manage the "Shared Responsibility Program." McNitt coordinates the involvement of student volunteers, dining service staff, and consultants in energy efficiency, waste reduction and other cost-saving programs.

Dining Service Waste Characterization Studies

Characterization studies conducted by half a dozen universities shed some light on dining service waste. A Tufts University analysis (which did not include rendered cooking fats or recycled cardboard) tallies dining service contributions as 10 percent of the total campus waste stream by weight. A UNC-Greensboro study estimates dining service contributions at double that. The precise percentage matters less than the understanding that feeding students, faculty, and staff generates a significant portion of campus waste—of which 30 to 50 percent by weight, and even more by volume, is readily recyclable and compostable.

Dining service waste reduction falls roughly into two categories: food and nonfood items. Nonfood items are most significant in terms of volume. By volume, a UCLA study shows plastic (51 percent) and cardboard (24.5 percent) as dominating dining service waste. A University of Michigan study characterized old corrugated cardboard (33 percent), metals (21 percent), and mixed paper (16 percent) as most significant by volume. By weight, however, food clearly dominates the dining service waste stream—accounting for an estimated 41.5 percent at Tufts and more than 63 percent at Dartmouth. (Tufts' exclusion of cardboard and rendered fats from their study may account for some of the discrepancy.)

Food can constitute almost 10 percent of campus waste by weight, according to data from four campuses who reported food waste composition in the University of Illinois' 1992 report *University and College Solid Waste Reduction and Recycling*. By volume, however, food contributes, on average, just over two percent

Glenn Hutchinson of UNC-Charlotte's honors program initiated the university's food-share program.

campus-wide. In "Trash and Recycled Material Streams at the University of Wisconsin-Madison," students Karma Geiger and Rob Walther calculated the percentage of food in waste from various areas of the campus. Their figures suggest food ranked first in the residence halls at 15 percent by weight (followed by paperboard, mixed office paper, and pizza boxes), second in the academic buildings at 13 percent by weight (after mixed office paper and glossy magazines), and third in both the libraries and the administration buildings, at 8 percent and 9 percent respectively (after mixed office paper and glossy magazines).

Managing Food

Donating unserved leftovers to local organizations in need and composting (a practice almost unheard of outside agricultural schools before the early 1990s) are gaining popularity as methods of reducing food and other organic waste on campuses. Recycling remains the method of choice for most inorganic materials such as metal cans and cardboard. While many campuses are cutting back on disposable food and beverage containers, changing food packaging is proving a more daunting task.

Food-Share

To keep food and waste disposal costs low, all campus dining service staff work hard to avoid leftovers. However, despite their uncanny ability to estimate the demand for particular dishes, something—be it half a tray of lasagna or a tray of vegetable sukiyaki—will invariably remain at the end of the day. Students and staff at several colleges and universities have discovered that these leftovers, though only a fraction of what is served on campus each day, can meet a considerable need in their communities. The University of North Carolina at Charlotte; Birmingham-Southern College in Birmingham, Alabama; Carnegie Mellon University; and Harvard University are among the campuses with ongoing services that provide campus leftovers to organizations in need.

Begun in December 1991, the food-share program at UNC-Charlotte provides a good example of how to start such an initiative and the problems encountered along the way. Glenn Hutchinson, the senior who founded the program, described the day he decided to get involved: "I saw some cafeteria workers dump a whole tray of cake," he recalled. When he was told that health regulations prevented donation of leftover food, Hutchinson investigated the matter further.

North Carolina, it turns out, had passed food-donor protection laws in 1989. An excerpt from General Statute 99B-10 of the North Carolina State General Assembly reads: ". . . any person including but not limited to a seller, farmer,

Thirty to 50 percent of dining service waste (by weight) is readily recyclable and compostable.

Food donor protection laws in some states help protect campuses that donate unserved food to organizations in need.

processor, distributor, wholesaler or retailer of food, who donates an item of food for use or distribution by a nonprofit organization or nonprofit corporation shall not be liable for civil damages or criminal penalties resulting from the nature, age, condition, or packaging of the donated food, unless an injury is caused by the gross negligence, recklessness, or intentional misconduct of the donor." When confronted with a true legal barrier, students at the University of Pennsylvania, with help from their administration, successfully lobbied the state legislature for passage of food donor protection laws. (See "Too Much Food," in *The Student Environmental Action Guide: 25 Simple Things We Can Do.*)

With this obstacle overcome, dining service staff welcomed Hutchinson and other volunteers from the Charlotte Honors Program, which requires 60 hours of community service, to collect food as often as three times a week. Hutchinson says that donations have been especially hefty before campus holidays, when the dining service empties its cupboards. Through much effort, he and other volunteers acquired a van for making deliveries to St. Peter's Soup Kitchen, where Hutchinson volunteered before entering college. According to an article in the *Charlotte Observer*, UNC-Charlotte donations cut St. Peter's food costs by 10 cents a meal per person.

Dr. Roald Hazelhoff, who coordinates Birmingham-Southern College's Environmental Programs, found that many organizations for the homeless or poor in the inner-city already received sufficient food donations. BSC's food-share program therefore concentrates on pre-holiday offerings to rural shelters, which are on call for pickups.

In its second year, UNC-Charlotte's food-share program faced a common challenge: leftovers were being donated that the food service director felt could have been served again on campus. There have been brief episodes of this, says McNitt, at Harvard's Phillip Brooks House, where student volunteers have pulled leftovers from Harvard's 22 food service operations for years. She simply clarified the distinction between food ready for donation and that still viable for campus use—a matter of aesthetics rather than quality. "It is not much of a problem now," she says. UNC-Charlotte's program was reinstituted after students signed petitions, the Student Government Association endorsed the program, and discussions took place between dining service management and staff.

As Hutchinson nears graduation, he is meeting with trustees and lobbying local residents to support the program. To become institutionalized, he says, the program will need a steady stream of volunteers. The Charlotte Honors Program, like the Phillip Brooks House at Harvard, provides a structure for community service which may sustain the food-share program.

Pre-consumer Food Waste

By composting organic food trimmings, paper towels, and napkins, college and university dining services can divert a significant portion of the waste stream and trim their operating costs. Between January and December 1993, for example, Bates College sent 167,533 pounds of pre-consumer food waste (more than half their total dining service waste) to a commercial composter, at a savings of $1,040. Dartmouth College composted 49,100 pounds of pre-consumer food waste, paper towels, and napkins between April and December 1992, saving $1,712 in landfill costs and another $9,702 in fertilizers. (See Chapter 7, Solid Waste.)

The role of dining service staff in composting is primarily one of separating pre-consumer food scraps into composting containers. Bates College separates trimmings into compostable bags tested by the American Society for Testing and Materials. The Johnson State dining service keeps 30-gallon, wheeled "compostainers" in the kitchen, within easy reach of the cooks. A dining service staffer empties one or two bins a day onto a holding pile—which sits, along with the compost and other holding piles, on a concrete slab on a small farm adjacent to the food service. Then a work-study student and student volunteers manage the compost. Peter Napolitano, dining service director at Dartmouth, devoted a walk-in refrigerator to 55-gallon compost containers, grease vats, and waste containers. Dartmouth Recycles, coordinated by Bill Hochstin, picks up and empties the compost bins and prepares the compost.

Dining service staff at Bates College may purchase compost derived from campus food trimmings at $3 a cubic yard for use on their own vegetable gardens. Both Frank Fortin, director of Johnson State's dining services, and Peter Napolitano of Dartmouth's dining services have considered using organic vegetables grown in campus gardens with the dining service-derived compost. Peter Napolitano has created slideshow presentations on Dartmouth's composting program and organic vegetable gardening for NACUFS and other environmental forums.

At Bates, kitchen scraps are separated into compostable bags.

Post-Consumer Food Waste

Post-consumer food waste—the leftovers scraped from diners' plates—is more highly regulated than pre-consumer food waste. Sending post-consumer food to pig farmers was the traditional solution on many rural campuses. This option is becoming expensive, however, as states adopt regulations requiring that post consumer food be sterilized before use.

Some campuses pulp and landfill post-consumer waste as an alternative to large garbage disposals which send ground food waste to sewage treatment plants and eventually to local bodies of water. The pulpers, or pulverizers, are juicers on a larger scale: they squeeze out liquid, greatly reducing both waste volume and landfill costs. Patricia Lee at Tufts receives several requests for information about the Tufts food pulper from staff at other campuses every year.

Single-Use, Non-compostable Materials

Dining service staff and students have several strategies for reducing the waste that is not, or cannot be, composted. Napkin waste, for example, is a pet peeve of many dining service staff, who employ any number of strategies ranging from posting signs asking students to limit the number of napkins they take (University of Richmond) to removing napkin dispensers from tables and placing them next to the condiments (Tufts). At Dartmouth, napkins are a source of carbon for the college's composting program.

Reducing the use of disposable food and beverage containers has been another focal point. The most visible initiative has been the "lug a mug" or "reusable mug" program. The program has spread so quickly that now there is scarcely a campus where students do not tote reusable mugs (often clipped to backpacks) emblazoned with a campus or organization logo. Several groups claim to have started the "lug a mug" concept, but the 1984 program initiated at UW-Madison is the earliest one in Campus Ecology Program records.

Today, "lug a mug" programs are launched as often by dining service managers as by students. Dining service staff will often invest in the mugs, giving students and others who use them a discount of 5–10 percent on beverages, in hopes that waste disposal savings will offset costs. At Dartmouth, the dining service hands out free mugs at the beginning of the year. At Tufts, the dining service subsidizes the mugs for the campus environmental group, which in turn sells them to students and uses the proceeds to fund their activities. Ron Inlow, dining service director at the University of Richmond, distributes "lug a mugs" to students through their campus environmental organization GREEN and also installed a mug rack for line cooks and other dining service employees, who otherwise would not have a place to put their mugs.

Jane Schimpf, director of food operations at Bowling Green State, estimated that disposable cup usage decreased by 16 percent the first year reusable mugs were introduced. UC-Boulder Recycling Coordinator Jack DeBell estimates disposables use decreased by 30 percent upon introduction of their recycled-plastic mug. Switching to washable dishware can result in even more dramatic waste reduction and savings. It cost $37,731 a year to buy paper cups at Bowling Green

Bowling Green State University's Jane Schimpf estimates the university saved $34,000 the first year it used reusable fiberglass trays instead of disposable ones.

State, but only $1,278 (.04 per rack of 36 cups) a year to wash glassware. When the initial cost to purchase new glassware ($4,454) and landfill savings ($251) are figured in, Schimpf estimates gross annual savings from the switch at $33,529. Bowling Green also saved $34,000 the first year they used reusable fiberglass trays instead of disposable trays. (Labor costs remained constant.) When Harvard made a similar shift from disposable beverage containers to washable plastic cups, McNitt says they saved $200,000 in one year, cutting their use of five million disposable cups a year to fewer than 500,000. Peter Napolitano at Dartmouth also switched to reusable beverage containers.

Analyses of the environmental costs and benefits of switching from disposable to permanent dishes and glassware compare the impact of manufacturing each product (e.g. energy, solid waste, water borne waste, water, atmospheric emissions) with the impact of recycling or washing (e.g. energy, water, detergent). One such report prepared in 1991 by Renne Harris, supervisor of environmental services for the Portland public schools, concluded that the conversion from polystyrene disposables to polycarbonate washables would result in an average energy savings of 2.18 billion BTU/year district-wide and a five-year savings in electricity of as much as $34,880. Solid waste, she reported, would be reduced an average of 50,000 pounds a year and atmospheric emissions by 12,000 pounds a year. Although water usage would increase by 2.11 million gallons a year (at a cost of $2,104) and water-borne waste by 7,893 pounds a year ($2,285 in sewer fees), the author deemed these vastly more benign than the costs associated with the manufacture of polystyrene.

Ron Inlow of the University of Richmond discusses waste issues with participants of a 1993 conference that brought together students from around the state to study the environmental impacts of their institutions.

Theft of dishware, which can cost dining services thousands of dollars each year, has vexed many institutions. The dining service at UW-Madison installed dish collection carts in the waste storage rooms on each floor of the student residence halls, using a little reverse psychology to help solve this problem. It even substituted chinaware for disposables in all of the campus take-outs. "There was little problem with theft because people were welcome to take dinnerware out of the dining area," says Neil Michaud, former Residence Hall House Fellow. Plus, he adds with a laugh, "they are really ugly, and I don't think anyone would want them in their home—even a college student."

Paper vs. Plastic

On most campuses, some customers continue to demand disposable food and beverage containers even after the dining service has shifted to reusable mugs and permanent dishware. Unless a campus were to decide not to offer disposable food and beverage containers when requested (which none to our knowledge has done), someone has to decide whether to purchase paper or plastic. This has proven such a controversial issue on some campuses that a few (George Washington University, Roanoke College, the College of William and Mary and, undoubtedly, others) have held forums at which industry and environmental experts make their case for various options.

The paper vs. plastic debate continues to be something of a red herring on campuses. It has frustrated staff and students alike who, nevertheless, have gained experience conducting life-cycle cost analyses which may be applied to other controversial projects later on. In making a decision, campuses have evaluated paper against plastic in all phases of production, use, and disposal, finding little consensus. Ultimately, it is the dining service director who generally makes the thankless choice.

Recycled/Chlorine-Free Paper Products

Cathy Moran, dining service purchaser at the University of Richmond, has made purchasing recycled products a high priority. Her files overflow with product samples and brochures from companies marketing themselves as environmentally-conscious, from tissue to recycling bin manufacturers. "More and more companies," according to Moran, "try to out-compete each other on the environmental front to win dining service contracts." After deciphering various claims and selecting a maker of recycled-content napkins and toilet tissue, Moran and other staff invited chosen vendors to display their wares in the dining hall and to speak with students.

Dining service purchasers have been among the first on campus to respond to concerns about the environmental and the suspected health hazards posed by dioxin and the other chlorine by-products used to whiten paper (see Chapter 6). By the fall of 1992, dining services at Rochester Institute of Technology and Bowdoin College had switched to chlorine-free napkins.

Packaging: Reducing, Reusing and Recycling

Most of the thousands of foods which campuses purchase each year come packaged in some way—eggs in egg cartons, sugar in packets, tomatoes individually wrapped and cushioned between cardboard shelves stacked in boxes, apples in shrink-wrapping. Packaging ranges from the highly functional to the patently comical, but packaging is no laughing matter for campuses; food packaging accounts for as much as 50 percent of dining service waste, and food packaging from dining services alone may total five percent of campus waste. In

Bowdoin College and Rochester Institute of Technology purchase chlorine-free napkins in their dining services.

the United States, product packaging accounts for 65 percent of the paper, 15 percent of the wood, and three percent of all the energy used each year. Yet thanks to overzealous wrapping, the United States has less food waste than many other nations.

Such trade-offs make reducing packaging waste more complex than it may sound. Attached to each seemingly obvious solution—eliminating wasteful packaging, purchasing in bulk, instituting vender take-back policies, and recycling—are both costs and benefits. Some solutions, such as recycling, reduce disposal costs but increase labor costs. Others, such as vendor take-back initiatives, reduce disposal costs and barely change labor costs, but increase storage needs. Reducing resource consumption and the pollution associated with the manufacture of packaging is the one universal benefit of all approaches to reducing, reusing, and recycling packaging waste. This benefit has driven programs at Dartmouth, Tufts, and Harvard.

Alexandra McNitt supplements Harvard's recycling efforts by purchasing in bulk and avoiding excess packaging.

Purchasing in bulk and eliminating unnecessary packaging were two of the first steps taken by Alexandra McNitt when she became Environmental Coordinator for Harvard Dining Services. Ketchup, Worcestershire sauce, mustard, soy sauce, and seasonings now arrive in jumbo-sized bottles. After phasing out 1,000 cases of sugar packets that had been ordered before her arrival, McNitt ordered glass sugar dispensers and began purchasing sugar by the 100-pound bag. From Bates College in Maine to Agnes Scott in Georgia, campuses have moved from mini cereal boxes to bulk cereal dispensers.

But bulk purchasing is not a panacea. There are limits to the weight dining service staff can comfortably and safely lift; anything heavier than 10 pounds presents a challenge for some. Larger sizes, moreover, are not always more efficient. McNitt found that several inches of tomato sauce usually remain at the bottom of 20-gallon dispenser drums.

Packaging take-back programs, whereby vendors reuse their own packaging, are still more a vision than a reality. Both McNitt and Napolitano have items they would like to see delivered in reusable containers. For McNitt it is coffee; instead of mylar bags, which can't be recycled or reused, McNitt wants to see coffee arrive in a plastic container that the supplier would take back and refill as needed. Napolitano would like Dartmouth's cleaning supply vendor to reclaim and refill pails of cleaning chemicals. (Bowling Green State staff wash and save five-gallon buckets, which campus residents use as recycling containers in their offices and rooms.) Vendors could also reclaim their own cardboard boxes. Only a few companies so far, says McNitt, have seriously investigated take-back programs in the dining service industry, but none that she knows of have implemented these programs. Like Kevin Lyons at Rutgers (who had more luck with his packaging take-back initiatives—see Chapter 1, Purchasing), McNitt has drafted letters to Harvard's vendors, alerting them to Harvard's interest in take-back and other waste-reduction opportunities.

The problem with take-back programs is that they require campuses to store and organize containers by vendor. Since storage space is expensive and scarce on many campuses, this can be a considerable deterrent unless vendors make frequent deliveries. Packaging could be housed in a central storage area on some campuses, but this would require vendors to make separate deliveries and pick-ups, increasing the cost and labor involved in serving a campus. The key seems to be selecting one or two vendors and types of packaging to target first—as McNitt has with coffee and Napolitano has with the plastic buckets in which chemicals arrive.

Who Does the Dirty Work?

Because of the relatively large volume of their waste, most dining services find it fiscally and environmentally responsible to recycle. Even where there are central recycling programs, many campus dining services have transformed themselves into mini-processing centers. Cleaning out, separating, and storing bottles, cans, and plastic—a process which adds several minutes to any task—is only part of the picture. Dining services often further process cardboard and cans,

Peter Napolitano poses with Dartmouth's "compostainers" and baled cardboard. At right, number 10 cans await crushing by student volunteers.

investing in their own balers and can crushers to do so. Breaking down and baling cardboard greatly enhances its commodity value on the recycling market, but increases labor requirements. At Dartmouth, one full-time staff position has been devoted to this task. At Tufts, two dedicated staff members perform the service on a voluntary basis.

Dining services are generally reluctant to involve students in cardboard baling and other aspects of recycling because of liability concerns. Cardboard balers are powerful and potentially dangerous pieces of equipment, and even glass is such an impediment to worker safety that Dartmouth switched all beverage contracts from glass to aluminum in fall of 1993. Central recycling programs run larger enterprises and therefore, the reasoning goes, are in a better position to train students through work-study programs and to address liability questions. Efforts to involve students as volunteers in other aspects of dining service recycling, such as can crushing, have been successful but spotty. Bags of number 10 cans at Dartmouth lie waiting, seemingly in vain, for the student volunteers who so enthusiastically crushed them the previous semester.

Overcoming Limited Staffing

Harvard's and Tufts' dining services benefit from unique institutional support. Harvard's Alexandra McNitt works full-time analyzing waste-reduction opportunities and coordinating environmental consultants. This support has enabled Michael Berry, Harvard's dining service director, to demonstrate that the fiscal and public-relations benefits of their waste reduction and other ecological initiatives have outweighed the costs.

Tufts' Patricia Lee emphasizes the role played by Sarah Creighton, Manager of the Tufts CLEAN! Program, which operated out of the Tufts Center for Environmental Management from 1989 until the spring of 1994. Creighton provided hours of free consultation, organized student volunteers to conduct research, helped organize Tufts' dining service conferences, and provided unquantifiable support and encouragement.

Campus dining services without such support or staffing have engaged in some creative compensation—such as forming alliances with on-campus recycling coordinators. The friendship cultivated between Peter Napolitano, director of dining services, and Bill Hochstin, head of Dartmouth Recycles, for instance, has made composting—and, undoubtedly, novel initiatives yet to come—feasible. Dining service staff have also become members of campus environmental committees, which link them with available resources and give them an opportunity to galvanize support. Ron Inlow, Peter Napolitano, and Robert Volpi (of Richmond, Dartmouth, and Bates, respectively) are active members of their campuses' environmental committees.

Dining service directors have reached out to state agencies and community groups for support. Purchasing from local, organic farmers at Bates would have been impossible if not for help from Russell Libby at the State Department of Agriculture. Dining service staff have also recruited faculty, who have made applied student research a part of their curricula; Molly Anderson supported Tufts local purchasing efforts in this way. Dining service staff serve on the NACUFS Environmental Committee and often network with staff at other universities.

No campus ecology initiative is complete without dining service staff. In recruiting dining service participation, however, campus activists need to be prepared to offer reliable support. Helping the dining service compost, recycle, or purchase locally grown foods may not be as glamorous as cleaning a local river, lake, or bay, but it may be more effective in the long run in preventing the pollution of these natural resources and protecting public health.

Dining service directors have reached out to state agencies and community groups for support.

BIBLIOGRAPHY

"27th Environmental Quality Review," *National Wildlife*, Feb/March, 1995, pp. 34–41.

"The Big Picture," *Farmer to Farmer*, Special Edition, Vol. III, No. 6, 1994, Ozark Small Farm Viability Project, P.O. Box 99, Mt. Judea, AR 72655.

Biotechnology and the Environment, Margaret Mellon, National Wildlife Federation, 1988. (See the Union of Concerned Scientists' publications office for a listing of Dr. Mellon's writings on biotechnology and the environment.)

Biotechnology's Bitter Harvest: Herbicide Tolerant Crops and the Threat to Sustainable Agriculture, Rebecca Goldburg, Jane Rissler, et al., Biotechnology Working Group, March, 1990.

"The Campus and the Biosphere Initiative at Carleton and Saint Olaf Colleges," Eugene Bakko and John Woodwell, *The Campus and Environmental Responsibility*, David Eagan and David Orr, Eds., Jossey-Bass Publishers, No. 77, Spring, 1992, pp. 89–102.

"Farm Herbicides Foul Tap Water for 14 Million," Gary Lee, *Washington Post*, October 19, 1994, A3.

"Financing a Local Foods Project with Energy Savings," Sean McCauley, Jennifer McWilliams, and John Woodwell, Department of Biology, St. Olaf College, Northfield, MN 55057. (507) 663-3399.

"Hendrix College Local Food Project," Gary Valen, *Campus Environmental Responsibility*, David Eagan and David Orr, Eds., Jossey-Bass Publishers, No. 77, Spring, 1992, pp. 77–88.

Kerr Center for Sustainable Agriculture Newsletter, Hwy. 271 S., P.O. Box 588, Poteau, OK 74953. (918) 647-9123.

Diet for a New America, John Robbins, EarthSave Foundation, 706 Frederick St., Santa Cruz, CA 95062-2205. (800) 362-3648.

"Bowling Green State—A Proposal," Jane Schimpf, University Food Operations, Bowling Green, OH 43403-0311. (419) 372-2891. (An annualized financial cost assessment of switching from disposables to glassware.)

"Eating Green: A Re-examination of Diet in Light of Environmental Concerns," Walter Simpson, Energy Coordinator, SUNY-Buffalo, Life Workshops. (716) 645-6125.

"Environmental Costs and Benefits of Switching from Polystyrene Disposable Ware to Polycarbonate Permanent Ware," Renne Harris, Portland Public Schools, Board of Education, April, 1991. (Contact Campus Ecology Program, NWF, see number below.)

"Environmental Stewardship in Tufts University Food Services," by Patricia Lee and Sarah Hammond Creighton, March, 1993. (Call Tufts University Dining Services or Campus Ecology, NWF at numbers listed below.)

"Farm Subsidies: Consequences and Alternatives," Rocky Mountain Institute, 1739 Snowmass Creek Road, Snowmass, CO 81654-9199.

Fertility on the Brink: The Legacy of the Chemical Age, National Wildlife Federation, 1994.

"Food Service Waste," *In Our Backyard: Environmental Issues at UCLA*, April Smith, et al., 1989, UC Regents, Publications Coordinator, Grad. School of Arch. & Planning, 1317 Perloff Hall, 405 Hilgard Ave., Los Angeles, CA 90024-1467.

The Four-Season Harvest, Eliot Coleman, Chelsea-Green Publishers, 1992.

"Special Report: Pesticides," *Farmworker Justice News*, Farmworker Justice Fund, Summer, 1990.

"Harvard University Begins Environmental Campaign," *Food Management Magazine*, Penton Publications, Dec., 1992, 1100 Superior Avenue, Cleveland, OH 44197-8146.

Friendly Foods: Gourmet Vegetarian Cuisine, Brother Ron Pickarski, O.F.M., EarthSave Foundation, 706 Frederick St., Santa Cruz, CA 95062-2205. (Brother Ron is a three-time Culinary Olympic Medal winner.)

"Growing Crops, and Wildlife Too," Greg Breining, *National Wildlife*, Dec/Jan, 1995, pp. 40–43.

The Guide to the U.S. Organic Foods Production Act of 1990, Stuart Fishman, Organic Foods Production Association of North America (OFPANA), P.O. Box 1078, Greenfield, MA 01301. (413) 774-7511.

Handbook of Toxicity of Pesticides to Wildlife, R. H. Hudson, et al., U.S. Department of the Interior, Fish and Wildlife Service, Resource Publication 153, 2nd ed., Washington, D.C., U.S. Government Printing Office.

"Natural Farming Harvests New Support," Michael Lipske, *National Wildlife*, A/M, 1990, pp. 18–24.

"North Carolina Laws Protecting Food Donors," *1991 Cumulative Supplement*, General Assembly of North Carolina, General Statute 99B-10.

"Paper Versus Polystyrene: A Complex Choice," by Martin B. Hocking, *Science*, Vol. 251, Feb., 1991, pp. 504–5.

Pesticide Alert: A Guide to Pesticides in Fruits and Vegetables, L. Mott and K. Snyder, Natural Resources Defense Council, 1987.

"Pesticides: Amounts Applied and Amounts Reaching Pests," D. Pimentel and L. Levitan, *BioScience*, 36, 1986.

"Pulling Utilities Together: Water-Energy Partnerships," Rocky Mountain Institute, 1739 Snowmass Creek Road, Snowmass, CO 81654-9199.

Silent Spring, Rachel Carson, Houghton Mifflin Co., 1962.

Solid Waste Reduction in Colleges and Universities: A Status Report, Sarah Hammond Creighton, et al., Center for Environmental Management, Tufts University, 1993, pp. 53–59. (Ms. Creighton, an environmental consultant, may be contacted at: 51 Orchard St., Byfield, MA 01922 for information on food service equipment energy efficiency and other issues of relevance to dining service waste reduction.)

"Too Much Food," *Student Environmental Action Guide: 25 Simple Things We Can Do*, Student Environmental Action Coalition, Earth Works Press, Berkeley, CA, 1991, pp. 15–17. (415) 841-5866.

"Trash and Recycled Material Streams at the University of Wisconsin-Madison: A Characterization and Analysis," Karma Geiger and Rob Walther, *Campus Ecology Research Project Report No. 6*, May, 1994, Appendices D-I.

University and College Solid Waste Reduction and Recycling, by Bruce Hegberg, et al., University of Illinois Center for Solid Waste Management and Research, 1992, pp. 23–30. (See Chapter 7, Solid Waste, for ordering information.)

NETWORKING

Campus

Bates College
Attn. Robert Volpi
Dining Services
Lewiston, ME 04240
(207) 786-6255
Purchasing local, organic foods; large-scale pre-consumer food composting program; wide variety of vegetarian recipes.

Bowling Green State
Attn. Jane Schimpf
University Food Operations
Bowling Green, OH 43403-0311
(419) 372-2891
Comparative cost-benefit analysis of dishware and disposables, showing dishware is significantly less expensive.

Carleton College
c/o Ed Buchwald
Department of Geology
Northfield, MN 55057
(507) 663-4403
For information about Campus and the Biosphere Program and related studies.

If you find that an organization listed here has moved or a contact has been replaced, let the Campus Ecology Program staff know. We'll help match you with the latest source for the information you need.

Colby College
Attn. Dining Services
Waterville, ME 04901
(207) 872-3168
Small-scale local and organic food purchasing.

Connecticut College
Attn. Matthew Fay
Dining Services
270 Mohegan Ave.
New London, CT 06320
(203) 439-2752
Uses low-phosphate detergents to prevent pollution of local water resources.

Dartmouth College
Attn. Peter Napolitano
Dining Services
Hanover, NH 03755
(603) 646-1110
Composting pre-consumer food waste, waste reduction.

Duke University
Attn. John Woodwell
School of Forestry and Env. Studies
Bio Sciences Building
Durham, NC 27706
Information about Campus and the Biosphere Program.

George Washington University
Dining Services
Washington, D.C. 20052
Sponsored forums on paper vs. plastic debate.

Harvard University
Attn. Alexandra McNitt
Dining Services
Cambridge, MA 02138
Alexandra McNitt serves as NACUFS Environmental Committee Chair. Dynamic food share program, comprehensive dining service greening efforts, energy and water efficiency initiatives, complete environmental auditing, hazardous waste minimization, air and water quality improvements, purchasing in bulk, packaging take-back, cost benefit analyses, use of outside environmental consultants, occasional organic meals.

Hendrix College
Dining Services
Conway, AR 72032
(501) 450-1362
Local foods purchasing program operated in late 1980s and first couple of years in 90s, see chapter by Gary Valen, former dean, listed above.

Johnson State College
Attn. Frank Fortin
ARA Services
Johnson, VT 05656
(802) 635-7751
Pre-consumer food waste composting; use of "compostainers," perforated PV-pipe for aeration, slanted concrete catchment for holding piles.

Rochester Institute of Technology
Student Union Food Services
Rochester, NY 14623
(716) 475-6631
Chlorine-free, recycled napkins; waste reduction.

St. Charles Community College
c/o Dr. Arlan Hinchee
Biology Department
P.O. Box 76975
St. Peters, MO 63366
(314) 922-8000 ext. 4340
Reusable mug video, area businesses give discounts on drinks served in the mugs.

St. Lawrence University
Attn. Dr. Alan Schwartz
Environmental Studies Program
Canton, NY 13617
(315) 379-5357
Food-waste composting program was abandoned, but is an interesting case study for anyone wishing to establish a similar program.

St. Olaf College
Attn. Gene Bakko
Department of Biology
St. Olaf College
Northfield, MN 55057
(507) 663-3399
Information about the Campus and Biosphere Program which included several campus food studies.

Tufts University
Attn. Patricia Lee
Dining Services
89 Curtis St.
Medford, MA 02155
(617) 627-3566
Long-range environmental planning, energy efficiency audits, waste reduction, food pulping, local organic foods research project.

University of California-Davis
Attn: David Orr
Office of Environmental Services
Davis, CA 95616
(916) 752-6970
dgorr@ucdavis.edu
Food composting and use of compost in on-campus organic gardens.

University of California-Santa Cruz
Attn: Monte Tudor-Long
Food Services
Santa Cruz, CA 95064
(408) 459-4415
*Tudor-Long piloted a composting
program in one of the university's
four food services; related studies
are available.*

University of North Carolina-
Charlotte
Honors Program
Charlotte, NC 28223
*Food-share program, donor
protection laws.*

University of Richmond
Attn. Ron Inlow
Dining Services
Richmond, VA 23173
*Chlorine-free, recycled products;
specifies 'dolphin-free' tuna in
vender contracts; extensive waste
reduction and recycling; bulk
purchasing; wide variety of
vegetarian meals; creative
signage.*

Regional and National

National Association of College
and University Food Services
(NACUFS)
1450 South Harrison Road, Suite 303
Michigan State University
East Lansing, MI 48824
(517) 332-2494
*Hosts active environmental
committee, regional conferences,
and electronic correspondence
group for members on waste
reduction, energy efficiency,
water quality and other environmental topics pertaining to
campus food services.*

AgriSystems International
125 West Seventh St.
Wind Gap, PA 18091
(215) 863-6700
*Policy primers and technical
assistance with organic food
purchasing, processing,
distributing and marketing.*

Agricultural Resource Center
Pesticide Education Project
115 W. Main St.
Carrboro, NC 27510
(919) 967-1886

Meadowcreek, Inc.
Attn. Gary Valen
Fox, AR 72051
(501) 363-4500
*Environmental retreat and
education center in the Ozark
Mountains of Arkansas.*

National Organic Marketing
Cooperative Project
Attn: Eric Ardapple-Kindberg
HC32, Box 40
Mt. Judea, AR 72655
*Project underway to research and
develop a model for a national
organic cooperative for marketing,
transportation, quality control
and distribution of organic
produce, field crops, dairy and
livestock products.*

Organic Foods Production
Association of North America
(OFPANA)
P.O. Box 1078
Greenfield, MA 01301
(413) 774-7411
FAX: (413) 774-6432
*Contact for organic food
brokerages and cooperatives near
you.*

National Wildlife Federation
Campus Outreach Division
1400 16th St., N.W.
Washington, D.C. 20036-2266
(202) 797-5435 (general
information)
(313) 769-9970 or
midwest@nwf.org (M.W.)
(202) 797-5468 or
noreast@nwf.org (N.E.)
(404) 876-2608 or
soeast@nwf.org (S.E.)
(503) 222-1429 or
western@nwf.org (West)
*Write for Food Issues Resource
Packet or call for help coordinating food related projects: organic
foods, vegetarian recipes, sources
for chlorine-free and recycled
products, energy efficiency
information, reusable mugs, case
studies, etc.*

National Organic Production
Program
USDA/AMS/TMD/MTRB
Room 2510-South
P.O. Box 96456
Washington, D.C. 20090-6456
(202) 205-7804
*Contact for updates on legislation,
federal programs and studies.*

NOFA Video Project
411 Sheldon Rd.
Barre, MA 01005
(508) 355-2853
*A project of the Northeast Organic
Farming Association; offers
dozens of videos on such subjects
as building organic soils, organic
weed controls, an overview of
organic practices in the Northeast,
the organic transition,
composting, school gardens, etc.*

State Departments of Agriculture
*Contact sustainable agriculture
departments for list of local
organic food cooperatives or for
help in forming one.*

CHAPTER 6

Communication Services
Office Equipment and Printing

Remember the indigo ink and nostalgic scent of copies made on ditto machines? Or the plunkety-plunk of typewriters? One need think back only a decade or so to realize how dramatically communication technology has changed. The vast array of equipment connecting people on campus and linking them to the larger world has become an essential aspect of academic vitality.

Advances in communication technology bring both unforeseen costs and opportunities. Campuses have seen financial savings from energy-efficient projects quickly offset in recent years by the rapid proliferation of personal computers and other office equipment. And despite the increase in electronic communications made possible by computers, the "paperless" university remains largely elusive in the U.S., which leads the world in paper consumption. From campus print shops to personal computers, producing documents is a resource-intensive business.

Even before a document is desktop published or photocopied, staff and students have numerous opportunities to reduce pollution through judicious use of computers, monitors, printers, fax machines, and other communications equipment. In this regard, SUNY-Buffalo (UB) sets a precedent. Walter Simpson, UB's energy officer, has collaborated with the EPA's Energy Star Program, student interns, and others, to launch the nation's first campus-wide Green Computing campaign, designed to cut the university's energy costs and to educate users of office equipment.

Although the printing industry is on the brink of fundamental reforms, it will be years before new technologies are accessible to most budget-constrained campuses. But even working with current technology, students and staff can choose from a

As a graduate student at MIT, Cyane Dandridge designed procedures for monitoring office equipment energy use.

CURTIS CROLEY

wide range of papers and a growing array of inks and printing processes that collectively lighten the environmental toll significantly. Printing staff at the University of Oregon and other campuses provide a glimpse of these opportunities.

SMART OFFICES

When Cyane Dandridge's graduate advisor encouraged her to apply her background in physics and electronics to an office equipment research project with the EPA's Energy Star Program, she jumped at the chance. It was a career-launching decision. While many of the other students in MIT's Building Technology Program analyzed heating and air conditioning systems, Dandridge was developing expertise in a nascent field. Her master's thesis, *Energy Efficiency in Office Technology,* has been included in the interactive CD-Rom *The Greening of the White House,* and is being published as a book by E-Source. Test procedures she wrote for her thesis may soon be used to satisfy certain provisions in the Environmental Policy Act of 1992. Her subsequent work as a researcher at MIT and, most recently, as program manager with the Energy Star Program, is helping to change the way office equipment is purchased and used on campuses and other institutions nationwide.

Office Equipment Offsets Energy Gains

Until 1990, says Dandridge, commercial electricity use was broken down into "heating," "lighting," and "other." "'Other' could include anything and was getting to be pretty big," she explains, "so people started trying to break it down, which is where studies on office equipment came in." When research showed that skyrocketing use of computers, monitors, fax machines, printers, and copiers had begun to offset efficiency measures in lighting and heating, office equipment emerged as a discrete and important category of energy use and general environmental accounting. Printing, xerographic and writing papers, for instance, are the largest category of paper waste in the U.S., equalling roughly the combined total of discarded newspapers and corrugated cardboard.

Office equipment is of particular significance in the federal government, which constitutes 10 percent of the U.S. market for such products. But academia is also an important market. The nation spent $1.8 trillion to power office equipment in 1989 alone. Without intervention, Dandridge says, this energy load is expected to double by 2011—to an annual expenditure of $3.6 trillion. The EPA's Energy Star Computers Program (which helped to finance Dandridge's research at MIT) aims to head off these cost and energy increases. By establishing energy efficiency guidelines for computers and monitors, labeling qualifying products, working

When it became apparent that computers were one of the fastest-growing electrical loads on campus, staff and students launched UB's Green Computing campaign.

with manufacturers, and educating purchasers, Dandridge estimates EPA's Energy Star Computers will reduce anticipated needs for new power plants from 6.4 plants by 2011 to 3.3, thus saving $1.7 trillion annually.

Manufacturers Help Consumers

It seems reasonable to expect office equipment manufacturers to provide energy consumption profiles for their products, as an aid to the individual consumer and to researchers in the field. The Energy Policy Act of 1992, in fact, requires manufacturers to provide such information, but there is no standard method of testing such energy use. Dandridge's timely research at MIT entailed developing procedures for measuring the energy requirements of specific types of office equipment. A committee under the Information Technologies Institute (formerly the Computer Business Equipment Manufacturers Association) is currently considering her procedures for use in satisfying the Energy Policy Act requirements. (For more information contact the EPA's Energy Star Program listed in the networking section.)

MIT, UB, and Other Campuses Get Involved

Dandridge has also worked with MIT staff, encouraging them to incorporate new specifications into their purchasing language for computers and monitors. She regularly receives calls from other colleges and universities where staff want information on reducing the cost and the environmental impact of office equipment. For example, when it became apparent to Walter Simpson, UB's energy officer, that computers were one of the fastest growing electrical loads on campus, he sought guidance from Dandridge and others in developing the university's Green Computing campaign—the first campus-wide energy conservation campaign in the country to focus on computers.

"People have developed extremely bad habits with respect to how they use their personal computers," says Simpson, who is aiming for a 50 percent reduction in the $300,000 annual cost of operating the estimated 8,000 personal computers on campus. To help improve computing habits, he and student interns Lisa DeFrancesco and Cindy Guguentz created the *UB Guide to Green Computing: How Your Choices Can Make a Difference*, which they distribute to all interested departments and provide at cost to other campuses (see ordering information in networking section).

Computers and Monitors

Computers and monitors deserve special attention, says Dandridge, because they represent the largest share of the office equipment energy load at most

To help improve campus habits, Simpson and two student interns wrote this guide, which they distribute to all interested departments.

PURCHASING ENERGY-EFFICIENT COMPUTERS, MONITORS, AND PRINTERS

The following specifications may be useful to campus computer purchasers:

1. Computer products must meet the EPA Energy Star requirements for energy efficiency. This means that personal computers (PCs), monitors, and printers shall be able to enter, and recover from, a low-power standby mode when not in use. For PCs and monitors, the low-power mode is defined as 30 watts or less (30 watts for the PCs and 30 watts for the monitor). For printers with speeds of less than 15 pages per minute, the requirement is 30 watts, and for printers with speeds of 15 or more pages per minute, the requirement is 45 watts. All high-end color printers must not exceed 45 watts in low-power mode.

2. All products should be shipped with the Energy Star low-power feature activated or enabled. This eliminates the need for users to configure the power management feature after delivery, and helps to ensure that the energy-saving feature is used.

3. Qualifying models must function similarly to equivalent non-Energy Star models. Functions should include but not be limited to:

a. the ability to run commercial off-the-shelf software both before and after recovery from a low power state, including retention of files opened before the power management feature was activated; and

b. full compatibility with specified network environments and, when in a low-power state, retained connection with the network—e.g. PCs resting in a low-power state should not be disconnected from the network. Many manufacturers are now testing their Energy Star equipment on networks and can report, for example, that they are Novell Certified.

4. Monitors should be capable of entering the Energy Star low-power mode when connected to the accompanying PC. Most Energy Star monitors must rely on some external input to trigger their low-power state. This is typically accomplished via one of the following: (1) VESA Display Power Management Signalling (DPMS), a signalling protocol that allows a PC equipped with DPMS to control a DPMS compatible monitor (both the computer and monitor must be DPMS compatible), or (2) the actual shut-off of power to the monitor via a special plug connected to the PC's power supply. Campuses may wish to specify one approach or the other. DPMS compatible PCs and monitors provide seamless power management and immediate recovery from the low-power state, but only when used with each other. PCs which employ the power-switch approach can shut off power to any monitor, not just an Energy Star monitor.

institutions—about 646 kilowatts per year for a conventional personal computer and a 15-inch color cathode ray tube (CRT) monitor. Computers and monitors consume more energy than other types of office equipment, says Dandridge, because there are more of them. Printers, copiers, and fax machines, although in some cases bigger energy guzzlers per unit, are typically shared by numerous users.

To reduce campus energy costs, Dandridge suggests buying more energy-efficient computers and monitors, and using existing computers more judiciously. The EPA's Energy Star Computers Program has thousands of qualified computers, monitors and printers which power-down or "sleep" to save energy when not in use (an estimated 50 percent of the time they are on). While a standard computer and 15-inch color monitor together use about 646 kilowatts or $52-worth of power annually, comparable Energy Star units cut those costs almost in half—to approximately 348 kilowatts or $28 annually. (Calculated savings are based on the average national energy cost of $0.08/kilowatt and estimated average computer on-time of 8.6 hours a work day.) Energy Star laser printers, also equipped with sleep modes, save an estimated 500 kilowatts or $40 per unit annually when compared to conventional equipment. Energy Star provides updated lists of certified computers, monitors and printers. Suggested purchasing language for Energy Star computers as well as the "Energy Star Purchasing Agreement" (which campus purchasers are encouraged to sign) are reproduced at the end of this chapter.

Sleep mode is an increasingly common, but nevertheless important, energy-saving feature in computers, but there are others. Notebook computers with liquid crystal display (LCD) screens use less than one-quarter the energy of Energy Star computers and CRT monitors. Color monitors use up to twice as much energy as monochrome monitors. And, in general, the higher the resolution and larger the screen, the more energy-intensive the monitor. (Screen savers, not to be confused with low standby, are not energy savers.)

The potential for significant savings increases in such places as campus administrative and computer centers, where the number of computers per capita is high and where the heat generated by office equipment and lighting begins to affect climate control costs. Heat gain from inefficient lighting, computers, and other office equipment accounts for much of the air conditioning needs of campus offices and administration buildings. Energy-efficient office equipment and lighting not only cost less to operate, but also radiate less heat, considerably reducing building cooling costs. On some campuses, the waste heat from computers and other office equipment is captured to heat buildings, but in many climates, the expense of cooling buildings far outweighs that of heating them.

Monitors and computers can be turned on and off throughout the day without damage to the equipment or loss of productivity.

Turn Them Off

Computers and monitors would consume much less energy if not for the myth that turning them off and on reduces their life expectancy. To the contrary, counters Dandridge, studies show that monitors can be turned on and off throughout the day without damage or loss of productivity. "You turn it back on and everything is right there again," she emphasizes; the computer can even be turned off and rebooted several times a day without damage to the switch or system. Since many people prefer not to reboot the computer, Dandridge suggests turning off just the monitor during short breaks, and both monitor and computer during lunch or long meetings. "It actually, in the long run, will probably add to their lifetime because they are off longer," she asserts.

Relying on behavioral change to curb the office equipment energy appetite, however, is a gamble. "Unfortunately, people will start out saying that they will turn off their computer and monitor, but after about two months of doing it," Dandridge has found, "they get tired of it and stop." Retrofitting computers with sleep devices or purchasing Energy Star equipment are ultimately the most reliable ways to conserve energy, she says. "We really need to go in the direction of having these things be automatic."

Radiation

Energy efficiency is not the only consideration when in the market for greener computer equipment. Many people worry about the long-term health effects of exposure to the high- and low-frequency magnetic radiation emitted by CRT monitors. Linda Latham, director of the Energy Star Program, says many Energy Star monitors are also low-radiation models. Those that specify "low radiation MPR 2" meet a standard established in Sweden to protect employees who work at computers all day. The *UB Guide to Green Computing* suggests that staff and students keep themselves at a reasonable distance from the screen (since radiation intensity is inversely proportional to the square of the distance from the source) and avoid the sides and backs of monitors, where emissions are usually higher than in front.

Printers and Copy Machines

Use Both Sides

The single most energy-conscious action anyone can take when using office equipment, says Dandridge, is to print or copy on both sides of the page. The energy consumption represented by paper is indirect, but substantial. "It takes about 20 watt-hours to produce a sheet of paper at the paper manufacturing

> The single most energy-conscious action anyone can take when using office equipment is to print and copy on both sides of the page.
> —Cyane Dandridge, EPA, Energy Star Program

plant," Dandridge found, "and it takes about two watt-hours for a copier to put an image on one side." Double-sided copying thus saves approximately 20 watt-hours per sheet (since it costs 44 watt-hours to print on one side of two sheets as opposed to only 24 watt-hours to print on both sides of one sheet), making the duplex feature on copy machines one of their most important energy-saving features. Double-siding also cuts paper costs in half, saving small companies or departments an estimated $700 annually in paper costs, says Dandridge, or more than 240 kilowatts annually in paper production. And, she says, the extra energy used by duplex document handlers is minimal, adding a maximum of five watts to models with reliable mechanisms.

Right-Sizing

Size and speed, after duplex features, are the next most important issues in selecting copy machines. "The copy machine should be appropriate for the need," Dandridge emphasizes. A midsize machine sitting idle will use 300–400 watts and an additional 100 watts or so when active. Large copy jobs can more efficiently be done on the large, high-speed copiers available in the printing and xerographic departments on most campuses. It is also useful to compare the energy use of comparable models. When comparing copiers, for example, Dandridge says, "I tested two that were exactly the same speed and had the same automatic document handlers for double-sided copying, but one used 200 watts when it was on and waiting to copy and the other used 350 watts." They had the same features, but their energy consumption was very different.

Ink Jets vs. Lasers

While paper use accounts for most of the indirect energy costs of copying and printing, most of the direct energy consumption comes from heat transfer around the fusing mechanisms in copiers and laser printers. For example, a 4 page-per-minute (ppm) ink jet printer, which sprays ink directly onto the page, uses only about 13 watts, Dandridge found, whereas a 4 ppm laser printer, which uses a hot roller and pressure to fuse an image onto the page, uses between 60 and 80 watts. Ink jet printers also re-feed old paper (facilitating the use of second sides for drafts) more easily than laser printers, and ink jet quality is often comparable to laser. "The color ink jets are definitely equal to laser quality," says Dandridge, "and use a lot less energy." In order to make copy machines more efficient, manufacturers and the students and faculty in Dandridge's former department at MIT are exploring fuser mechanism innovations.

Where laser printers are required, Dandridge suggests selecting Energy Star models with "low standby" states and with draft modes that use less toner. En-

Copiers with the same features often do not use the same amount of energy.

ergy Star laser printers consume about 227 kilowatts per year, 500 kilowatts or $40 less than conventional laser printers. Dandridge has found standby states less effective in copiers than in printers—especially if copiers are in nearly continuous use. Depending on the copier, recovery time can be longer than 15 seconds, the maximum wait most people will accept. Although studies have shown people will not tolerate long recovery times, says Dandridge, who has researched issues of productivity in connection with energy efficiency, "it's not as imperative for a printer to have immediate recovery," she says, because more of the process is automatic, requiring less time away from one's desk.

Fax Machines

The least energy-intensive way to send and receive a fax is by computer modem. A fax machine uses as much as 100 watts, but a fax modem adds only a couple of watts to a computer's energy consumption. "Unless you will need to leave your computer on to accept faxes at night," says Dandridge, using a fax modem makes the most sense. If receiving faxes at night is important, fax machines can be turned on at night when computers are turned off, or many computers can "wake up" when receiving incoming faxes. Fax modems also reduce paper use, since you can fax directly from the computer. If a fax machine is necessary, ink jet faxes, like ink jet printers, consume much less energy than their laser counterparts, and can reuse paper for incoming faxes.

Computer "Take-Back"

Purchasers should also consider the recyclability and reusability of computer parts, says Dandridge, whose research covered "take-back" programs in the U.S. and in Europe. Sending toner cartridges from laser printers and copy machines back to manufacturers for refilling has become commonplace, and saves campuses thousands of dollars each year. (It also helps support conservation organizations; e.g. Canon USA, Inc. donates 50 cents from each of its recycled cartridges to the National Wildlife Federation and other nonprofit organizations.)

The recycling and reusing of computer parts is still relatively new. In many European countries, laws require that manufacturers take back used appliances, including computer equipment, but Dandridge has found only a couple of take-back centers in the U.S. do more than salvage copper wiring or other parts with high market value. Full-scale take-back centers reuse and recycle a substantial portion of the components and casing. "They may take reusable parts from a 286 computer, for instance, and put them into other products or recycle the glass, metal or plastic," explains Dandridge, "or sometimes they will sell old chips to toy or car manufacturers." If it doesn't have significant burn-in, the CRT, she

In many European countries, laws require that manufacturers take back used appliances, including computer equipment.

says, is often placed in a different casing.

Campuses interested in renovating their old computers someday, says Dandridge, should keep in mind that computers and monitors with only one or two different types of clearly numbered plastics and a single screw size can be disassembled and rebuilt more easily than equipment with less standardized fastenings and casings.

Campuses might also consider donating their old computers to organizations in need. The East-West Educational Development Foundation in Boston is one organization which facilitates such exchanges, channelling hundreds of donated personal computers to Eastern Europe and elsewhere each year.[1]

Watching Watts on Campus

Computer users often say their machines use only about as much energy as a light bulb—but those light bulbs are the outmoded incandescent types, which gobble up 100 watts or more and which campuses are rapidly replacing with 15- and 18-watt compact fluorescents. Although any single piece of office equipment may seem as innocuous as "one of those old light bulbs," they all add up: 200–300 watts for a computer and monitor, another 50 for a fax, another 200–1,000 for a copier, and 100 or more for most laser printers. UB's *Green Computing Campaign* is proof that campuses have caught on to this fact. With Energy-Star labeling on computers, it is finally easy for students, faculty, and staff to compare brands and models, casting their dollars like votes for energy-efficient communication technology.

PURCHASING POLICY
In Support of Purchasing Energy Star Computers

....

Policy

Our organization supports the concept of voluntary programs that reduce air pollution and enhance environmental protection.

Our organization agrees that the use of energy-efficient computers and printers will reduce energy use, save money, and prevent pollution.

To demonstrate our commitment to saving energy, we agree to do the following:

- Revise our purchasing or procurement specifications to require that all purchases of new computers, monitors, and printers meet the EPA's Energy Star requirements, so long as performance needs are met, and there is no significant cost difference;

- Investigate the profitability of purchasing after-market devices or software designed to help us reduce the energy use associated with our current stock of computers, monitors, and printers;

- Encourage our employees to turn off their individual computers, monitors, and printers when they leave for the day, where applicable;

- Educate our employees about the economic and environmental benefits of using Energy Star computers (with the assistance of EPA-provided materials).

_____
Signature

_____
Title

_____
Name of Organization

Please return signed copy to:
Linda Latham
MC 6202J
US EPA
Washington, DC 20460

Signing this pledge can be the first step in curtailing computer-related energy use.

---

1. *Global Network*, 1993, p. 46. See bibliography.

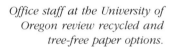 PRINTING

While they may not always match the convenience and flexibility of personal computers, printers, and copiers, central reprographic and printing services typically produce the most cost-effective and energy-efficient documents and publications. Using central services is, in itself, often an environmentally prudent choice. This is especially true at such campuses as Pennsylvania State, Oregon State, and the University of Oregon, where print shop staff and customers are helping to broaden markets for environmentally friendly paper, inks and printing methods.

Offset and Copy Paper

J.R. Gaddis, director of printing services at the University of Oregon, has been in the printing business for 32 years. He began using recycled paper and lobbying paper manufacturers for better recycled sheets in the early 1970s, when he worked in private industry. By the time he arrived at Oregon State University (OSU), the quality of recycled paper had improved significantly. Gaddis joined a waste management committee on which, he says, as production manager, it was easy for him to counter the arguments popular in the mid-1980s that "recycled sheets didn't run well through the copiers or presses." When Gaddis transferred to the University of Oregon in 1994, OSU was using recycled paper for most of its work. "We even used recycled glossy paper," Gaddis says.

Gaddis's predecessor at the University of Oregon had already introduced a wide variety of papers with recycled content. The University of Oregon now aims, says Gaddis, to have at least some recycled content in all paper used on campus. But environmentally friendly paper is more than the sum of its recycled content, recognizes Gaddis, who says the university's specifications for paper have become more exacting over time, addressing such issues as post-consumer content, bleaching, deinking and alternative fibers.

Office staff at the University of Oregon review recycled and tree-free paper options.

TERRA MONTGOMERY

Post-Consumer Content

"Students increasingly ask for post-consumer paper and printers are becoming more accustomed to working with it," says Bill Meyer, president of the American Association of College and University Printers and director of printing at Pennsylvania State.

Not to be confused with the "recycled content" made from paper mill waste, "post-consumer" pulp is made from residential, retail and office paper waste. By purchasing paper with high post-consumer content, campuses are creating markets for their own recyclable paper.

Pennsylvania State, the University of Oregon, SUNY-Buffalo and other campuses use 100 percent recycled, 50 percent post-consumer dual-purpose (meaning it can be used in copy machines or printing presses) paper throughout much of their campuses. Though some campuses have found it difficult to recycle because of its high groundwood content, Gaddis says the 50 percent post-consumer paper is the most popular paper at the University of Oregon. "We are trying to get to at least 50 percent recycled, 10 percent post-consumer paper, but many customers request paper with even higher post-consumer content," says Gaddis. The other paper-related issue Gaddis often encounters is paper bleaching.

Bleaching

"We are using a lot of unbleached bonds now to get away from chlorine," says Gaddis, who voices concern about the process of whitening paper, which often releases organochlorines and other toxic chemicals into the environment. Many of these chemicals are thought to imitate estrogen, confusing the human and animal endocrine and reproductive systems—a phenomenon associated with a variety of serious health problems in humans and wildlife.

It is now possible to purchase non-recycled, *totally chlorine free* (TCF) paper. TCF means that no chlorine or chlorine compounds have been used in the bleaching process. When recycled fibers are mixed with TCF pulp, the resulting product is deemed *secondarily chlorine free* (SCF) because most recycled pulp is not TCF. Purchasing SCF paper increases the percentage of TCF fiber in the waste stream, while maintaining markets for existing post-consumer paper waste. (See "Why Ask for Chlorine-Free Paper?" on 124.)

Deinking

In addition to requesting post-consumer content, customers are addressing problems associated with deinking by using flecked paper (when acceptable from a design standpoint) or less toxic inks. Deinking is a multi-phased process in which printed inks and applied finishing materials are removed from the reusable cellulose fiber of the paper. The heavy-metal content in ink pigments renders the sludge by-product from deinking hazardous. (Inks are explored more fully later in this chapter.)

Tree-Free

Some purchasers and consumers are exploring alternatives to trees as a source of paper. The University of Oregon print shop, for example, began offering half-straw, half-hemp paper in the fall of 1993. Hemp is a particularly tough, fibrous

A lot of schools are providing unbleached paper with high post-consumer content in their coin-op copiers. The contamination levels in the equipment are a little higher, but it is still acceptable paper and it is less expensive than virgin.

—William Meyer, President, ACUP

WHY ASK FOR CHLORINE-FREE PAPER ?

When paper mills use chlorine to bleach and brighten paper, they discharge dioxin—one of many of the chlorine compounds—directly into rivers. These pollutants, which resemble such hormones as estrogen, trick the body into accepting them as natural hormones, with severe results. Scientists have linked reduced sperm counts, rising rates of endometriosis, testicular and prostate cancer, reproductive deformities and other health problems in humans and wildlife to chemical hormones. Industries often refer to emissions of "trace" amounts of dioxin—in the parts per billion. Our bodies, however, respond to natural hormones in quantities as small as parts per quadrillion. The National Wildlife Federation publication *Fertility on the Brink: The Legacy of the Chemical Age* documents current knowledge about the effects of hormone-mimicking chemicals on wildlife and humans.

In part because of the switch by many mills away from elemental chlorine to chlorine compounds, dioxin levels in the environment are lower now than they were 20–30 years ago. But this is only an intermediate step. An elemental chlorine pulp mill produces some 35 tons of organochlorines every day. The elemental chlorine-free (ECF) paper such mills produce has not been bleached with elemental chlorine gas, but with a chlorine-based compound, i.e., chlorine dioxide or sodium hypochlorite. While less harmful than elemental chlorine, this ECF technology produces an alarming amount of dioxin and other chlorinated organic compounds.

Several mills in the U.S. now manufacture "totally chlorine-free" (TCF) paper, which has not been bleached with chlorine or any chlorine-based compound. Worldwide, there are 55 mills now producing totally chlorine-free paper, most in Scandinavia, a few in Spain and Portugal, seven in Canada, and four in the United States. Some of them use alternative bleaching technologies such as hydrogen peroxide, calcium carbonate and ozone gas bleaching. Other mills simply do not bleach or rebleach the papers they produce. TCF papers are currently made only from virgin fiber (i.e. they have no recycled content), but it is possible to purchase secondarily chlorine-free (SCF) paper in which the non-recycled portion of the paper is TCF while the recycled portion has not been re-bleached with chlorine compounds.

Pennsylvania State University, the University of Michigan, the University of Oregon, and SUNY-Buffalo are among campuses that have switched to chlorine-free paper for many uses, and many dining services have switched to chlorine-free napkins and other paper products. For more information, please consult the Campus Chlorine-Action Information Packet available through NWF's Campus Ecology Program (see bibliography and networking sections).

plant often used to make rope, sailcloth, clothing, and other durable materials. Although the paper is popular with only a few departments, Gaddis and staff work hard to promote it. "We took this paper and actually printed the notice—'This is the new Eco-Paper'—on it, and got it out to all departments on campus" says Gaddis. However, "it has a little bit more of an oiled finish to it," he admits. "It doesn't run really well yet."

Kenaf, a tropical, Asiatic plant, also grown for its fiber, is another tree-free alternative. Ecoprint of Silver Spring, Maryland, a printer serving the Washington metropolitan area, is a front-runner in the use of kenaf. "It actually runs well through the presses and is a very durable sheet," says Amy Peacock, an Ecoprint representative. As did recycled papers before demand swelled, kenaf and hemp-straw papers cost more than recycled or virgin tree-based paper. "As you start achieving economies of scale," anticipates Gaddis, "the cost will come down." For now, says Peacock, "many people use the tree-free paper for flyers and smaller jobs."

Kenaf and straw/hemp papers have several advantages that make their further research and development appealing—chief among them that kenaf, straw, and hemp plants all produce more fiber per acre than do trees. The USDA found that kenaf produces six to ten tons of raw fiber per acre—three to five times more fiber than an acre of southern pine.[2] Reducing the acreage used for paper production will alleviate the pressure to replace biologically diverse forest habitat worldwide with tree farms.

Currently, "more than half the cubic volume of trees harvested in our national forests is used to manufacture pulp and paper," reports Conservatree, a nonprofit recycled paper advocacy organization. The demand for wood pulp, they report, is expected to increase by 25 percent between 1986 and the year 2000. To meet this demand, clearcutting on public lands will increase considerably, resulting in further diminished habitat, destroyed fisheries, and other serious ecological damage.[3] As the demand for paper outpaces the availability of post-consumer fiber, tree-free paper presents a heartening alternative.

Beyond Paper

Gaddis thinks universities have targeted paper because it is one of the largest expenditures on campus. "If you want to take a simplified formula, a third of our [print shop] cost is administrative overhead—sales, expenses, salaries and so forth, a third of it is paper, and a third of it is labor," explains Gaddis. "With some of the big jobs," he adds, "as much as 50 percent of your cost is paper." But there

> Kenaf produces three to six times more fiber per acre than trees do.

2. *Sustainable Publisher*, Nov., 1993.
3. *Conservatree Fact Pack 5:5:1*, 1992, p. 3.

is more to improving the environmental profile of a print shop, says Gaddis, than introducing earth-friendly papers.

Inks

New inks are probably the biggest news, after paper, in environmentally-responsible printing today. Two components of ink pose problems: their base and their pigments. College printers increasingly use inks with vegetable oils (soy, canola, linseed, chinawood) in their base. Replacing petroleum distillate in inks with greater percentages of soy and other vegetable oils reduces the emission of volatile organic compounds (VOCs), which are regulated by the Clean Air Act. But it also increases drying time, says Gaddis, who uses soy and other vegetable bases for roughly 30 percent of his inks. "There are some trade-offs," he says. "The ink doesn't set up hard and flash dry like the old petroleum inks."

Oregon State (where most of the inks used are soy-based) held a printing conference in 1992 at which ink manufacturers and paper mill representatives were asked by Gaddis and other staff to address the drying problems associated with soy-based inks. Technical representatives could scarcely resist pointing the finger at one another, Gaddis recollects. "When you have four or five things that interact," he says, there is a lot of room for error. Compatibility issues—of paper with inks, inks with fountain solution and so on—pose some of the biggest obstacles to pollution prevention in printing. But as paper, printing plates, and vegetable-based inks become increasingly compatible, the percentage of soy and other vegetable oils in ink should rise.

The American Soybean Association (ASA) has established minimum content requirements for soybean oil in ink bases (20 percent for sheet-fed press ink, 7 percent for heat-set ink, 30 percent for cold-set ink, and 40 percent for black news ink). Only ASA certified inks may use the "SoySeal" trademark.[4]

Ink pigments pose another environmental challenge. Most of the printing industry, public and private, currently uses pigments with relatively high concentrations of heavy metals. The sludge by-product from the deinking and recycling of paper—which could otherwise be composted—is made toxic by the high concentrations of heavy metals in these inks. "Understandably, potential buyers like farmers and developers won't take it until these concentrations are reduced or eliminated," says Roger Telschow, founder of Ecoprint. By the spring of 1994, Ecoprint, working in collaboration with Alden & Ott Inks, had developed a line of non-heavy-metal inks which brought the concentration of heavy metals below 100 parts per million (ppm) for all but one shade of red, for which alternative pigments were not available. Notable examples of reduced toxicity include pro-

> High heavy metal content in many inks renders the sludge by-product from paper recycling toxic. Ecoprint's reformulated inks are free of environmentally toxic metals.

4. *Recycled Paper News*, 1994, p. 4.

cess blue (a bright blue used in all four-color printing) and green, in which concentrations of copper sank from 3,800 ppm to 10 ppm and 3,300 ppm to 11 ppm, respectively.

Reducing ink waste by recycling is not common practice, but sometimes black ink can be created from a mixture of inks and toner, and the newspaper industry often mixes used high-grade inks into low-grade newsprint ink. Gaddis says he is reluctant to reuse inks because "after a run in an offset press, water eventually transfers to ink rollers and pieces of the fiber come off paper that is streaming through at 5,000 sheets an hour, so after two or three hours you get fuzzy paper dust and water emulsification, which create hickeys and blemishes on the sheet."

Black ink is also two or three times less expensive than many colors, so the purchase price creates little incentive to create black from old inks. And while inks represent less than one percent of Gaddis's budget (or about $3,000 a year), Gaddis feels staff is inherently conscientious about conserving them. "I would say 90 percent of what is put in the fountain is used up on the printed sheet," he says. Nevertheless, the small amount of leftover ink accumulates with each job, and its disposal as hazardous waste can be two or three times more expensive than procuring the inks in the first place. Disposal costs prompted Ecoprint to reblend and reuse most of its leftovers.

TERRA MONTGOMERY

For Dar Walen at the University of Oregon, vegetable-based inks and recycled paper are the norm for print jobs on this two-color Heidelberg press.

Processes and Equipment

Beyond paper and inks, there are opportunities at every stage in the printing process to prevent pollution and improve worker health and safety. Innovative private-sector print shops have taken the lead, but the Association of College and University Printers and other printing associations are awakening campus print shops to these possibilities as well—both for their in-house print and copy jobs, and for the specifications they give outside contractors.

Most campuses offer xerographic or copying services and contract out for print work, though a steadily decreasing number still offer full printing services as well. (The University of Oregon is the last full-service print shop in the Oregon higher education system. Gaddis is limited to two-color presses, must have his purchases approved by the State Printer, and can accept work only from the public sector.) Whether a campus prints on- or off-site, however, the equipment and processes used, as well as the waste reduction opportunities, are similar.

The University of Oregon's printing equipment includes scanners and computers, a complete darkroom facility, three large presses, a perfecter (a press that can print both sides of the paper simultaneously), small duplicators, a complete bindery, three folding machines, collators, stitchers, a trimmer, a multi-color copier, five high-speed copiers, and mailing equipment. Together, this equipment moves projects through the four major stages of the printing process: image processing, plate processing, printing, and finishing.

Image Processing

In conventional image processing, images and text on art boards or computer diskettes are transferred to negatives. The negatives are used to imprint pre-sensitized printing plates (these are generally aluminum plates coated with light-sensitive chemicals). Disk-to-plate technology and the scanning of photographs, which Gaddis says are becoming *de rigueur* in industry, reduce some of the labor but not much of the waste associated with image processing. What is increasingly eliminated are the camera and physical stripping stages, whereby images were photographed and the resulting negatives cut by hand and formatted onto large flats. (The chemicals in the developer, stop bath, and photo fixer are treated as hazardous waste in many states. The silver in film is widely recovered. See Chapter 8, Hazardous Waste, for more on photo-processing.) The disk-to-plate approach does eliminate the paper and chemicals used to create camera-ready mechanicals—the hard copy which printers still photograph when they cannot generate a negative image straight from a computer file.

Plate Processing

In the plate processing stage, the printer shines an arc light through the negative, transferring the image to the plate. Plate development chemicals then remove everything but the burned-in image. Printing plates, which average two by three-and-a-half feet in size, are widely recycled at the market rate for aluminum. "You can get quite a volume and quite a bit of weight in aluminum," says Gaddis, whose print shop regularly generates a stack of plates three or four feet high. The University of Oregon is replacing its hazardous plate-developing chemicals with aqueous plate systems, in which pre-sensitized plates are developed solely with water.

Printing

The most common printing process is "offset" printing—as opposed to letterpress printing, photocopying, or the emerging techniques outlined below. The terms *offset* and *lithographic* printing are interchangeable. "The majority of ink going down on paper in this country is lithographic," says Gaddis.

In the first phase of offset printing, ink and fountain solution (a chemical compound called "water" in the printing trade) is run on a plate in the printing

> The University of Oregon is replacing its hazardous plate-developing chemicals with aqueous plate systems in which pre-sensitized plates are developed solely with water.

press. The image on the plate, which attracts inks and repels "water," is then offset to a rubber blanket. As the paper passes between the rubber blanket and an impression cylinder in the second phase, the rubber blanket gently presses or "offsets" the image to the paper. Campuses and industry pollution prevention efforts have altered the inks (as discussed above), fountain solution, and cleaning solvents used in this basic process.

Fountain Solution

The image on a plate attracts ink and repels water. The "water" is actually a mixture of water and chemicals (usually with between five and 25 percent isopropyl alcohol), otherwise known as fountain solution. Printers mix several ounces of fountain concentrate with several gallons of water for each press each day.

Isopropyl alcohol, another VOC, has been the source of considerable air emissions from print shops. But Ecoprint reports that improvements in fountain solutions have cut these emissions significantly. "The newest fountain solutions do not even contain chemicals that are reportable as toxic, and have no volatile emissions whatsoever," they say, "which may eliminate them as an environmental consideration altogether."

Cleaning

Printers clean their rubber press rollers and blankets between print jobs. Especially thorough cleaning is needed when moving from dark to lighter inks. As former pressman Gaddis recalls, "You get blue ink on a press (cyan or blue are the world's worst in pigments) and they get into your rollers, and I don't care how well you wash that press up, if you go to yellow ink, you are going to have some real problems. It sometimes takes a couple coatings of yellow, and you have to wash it off to pull the blue pigment out of those rollers."

Environmentally, solvents are a secondary concern, after alcohol in fountain solution, says Telschow. Ecoprint uses a solvent free of chlorinated hydrocarbons and low in VOCs, thus reducing by 60 percent the air emissions associated with their press cleanup. The new product is still petroleum-based and doesn't evaporate as quickly as other solvents, but the Ecoprint staff prefer it to the citrus-based alternatives they have tested. Telschow says the shop found citrus-based printing solvents to be "higher in overall VOC content than alternatives because they typically contained only a small amount of citrus."

Dedicating presses to a specific range of ink colors, using cleaning rags efficiently, and laundering solvent-soaked rags are methods adopted by print shops to reduce solvent use and the resulting hazardous waste. Dedicating presses

Ecoprint uses a solvent free of chlorinated hydrocarbons and low in VOCs, thus reducing by 60 percent the air emissions associated with their press cleanup.

to light or dark inks can reduce cleaning between jobs, but Gaddis thinks most campuses can scarcely afford this approach. His department's three large presses handle rush jobs every hour of the day, each running three or four jobs daily. "Most jobs require black ink and, at $65 to $80 dollars an hour, reserving a press for light inks," he says, "wouldn't be cost-efficient for the taxpayers of Oregon."

Proper use and laundering of cleaning rags, however, strikes Gaddis as a more practical suggestion for campuses. Instead of using freshly-cleaned rags at the start of a cleaning job, his staff uses rags from previous jobs until these are thoroughly soaked. The soaked rags are then laundered and reused. Laundering reduces hazardous waste, disposal costs, and the need to purchase new rags.

Technologies of Tomorrow in Use Today

Echoing a sentiment common among veteran printers, Gaddis reflects: "I am a third-generation printer . . . and the [changes] I have seen have been mind-boggling just in the last 30 years."

In digital plate imaging, information sent directly from computers to plates via lasers eliminates the need for film processing, stripping negatives, and burning plates. This saves time and reduces the use of hazardous photo- and plate-processing chemicals. In digital printing, images are transferred directly to presses, eliminating plates altogether. Manufacturers of "waterless" printing technology cite the absence of alcohol-based fountain solutions and the improved compatibility with recycled papers as proof that their new system is superior to conventional printing.

Are these developments environmentally beneficial? On balance, most appear to be, but the answer is qualified and complex. Digital printing, on the one hand, is less energy-intensive and produces less hazardous waste than lithographic offset printing, but it is still a relatively slow process. Waterless printing, on the other hand, provides less clear-cut environmental benefits. When solid waste, energy use, and toxic substances used in pre-press are tallied, the advantages of waterless printing become less definite. As currently conceived, reports Ecoprint, waterless systems are more energy-intensive, double plate consumption, and still use toxic plate processing chemicals.[5]

As a large market for printing, colleges and universities play an important role in ensuring environmental impacts are reduced as technology becomes more sophisticated. At the University of Oregon, putting customer service first does not preclude a little environmental education in the print shop. Through offering alternatives and publicizing them well, Gaddis and staff have made it as easy as possible for customers to support pollution prevention on campus.

5. Ecoprint, May-June, 1994.

Colleges and universities play an important role in ensuring environmental impacts are reduced as technology becomes more sophisticated.

BIBLIOGRAPHY

"American Soybean Association Lowers Requirement for Use of Its SoySeal Logo," *Recycled Paper News*, Feb., 1994. (703) 451-0688.

"A Good Working Environment," Heidy Steidlmayer, *Instant & Small Commercial Printer*, April, 1994.

"Conservatree Fact Pack 5:5:1," Conservatree, Sept/Oct, 1992, 10 Lombard St., Ste. 200, San Francisco, CA 94111. ("5:5:1" covers the connection between recycled paper and forests/biodiversity.)

"Dioxin's Toll on Wildlife," Vicki Monks, *National Wildlife*, A/S, 1994, p. 9.

"Energy Efficient Office Technology," Cyane Dandridge, Building Technology Program, MIT, 1994.

Fertility on the Brink: Legacy of the Chemical Age, National Wildlife Federation, 1994. (202) 797-6800. (Details scientific studies indicating that hormone-imitating chemicals such as dioxin and other chlorine by-products are building up in animals and humans and disrupting reproduction, immune systems, behavior, and metabolism.)

"Global Network: Computers in a Sustainable Society," John E. Young, *Worldwatch Paper 115*, 1993, Worldwatch Institute, 1776 Massachusetts Ave., N.W., Washington, D.C. 20036-1904.

Guide to Energy-Efficient Office Equipment, American Council for an Energy Efficient Economy, 1993. (501) 549-9914.

"Printer Removes Heavy Metals from Ink," *Recycled Paper News*, February, 1994. (703) 451-0688.

Recycled Products Guide, General Services Administration, Centralized Mailing List Service, P.O. Box 6477, Fort Worth, TX 76115. (817) 334-5215.

"The State of Plates," *American Printer*, February, 1992.

"Student Newspaper Distribution," Suzanne Tegen, 1994, Campus Ecology Research Project, UW-Madison, Rm. 120, WARF Bldg., 610 Walnut St., Madison, WI 53705. (608) 265-3417.

"Tree-Free Paper," *The Sustainable Publisher*, Center for Children's Environmental Literature, November, 1993. (202) 966-6110.

"The Truth About Dioxin," Vicki Monks, *National Wildlife*, A/S, 1994, pp. 4-13.

UB Guide to Green Computing, University of Buffalo, 1994. (To receive: send $2 check made out to "SUNY Buffalo" to Walter Simpson at address listed below.)

"Waterless Pros and Cons," William Lamparter, *American Printer*, October, 1994, pp. 43-46.

NETWORKING

Campus

Massachusetts Institute of Technology
Attn. Professor Les Norford
Building Technology Program
77 Massachusetts Ave.
Cambridge, MA 02139
Research and development of energy-efficient computers and other office equipment.

Pennsylvania State
Attn. William Meyer
Printing Services
University Park, PA 16802
Short-run or "just in time" printing, heavy use of unbleached paper with high post-consumer content; Meyer is also president of the Association of College and University Printers.

Rochester Institute of Technology
Attn. Dave DuBrowsky
Printing Management and Sciences Department
Rochester, NY 14623
(716) 475-2880
Research and development of sustainable printing technologies.

If you find that an organization listed here has moved or a contact has been replaced, let the Campus Ecology Program staff know. We'll help match you with the latest source for the information you need.

St. John's University
Attn. Peter Taras
Printing and Reproduction
Jamaica, NY 11439
Printing staff involved in wider campus ecology initiatives.

SUNY-Buffalo
Attn. Walter Simpson, Conserve UB
University Facilities
120 John Beane Center, North Campus
Buffalo, NY 14260
(716) 645-3636
"Green computing" campaign and other campus energy conservation activities; to receive UB Guide to Green Computing, send check made out to SUNY Buffalo for $2/copy to Walter Simpson.

University of Oregon
Attn. J.R. Gaddis
Printing Services
Eugene, OR 97403
For information on use of tree-free paper and chlorine-free post-consumer paper.

Regional and National

Association of College and University Printers (ACUP)
Contact William Meyer, ACUP's president at Pennsylvania State University address listed above for information on environmental forums at annual printing conference or for latest ACUP address.

Chlorine-free Products Association
(708) 658-6104
Contact Archie Beaton for dates and locations of regional and national conferences.

Graphical Arts Technical Foundation (GATF)
4615 Forbes Ave.
Pittsburg, PA 15213
(412) 621-6941

National Wildlife Federation
Campus Ecology Program
1400 16th St., N.W.
Washington, D.C. 20036-2266
(202) 797-5435 (general information)
(313) 769-9970 or midwest@nwf.org (M.W.)
(202) 797-5468 or noreast@nwf.org (N.E.)
(404) 876-2608 or soeast@nwf.org (S.E.)
(503) 222-1429 or western@nwf.org (West)
Contact for Campus Chlorine-Dioxin Action Kit, Campus Energy Efficiency Issue Packet, Campus Year in Review, and updates on campus involvement in recycled and chlorine-free paper and products procurement, use of tree-free paper, use of soy and low heavy-metal inks, etc.

Rocky Mountain Institute
1739 Snow Mass Creek Rd.
Snow Mass, CO 81654
(303) 927-3851
Contact for publication list of guides, articles, and other resources on energy-efficient office equipment and other cutting edge topics in energy efficiency and renewable energy.

U.S. Environmental Protection Agency
Energy Star Computer Program (MC:6202J)
Washington, D.C. 20460
(202) 233-9114
Contact for updated lists of Energy Star computers, monitors, and printers.

Other Resources

CARTRIDGE RETURN CENTERS

Canon USA, Inc.
400 Valley Drive
Brisbane, CA 94005
(800) 962-2708

Lasertronics, Inc.
6075 Roswell Road, N.E.
Suite 425
Atlanta, GA 30328
(800) 723-6394

Toner, Etc.
210 West Road
Portsmouth, NH 03801-9879
(800) 370-8663

LOW HEAVY-METAL CONTENT INKS

Alden & Ott Inks
(708) 956-6830

TCF (TOTALLY CHLORINE FREE) PULP OR PAPER

American Paper Sales
10 East 40th St.
New York, NY 10016
(212) 889-3001

Classen Papertronics
13601 Preston Road
Suite 700 West
Dallas, TX 75240
(214) 490-5128

Crosspointe
1295 Bandana Blvd. N
St. Paul, MN 55108
(612) 644-3644

Hayden-Cary & King
777 Post Road
Darien, CT 06820
(203) 656-3111

Lyons Falls Pulp & Paper
Center St.
P.O. Box 338
Lyons Falls, NY 13368
(315) 348-8411

MD North America
108 Wilmot Rd.
Deerfield, IL 60015
(708) 317-0180

MoDoCell, Inc.
1 Selleck St.
Suite 460
Norwalk, CT 06855
(203) 854-9447

Mohawk Paper
465 Saratoga St.
Cohoes, NY 12047
(800) 543-4776

National Pulp and Paper
3010 Westchester Ave.
Purchase, NY 10577
(914) 253-8377

Niagara Paper Company
11-1 Mill St.
Niagara, WI 54151
(612) 644-3644

Perkins-Goodwin
300 Atlantic St.
Stamford, CT 06901
(203) 363-7800

Portage Paper Co.
2030 Portage St.
P.O. Box 2048
Kalamazoo, MI 49003-2048

Repap
433 N. Main St.
Kimberly, WI 54136
(800) 558-3331

TREE-FREE PAPER

EcoPaper
121 SW Salmon, Ste. 1100
Portland, OR 97204
(800) 775-0225

KP Products
P.O. Box 20399
Albuquerque, NM 87154

CHAPTER 7

Solid Waste Management

I n just the last few years, campus recycling has become a bona fide profession, more institutions are reusing materials and reducing waste, and composting has moved from the fringes toward the mainstream. Case studies of several of the colleges and universities at the forefront of these trends illustrate the hurdles and rewards inherent in the effort to protect natural resources by transforming solid waste into a valuable commodity.

🍀 RECYCLING

Nobody better embodies the campus recycling phenomenon than Jack DeBell, the recycling coordinator for the University of Colorado at Boulder. Upon graduating in 1984, he created and found funding for his own position as one of the first full-time campus recycling coordinators in the country. In 1982, when CU hosted the second National Recycling Conference and DeBell was still a student volunteer, only four universities were known to have established recycling programs with funding, an office, and a sense of institutional commitment: Colorado University, Stanford University, the University of California at San Diego, and Cornell University. Tracing the development of recycling at CU provides a virtual how-to manual for campuses launching or enhancing their own recycling programs.

When asked to explain the evolution of his job at CU and his role in the national campus recycling movement, DeBell replies with a quote he attributes to the Grateful Dead: "What a long strange trip it's been."

"In retrospect," he laughs, "I was asked to jump in as an expert before I was out of Boy Scouts." All the same, he feels his self-structured academic career

Jack DeBell, one of the first campus recycling coordinators in the country, created his own position at the University of Colorado at Boulder.

prepared him for just about anything. With the late Buckminster Fuller as an advisor, he delved into what he refers to as "Comprehensivism"—the study of human judgment. "We worked with cybernetics and general systems theory," he elaborates, "using mathematical constructs to explain and predict decision-making."

A Growing Effort

Since the early 1980s, says DeBell, the campus recycling movement has come a long way. Each year for 15 years, the number of campuses represented at the National Recycling Coalition Conference has increased. When DeBell helped UCLA and Washington University conduct a national survey of campus recycling in 1990, he found that more than 78 percent of U.S. institutions of higher education had fairly well-established recycling programs. Many of the rest had at least fledgling volunteer efforts. During the year of "Earth Day 1990," DeBell was besieged by requests from campuses in every part of the country for presentations on managing recycling programs.

Student involvement and pressure, believes DeBell, have been the primary forces behind the high level of campus commitment to recycling. If legislative compliance were the main motivation, he reasons, why do so many campuses exceed their states' targeted recovery rates for recyclable materials? While 30–40 percent recovery rates are not unusual on campuses, mandates seldom exceed 25 percent. Many of the institutions with high rates of recovery, moreover, are outside the 12 states (at the time of this writing) with legislated mandates. And on a national level, the 25 percent diversion rates set by EPA have remained targeted goals, rather than legal mandates.

If anything, campus recycling has helped drive municipal mandates, believes DeBell. Two other strong inducements for campuses to recycle, he says, are reducing costs and positive community relations. "Solid waste," he notes, "is a real town-gown issue."

Roles for Students and Staff

Financial savings, while not the motivating force behind the start-up of college recycling programs, has been the determinant, says DeBell, in the shift of responsibility for recycling from students and other volunteers to full-time facilities and custodial staff. Physical plants "are revising job descriptions; they are retooling their capital equipment purchases; they are allocating space on campus." This would seem quite a victory to many in the movement who have long argued that college administrations should integrate recycling into traditional solid waste management. To DeBell, it is not that simple. A motto originated at CU

Each year for 15 years, the number of campuses represented at the National Recycling Coalition Conference has increased.

BRENDA GILMORE AT VANDERBILT: Recycling & Beyond

Brenda Gilmore has gone all out to green her campus. Primarily responsible for the campus Direct Mail Service, she has been tapped to coordinate an office paper recycling pilot program and to help set up mobile recycling stands—as well as to serve as a liaison between the administration and student environmental groups. An active participant on the Resource Conservation Advisory Committee, she has played a role in Earth Day activities and an annual Rite of Spring; an end-of-semester "Build a Clothing Mountain" Campaign, during which students pile up unwanted clothing for donation to a rescue organization; a campus tree planting ceremony with local elementary students; the "lug a mug" discount program in the dining halls; and a "t-shirt exchange" in which students received a 20 percent discount on new t-shirts at the campus bookstore when they brought in a used shirt. When Gilmore met with other campus recycling coordinators at the National Recycling Coalition's Annual Congress & Exposition in September 1993, she had this to say: "I think the challenge to all of us is what to do with the student part of recycling. In addition to our emphasis on the academic side of environmental issues, we probably need to include the students in the operational side also, so that they can get some hands-on experience of what it actually takes to get materials from point A to point B, as well as experience in looking at markets and doing economic analyses."

Brenda Gilmore (below center) works to ensure student involvement in recycling and related programs at Vanderbilt. At left, students build a mountain of discarded clothes.

which DeBell is promoting at other campuses: Institutionalization Without Disenfranchisement. "The trend I am seeing is that physical plant operations are taking over recycling," says DeBell, "cutting students out of the loop operationally, managerially, emotionally, as well as academically."

The debate in professional recycling circles on the relative merits of facility-run versus student-run programs is, in DeBell's view, one of great consequence to the future of recycling—and environmentalism in general—in the U.S.

One incentive for including students, admits DeBell, is the low-cost labor they provide. All student recycling employees at CU are paid through the work-study program. Recycling is one of the best paying jobs on campus, and students are eager for the work experience. An additional 2,000 hours of assistance for the program come from the county's community service program, which provides opportunities for students with first-time misdemeanors to do restitutional work.

The best reasons to involve students, however, tend to be less quantifiable—public relations, for example. Publicity for recycling programs works best from within peer groups, says DeBell, so students, faculty, and staff all have important roles to play. Jim Rice, solid waste manager at Appalachian State University, has said much the same thing; recognizing that students publicize better to students, he has tailored a lighthearted newsletter and other incentives to staff and administrators, who have cooperated to the point of tearing sticky parts and windows out of envelopes. At Appalachian State, the residence hall recycling program is coordinated separately.

"The bottom-line reason for keeping students involved," says DeBell, "is that they are future leaders." He sees recycling as part of the educational mission of the university: "It enhances their undergraduate academic experience. We call it service learning, task-based learning, applied research. Call it what you will. Students can learn the operations, management, and the education or promotion of recycling . . . and prepare themselves to be future leaders of this booming field."

It is hard to counter the argument, however, that institutional facilities tend to run more efficient programs than students can on their own. DeBell admits that staff-run programs "have the potential for instituting disposal savings and avoided cost mechanisms, which is the real economic future of recycling on campus." Students lack direct access to purchasing and custodial staff, making it difficult for them to influence contracts and "institute the accounting programs that are necessary to balance the ledger." Students are also frequently unaware of the fire and egress codes which require that bins be fire-retardant and placed away from halls and entryways. The picture DeBell paints of the more

> The trend I am seeing is that physical plant operations are taking over recycling, cutting students out of the loop operationally, managerially, emotionally as well as academically.
>
> —Jack DeBell,
> University of Colorado-Boulder

sophisticated student-run programs, however, is not one of unsightly cardboard boxes spilling over in dorms. Student-run programs have come a long way with regard to aesthetics and efficacy—with tidy bins in the most convenient, if not always the safest, places.

So who should run recycling programs—students or facilities staff? The answer, says DeBell, is to retain the strengths of each by forming a partnership. CU's program had expanded to the limit, he recalls, and could not get more material without facilities management help. "Eighty percent of my budget was going to collect materials, to hire students, to buy barrels and paint for the barrels," says DeBell. "All those operational costs were requiring over three quarters of my budget." He did not have sufficient people-power or financial resources, he found, to get to those smaller amounts of desk-side recyclables.

For these reasons, and because the Student Government Association at CU was adamant that any proposed recycling model include students (who had contributed the fees and organization that had sustained the program for 15 years), DeBell and staff successfully negotiated for staff help in expanding recycling, while retaining the student-based program and its managerial autonomy. With physical plant approval, the Chancellor announced the formation of an official CU Solid Waste Task Force on Earth Day 1990.

The first challenge, recalls DeBell, was to assemble "an informed group of diverse yet committed individuals, representing the different stakeholders." Custodians and participating work-study students were obvious candidates. Recruiting administrators with a working knowledge of legislative compliance issues (RCRA, OSHA, local regulations, etc.) and who could enlist financial support proved relatively easy, says DeBell: "They all wanted to see recycling succeed in one way or another, which is an important element—getting a group of people who have already gotten to 'Yes!' and have already committed to seeing something happen."

Once the committee was assembled, its first task was to figure out how to allocate responsibilities for recycling in a way that would balance student and staff involvement in a cost-effective manner. "Who is doing what, by when, at what costs, for which ends?" were the formative questions, recalls DeBell. "It sounds kind of cute, but it really helped us define the relative roles and responsibilities of the new partnership model we were forming." It also resulted in the identification of five areas the task force deemed integral to a successful recycling program: (1) procedural training, (2) collections, (3) processing, (4) marketing, and (5) program development. With appropriate staffing, the task force anticipated, this combination of programs would yield the highest economic and environmental returns.

DeBell and staff successfully negotiated for staff help in expanding recycling, while retaining the student-based program and its managerial autonomy.

Procedural Training

In the spirit of "service learning" which undergirds CU's program, students themselves conduct training on recycling procedures for staff, administrators and other students. To qualify as trainers, students must first complete a semester-long course offered for independent-study credit. DeBell and other CU recycling staff teach the course, which requires that students volunteer four hours a week in the recycling office, where they respond to inquiries from the public. They also study an exhaustive manual prepared by staff, make a public presentation, produce a professional poster, write a letter to the editor, and prepare a research paper on some aspect of recycling. After completing these tasks and passing the final exam, each student receives a coveted certificate of accomplishment and is qualified to conduct trainings and perform other recycling office duties in return for payment through the work-study program.

The program is so popular that DeBell has had to institute a selection process, since on a first-come-first-serve basis, qualified and interested students were being turned away. "It is an interesting 'Catch-22' quandary," admits DeBell. "We want a professional program, but we also want to give a student without any experience the opportunity to do something professional." DeBell now accepts students on the basis of four criteria: experience, commitment, schedule and cultural diversity. To meet these criteria, he recruits students from such nontraditional sources as the journalism and business schools, as well as from more predictable places like the environmental science programs.

Recycling efforts at Vanderbilt include reclamation of phone books.

Custodial Staff

While custodians at CU and a growing list of other campuses willingly accommodate recycling, some campuses continue to wrestle with this end of the staffing issue. The trend is towards facilities staff control of recycling, says DeBell, but many campuses do employ off-campus collection companies or rely solely on volunteers, work-study, or non-custodial staff, especially where personnel guidelines and custodial unions have opposed shifting custodial tasks. Negotiation with custodians, custodial involvement in the planning process, and custodial incentives are among the most important characteristics of CU's recycling program. CU Recycling has translated several recycling brochures into Spanish and Hmong (the two prevalent languages spoken by CU custodians), and launched a "multicultural campaign" which, DeBell reports, "does a number of things to express appreciation for custodian involvement."

Collections

In order to achieve economy of scale, CU needed to integrate its recycling program into its regular solid waste collection. Custodians proved amenable to this and worked with the task force to redesign the collection process. In order to avoid increased labor costs (one of the university's chief concerns), they chose to collect recyclables one day a week and reduce regular waste collection from five days to four. They also designed special recycling collection carts, distributed 10,000 desk-side recycling containers, bought three small recycling trucks, and transformed an old warehouse into a recycling facility.

Even with recyclables collection only once a week, CU is diverting about 40 percent of its waste. "Those desk-side recycling containers are pretty well packed," explains DeBell, "whereas the trash containers are not." Health considerations, he says, account for the more frequent garbage collections.

CU Recycling has translated several recycling brochures into Spanish and Hmong— the two languages most commonly spoken by CU custodians.

Processing

CU Recycling trains and hires students to process recyclables. Because of liability and other concerns, says DeBell, many campuses have relegated students to outreach and publicity roles. At CU, however, for a starting salary of $6.00 an hour, work-study students "upgrade" and "densify" collected materials. They bale cardboard and remove contaminants—a tough job at CU, where white paper, computer printout, mixed office paper, newsprint, and corrugated cardboard must be kept separate to maximize revenues.

Work-study students can opt to take the certification course offered by CU recycling staff, working one day a week in the recycling warehouse, passing a 3-hour competency exam on operational issues and concepts, and making two field trips to area recycling facilities.

Marketing Recyclables

DeBell handles marketing of the recyclable materials CU collects—an "increasingly complex, difficult, and important" component of campus recycling, he says. DeBell is surprised by how few campuses have contracts with buyers, even though campuses have a competitive advantage over many other institutions because of the steady volume and high quality of their materials. Even in depressed market conditions, he says, "schools, colleges and universities will still probably be the best source of recyclables for the buyer. If that buyer is buying any recyclables at all, they should be buying from colleges and universities . . . . I am shocked at just how many schools don't realize they are sitting on a gold mine of high-grade recyclables—not only a lot of aluminum cans, but tons of high-grade white paper that make it a really lucrative account for area buyers."

DeBell has helped other campuses design competitive requests for proposals (RFPs) and contracts. When possible, he suggests that campuses ask for an indexed price per ton. "By that I mean it is indexed to the market journals," explains DeBell, "so there is a commodity listing and we know when the prices change." Contracts should also guarantee a minimum revenue by offering floor prices below which prices cannot drop. Contractors may also provide some of the necessary equipment, says DeBell. Drums, trailers, roll-offs, etc. can be provided to decrease capital equipment costs and ensure containers will work at the buyer's plant. "You don't want apples and oranges when it comes to types of equipment," DeBell cautions. "It has to be compatible at each step of the line." Containers in which recyclables are collected on campus, for instance, should be easily emptied at the recycling facility.

Service is another consideration. Contract provisions should address frequency of pickup and the availability of emergency pickups, as well as educational services. Material downgrading policy, or how clean the materials must be, can also be specified. The idea, says DeBell, is to control as many variables as possible.

DeBell explains that "research has shown that marketing should be done by a person who has experience, who can monitor the contract for compliance and really stay dedicated to it." Several recycling coordinators—Jon Miller at Georgetown University and Stephanie Finn at Duke University, to name two—broker recyclable materials themselves. Serving in the role that contractors often play for campuses, these coordinators use university vehicles to deliver materials to whichever facilities offer the best prices at the moment. These coordinators must maintain up-to-the-minute information on markets for specific commodities, and they shoulder more of the capital costs for recycling.

The availability of service and the local market conditions will determine whether contracting or self-brokerage is the more cost-effective marketing method. The best approach, says DeBell, is to evaluate alternatives, drawing from existing campus recycling models and conducting a cost-benefit analysis based on local factors. (See bibliography for more information.)

Program Development

Buying recycled products, minimizing waste, and designing buildings to accommodate recycling—anything that pushes the envelope of recycling—falls under "program development" at CU. DeBell and students, who research such

FRITZ MYER

Georgetown University hauls and brokers its own recyclables. Many other campuses contract out for these services.

Arkansas State University
Environmental Benefits of Recycling
1993

	Percent Recyclable	Tons	Cubic Yds.	Energy KWH	Raw Materials	Water Pollution Gallons	Air Pollution Pounds
Aluminum	100%	1.3	43.3	66,365.4		97% less	95% less
Glass	100%	1.7	6.3	161.8	1.9 Tons	n/a	7.8
Paper	100%	54.8	252.3	224,475.0	4,289 Trees	383,250	3,285
Plastic	100%	1.3	51.7	88–97% less			
Steel	100%	4.9	59.3	14,241.6	9 Tons	76% less	47–74% less
TOTAL		64	412.9	305,243.8			

Starr Fenner of Arkansas State carefully documents the benefits of recycling.

ARKANSAS STATE UNIVERSITY
Recycled Products
1993

	Cartridge Recon'ed (No.)	Paper Bags (lbs.)	Card-B Flats (lbs.)	White Paper (lbs.)	Comp. Paper (lbs.)	Card-board (lbs.)	Pallets (lbs.)	Plastic (lbs.)	Tin Cans (lbs.)	Soda Cans (lbs.)	Clear Glass (lbs.)	Color Glass (lbs.)	TOTAL (lbs.)	TOTAL ($)
January	24*	☼	☼	8,120	1,800	3,400	☼	212	640	233	450	☼	14,855	$338
February	14*	☼	☼	1,800	250	3,400	☼	246	1,160	244	210	☼	7,310	$173
March	22*	11	☼	☼	☼	3,500	☼	293	520	229	275	☼	4,828	$178
April	17* 10	34	556	4,000	2,100	4,120	☼	379	1,840	347	572	☼	13,948	$380
May	27	☼	455	5,390	2,184	2,110	☼	297	700	195	629	☼	11,960	$252
June	11	114	210	6,010	1,505	1,850	☼	296	580	145	☼	☼	10,710	$216
July	14	57	193	170	1,925	1,900	☼	223	540	☼	☼	☼	5,008	$129
August	9	☼	298	6,640	2,164	4,320	☼	365	☼	210	☼	☼	13,997	$246
September	6	☼	350	4,980	3,285	4,015	☼	223	☼	329	☼	☼	13,182	$315
October	24	☼	☼	☼	835	1,065	1,120	☼	1,360	407	☼	1,200	5,987	$175
November	28* 17	171	☼	7,885	1,460	8,690	1,000	☼	880	171	☼	☼	20,257	$466
December	35* 23	☼	☼	5,060	☼	1,120	☼	☼	760	178	☼	☼	7,118	$381
Total (Pounds)		388	2,061	50,055	17,508	39,490	2,120	2,534	8,980	2,688	2,136	1,200	129,159	
Income	$700	$48	$118	$523	$776	$109	$20	$25	$81	$590	$21			$3,010
Cost Avoidance	$4,523	$5	$26	$626	$219	$494	$27	$32	$112	$34	$27	$15		$6,137
Total Benefit														$9,148

* Recycled ☼ None sold this month

topics as part of their certification in procedural training, find themselves increasingly preoccupied with program development. Students have measured costs per ton and per route; made maps of the campus, identifying existing recycling locations and recommending additional ones; conducted recycling surveys; and collected literature on recycling bins and other equipment.

Most recently, DeBell has integrated code-compliance provisions (such as the appropriate sites and square footage for recycling bins) into the campus master plan. This formidable task yielded precedent-setting results; architects must now win recycling office approval of their plans, says DeBell: "Going through the Boulder Campus Planning Commission was a very big challenge . . . , but it was worthwhile because we found that when a building 'designs in' recycling provisions, the collections are more convenient, they are safer [and] more attractive looking, and they just make for a better recycling and collection program."

DeBell hopes next to include provisions for purchase of recycled plastics and rubber in the campus master plan. Colorado law requires all state agencies to buy a phased-in percentage of recycled products, reaching 50 percent by 1995. Colorado is one of many states with a 10 percent price preference program, requiring purchasers to buy recycled products whenever they exceed the price of comparable virgin products by less than 10 percent.

Financing

Funds for CU Recycling come from four sources: the students, the administration, avoided costs, and revenues from the sale of the materials. Student activity fees contribute $50,000 a year to the program—about one dollar per CU student, or 20 percent of what students indicate on surveys they are willing to pay. CU Recycling also lobbied for and received a half-million dollar loan, which it repays not through its revenues (amounting to $35,000 annually), but through disposal savings (about $60,000 annually). "When we went in there with this proposal that would retire a loan within five to seven years," says DeBell, "they were really impressed. We have met and in some cases exceeded our projections."

By repaying its loan through avoided costs, CU Recycling sets a precedent that can be applied not just to recycling, but to myriad other environmental initiatives, from energy efficiency to transportation management. DeBell admits this financing mechanism was one of the most professionally challenging aspects of the program. It meant working with the purchasing office to write new collection schedules into contracts with solid waste haulers. Removing dumpsters, scheduling less-frequent collections, and replacing larger dumpsters with smaller ones all contribute to disposal savings. And it meant working with the accounting office to track and allocate the savings generated by recycling back into the

It has been suggested we fund a literacy program or subsidize faculty salaries. Recycling is one of the few waste management options that does generate some revenue, but ninety percent of the value of our program is the avoided cost. It is not to be thought of as this cash cow.

—Jim Rice, Appalachian State University

program. "That is probably the challenge of environmentalism in the '90s," says DeBell, "to make sure that those savings pay off. Otherwise, they are just paper savings or they disappear into the black hole of the general ledger—which on campus is a real problem because you either use it or you lose it."

Future Initiatives

Now that CU Recycling is a well-established program, much of DeBell's effort centers on working with a handful of other campus recycling coordinators to establish a College and University Recycling Caucus for the National Recycling Coalition (NRC). Caucus objectives include reporting campus waste diversion and procurement rates at annual NRC meetings, identifying and developing models for integrating solid waste issues into diverse curricula, creating electronic mail conferences on the Internet and other networks, and organizing a Technical Council to address challenges unique to college and university recycling programs.

DeBell reports that the caucus is in a position to "define expectations for college waste diversion and procurement programs. [The caucus] has developed criteria for evaluating programs and helping to bring them up to speed." Evaluation of a an institution's diversion rates, recycled-content purchasing, and academic integration would lead to a rating of "below compliance," "in compliance," or "proactive." The goal, says DeBell, is to see every school qualify as proactive, which would mean they had higher diversion and purchasing rates than their states' goals. It would also mean integrating academic work with on-campus and local recycling efforts.

🍂 COMPOSTING

If you were to ask Clark Gregory from Atlanta, Georgia, what one thing you should do to protect the environment, he would tell you to compost. Affectionately known in Georgia as the "Compost Man," Clark is part of a growing nationwide movement striving to keep leaves, yard trimmings, wet paper towels and even some food scraps out of our landfills.

When it comes to small-scale composting, elementary schools appear to be setting the standard for the academic community. With the support of Governor Zell Miller of Georgia, Gregory and other local activists have worked with the Georgia Department of Education to integrate composting issues throughout K-12 curricula. Gregory has helped numerous elementary schools in Georgia establish composting programs, and has set up 12 demonstration sites across the state. The New York Department of Environmental Conservation has also devel-

Recycling handbooks such as these from Dartmouth and Georgetown University help educate members of the campus community while codifying procedures.

oped several innovative composting curricula for elementary schools. And the February 1991 issue of *BioCycle Magazine* reports that the Alcott Elementary School in Concord, Massachusetts—one of the first schools in the United States to start a food waste composting program—has processed more than 3,000 pounds of food, paper napkins and lunch bags.

Colleges and universities are becoming part of the leadership, however, as administrators from Rutgers University in New Jersey to the University of California begin to view composting as an attractive alternative to costly waste handling and fertilizers.

The Dartmouth Model

Such is the case at Dartmouth College in New Hampshire, where Bill Hochstin, head of Dartmouth Recycles, has managed campus composting since 1992 with the assistance of Dining Services Director Peter Napolitano, Grounds Foreman Bob Thebodo, and other staff. Before developing a full-scale program, Hochstin spent about a year filing permits with the College Office of Real Estate and the Department of Environmental Services, and then ran an eight-month pilot program.

Hochstin and his crew use a tractor to form two long windrows (long narrow piles of compost, in this case about 230 feet long, six feet wide and five feet tall) on a loamy area fenced off from the rest of the campus. The windrows consist of layers of cow manure, pre-consumer food scraps, napkins, and newsprint, turned by a tractor semimonthly for aeration and moisture distribution. The crew regularly monitors moisture content and nutrient ratios. Decomposition is most efficient when moisture levels hover around fifty percent and the ratio of carbon (from leaves, napkins, newspaper, or other bulking agents) to nitrogen (from grass, vegetable and fruit trimmings) is approximately 30 to 1.

Dartmouth's Bill Hochstin describes windrow composting.

Savings

The dining service and the buildings and grounds department help cover the minimal costs of Dartmouth's composting program. In return, each department saves money through reduced tipping fees. The dining service contributes several sealed 32-gallon plastic barrels (200 to 400 pounds) of vegetable and fruit trimmings daily, saving approximately $1,700 in tipping fees over the eight-month trial period. Various administrative offices also contribute their paper towel waste, collectively adding about 15 pounds per day. A dairy farmer trucks 1,000 pounds of cow manure to Dartmouth every two weeks, in exchange for which the college transports a truckful of newspapers to the dairy farm for use as animal bedding. Coffee grounds and unbleached paper filters are also added to the mix. Hochstin is considering the addition of certain post-consumer food scraps.

The resulting compost is used on athletic fields and in various other landscaping projects. The 20,000 pounds of compost generated during the trial period replaced fertilizers which would have cost approximately $9,700 ($8.50 per 50 pound bag) over the trial period. After subtracting program costs of $1,200 and adding tipping fee savings, Hochstin figures the pilot resulted in net savings of more than $10,000 dollars over eight months.

Quality Control

Hochstin works hard to ensure there are no pesticide residues on materials coming into the yard waste compost. The grounds crew has implemented an Integrated Pest Management (IPM) program (see Chapter 2, Landscaping), which minimizes their use of pesticides, and consults with the campus Biosafety Committee before applying chemical controls of any kind. "We test and come out absolutely clean," says Hochstin, who cautions, "you don't want organic matter that has been contaminated with pesticides, fungicides, any kind of weed killer or other toxic . . . . Otherwise, when you do testing on your compost before application, you'll find the material is suitable only for landfill, especially if you are going to grow food on it. We control from start to finish."

Staff are instructed to properly dispose of any chemically treated materials rather than add them to the compost. After testing by the Woods End Research Laboratory in Maine, which specializes in composting research and development, Dartmouth's compost was found to be free of toxins and to have a good nutrient balance. With student help, Hochstin has begun growing organic vegetables in the nutrient-rich compost with the idea that one day they may be able to supply vegetables to the dining service, creating a closed-loop system.

Scaling it Down

Johnson State College in Johnson, Vermont, also composts pre-consumer food wastes from the cafeteria, but uses a passive system on a smaller scale. Johnson State is not an agricultural school, but the compost program established in 1991 has been part of a three-pronged project to reclaim a small farm on campus land: maintaining rotational heifer grazing, an organic community garden, and the composting project. Founders of the 2001 Club, students D.J. Donahue and Shahab Farzanegan, envisioned the project and, with the support of faculty, won two start-up grants. The Vermont State Agency of Natural Resources funded the creation of a composting facility for pre-consumer food waste. The Regional Solid Waste Management District funded the development and test-

Composting saved Dartmouth more than $10,000 in fertilizer and disposal costs over an eight-month trial period.

ing of home composting units, along with demonstrations of composting techniques in workshops for the local community.

Though he has graduated, Donahue continues to volunteer on the pilot farm along with faculty and new 2001 Club members. He and the other program founders credit Frank Fortin, director of the dining service, with sustaining the program after the grants ran out. Fortin has lobbied other administrators, helped secure a work-study student manager for the composting site, and instructed dining service staff to separate pre-consumer vegetable and fruit waste into the 32-gallon drums they call "compostainers," which they store in a walk-in refrigerator and empty daily at the composting site. He has also approached the business office about purchasing vegetables from the organic garden during the short summer growing season.

Johnson State has several holding piles for pre-consumer waste, sawdust, shredded paper (from the office services department), and cow manure. These and the compost pile rest on a 30-by-30-foot concrete slab, which slopes toward a catchment wall where moisture runoff can pool and evaporate. The compost pile is not tilled, but is aerated passively via PV pipe running through its center. Donahue deems the passive system efficient—and cheaper than his original approach of hiring the labor and machinery to till the pile.

The use of compost and the initial planting of cover crops has improved soil conditions at the community garden site, which had an active planting and harvest season in 1993. The site has been used by 12 groups, including a student volunteer program supplying a local food bank, and a small, student-run market which sells organic produce to local restaurants. Participants are seeking organic certification for the garden through a Vermont subsidiary of the National Organic Farmers Association (NOFA).

Composting efforts at Johnson State (below, right) and Miami Dade Community College in Miami, Florida (left).

The Power of Worms

Johnson State students also built a large dual-compartment vermicompost (worm composting) bin as part of their research on various home composting systems, of which they run about a dozen for use in community demonstration projects. They purchased red wrigglers, the recommended earthworm for vermicomposting, and poured them over a bed of silage (dairy animal feed) and vegetable scraps in one of the three-by-three-foot compartments. They continually add vegetable scraps until the pile has turned to rich, black compost, at which point they create a bed of silage and vegetable scraps in the other empty compartment. The red wrigglers migrate from the finished compost—which is removed and used on the organic vegetable garden—to the new bedding. The rotation of red wrigglers and compost continues throughout the year.

Scaling Down Even Further

It is not necessary to start out on the level of large windrows or even small holding piles on concrete slabs. For groups wishing to start very modest composting systems—perhaps encouraging departments or residence halls to manage their own piles and use compost in adjacent landscapes—there are several low-tech options. The most popular bin in Georgia, according to Clark Gregory, is made of a three-dollar piece of fence wire looped into a one-cubic yard composting hoop.

Johnson State students check their large vermicompost (worm composting) bin.

Gregory's favorite bin, and the one he recommends most often for elementary schools, is the five-pallet model. Using shipping pallets reduces waste of precious timber and costs nothing; the pallets pile up on campuses and at business sites and are usually landfilled or incinerated. The five-pallet model is attractive (high-quality oak is still used to make many pallets) and effective. One pallet rests flat on the ground, allowing for aeration from below, and four pallets attached by wire form standing walls around it. With a little turning, composting happens as rapidly as in the most expensive bins.

These simple, inexpensive approaches make composting a practice that campuses can hardly afford not to try. (Additional campus composting programs are listed in the networking section.)

SOURCE REDUCTION: THE NEXT THRESHOLD

From instituting reusable mug programs to renting out cloth bags in bookstores, hundreds of campuses have initiated innovative source reduction efforts. Source reduction takes waste reduction measures such as recycling and composting a step further. By reducing the amount of material discarded for eventual recycling or composting, source reduction shifts some of the labor off already overworked campus recycling and waste management staff. Source reduction programs eliminate single-use items, encourage reuse of materials, use more durable materials, and/or eliminate unnecessary usage. This is the next threshold for campuses, most of which focused first on establishing recycling programs.

Two of the more comprehensive source-reduction efforts on campuses address the problems of junk mail and students' end-of-semester cast-offs. Appalachian State University, Yale University, the University of Arizona, and the University of Minnesota each have aggressive junk mail reduction programs, which range from providing forms for deletion from mailing lists (see box below) to returning used catalogs to vendors for recycling (see Chapter 1, Puchasing). The University of Michigan's "Student Move-Out Project" collects furniture, carpets, food, and clothing at the end of each semester. Paul Smiths College uses a regional waste exchange database operated by the Adirondack North County Association to share materials.

More modest source reduction efforts can also have impressive cumulative effects. The hundreds of campuses now offering reusable mugs and drink discounts, for instance, have seen disposable waste decrease by as much as 30 percent (University of Colorado-Boulder). Then, too, many campuses now offer incentives for, or require, double-sided copying—cutting paper use *and* costs almost in half. Others, such as the Rochester Institute of Technology, Highline Community College, and Tufts University, make note pads by cutting and binding paper that has been used on only one side.

One of the best places to share campus source reduction tips is "RECYC-L," an Internet "listserv" or electronic correspondence group run by Kurt Teichert, Coordinator of *Brown is Green* at Brown University. To tap this resource, send the following message to Listserv@BROWNVM.BROWN.EDU: subscribe RECYC-L "your name". Subscribers are immediately plugged into

Many campuses are grabbing junkmail by the horns. Appalachian State encourages staff to use the following de-subscription form.

Junk Mail Form

Mail to: Mail Preference Service
Direct Marketing Association
6 E. 43rd St.
New York, NY 10017 USA

Dear Folks:

I'm tired of junk mail, and I don't want my name sold to mailing list companies any more. Please remove it from your files right away. Thank you.

_____
name

_____
street

_____
city/state/ZIP/country

some of the more creative minds in the campus solid waste business.

One of the myths of the campus environmental movement was that once a recycling coordinator was hired, a campus had met its obligation to reduce waste. But students and staff on many campuses have realized that recycling coordinators, as critical as they are, can only do so much. Working as they do at the end of the campus waste stream, recycling coordinators are, in fact, rather poorly positioned to prevent waste on their own. As UC-Boulder and other campuses have demonstrated, in order to truly succeed, recycling coordinators need to be part of leadership teams in which purchasers, accountants, students, custodians and others are equally motivated to create and implement both source reduction and recycling on campus.

BIBLIOGRAPHY

"Coming of Age: Recycling on Campus," Jack DeBell, *Resource Recycling*, September, 1994.

Community College Waste Reduction and Recycling Guide, Pacific Energy Institute, Seattle, WA, 1991. (206) 628-0460.

"Compost Update," Russel Roe, *Environ-Mental-List: SFSU Recycling Center's Newsletter*, fall, 1994, San Francisco State University Recycling Center, 1600 Holloway, San Francisco, CA 94132.

Composting: Returning Organic Waste to the Soil, Campus Ecology Program Issue Packet Series, National Wildlife Federation, 1993.

"Dartmouth: 100 People Try to Learn More About Refuse," Campus Life, *New York Times*, Sunday, November 19, 1989, p. 51.

Enchiridion Renovandi: The Georgetown Recycling Handbook, Joshua D. Edelstein, Georgetown Recycles, Georgetown University, 1994.

Four R's: Refuse, Reduce, Reuse, and Recycle, Campus Ecology Program, National Wildlife Federation, 1994.

"Brown University Recycling Program," Kurt Teichert, Brown is Green, Brown University, 1993. (401) 863-7837.

"Closing the Loop: A Guide to Responsible Waste Management Policy at the College of William and Mary," Katherine O'Neill and Alexandra Scott, 1991.

Creating Local Recycling Markets, Tom Martin, Institute for Local Self-Reliance, 1994. (202) 232-4108.

"Federal Government Gets Serious About Recycled Paper," *Greenline*, January, 1995, Conservatree, 10 Lombard St., Ste. 200, San Francisco, CA 94111.

"Getting Started: A Recycling Kit for the Office," Office Paper Recycling Program, University of Michigan.

"Limestone Receives Recycling Grant," Lori Gwyn, August, 1993, Limestone College, 1115 College Drive, Gaffney, SC 29340. (803) 489-7151 ext. 438.

Making Less Garbage: A Planning Guide for Communities, Bette K. Fishbein and Caroline Gelb, INFORM, Inc., 1992. (212) 689-4040.

Pilot Composting Facility, Department of Environmental Sciences, Rutgers University, Cook College, P.O. Box 231, New Brunswick, NJ 08903-0231. (908) 932-9735.

"Precycled Scratch Pads," Paul Branca and William Hanna, Final Class Report, May, 1993. (Call Campus Ecology for details.)

"Recycling 101, Dartmouth College," *New England Waste Resources*, February, 1991.

Recycling Economic Development through Scrap-Based Manufacturing, Michael Lewis, Institute for Local Self-Reliance, 1994. (202) 232-4108.

"Recycling and Sanitation at Duke University: Report of Evaluation of Duke University's Long Term Solid Waste Management Alternatives," Stephanie Finn and Randy Bowen, Duke University, 1994.

"Resident Staff Members' Guide to Recycling," University of Michigan, Housing Division and University Unions, 1500 Student Activities Building, Ann Arbor, MI 48109-1316.

"Rot is Hot," William Bryant Logan, *New York Times Magazine*, September, 1991.

"Solid Waste," Dr. Alan Schwartz, et al., *Environmental Audit of St. Lawrence University*, May, 1993, pp. 35–55. (313) 379-5357.

"Starting Our Fifth Year of Recycling," Appalachian State Recycling Update, Appalachian State University, February, 1994.

"Trash and Recycled Material Streams at the University of Wisconsin-Madison: A Characterization and Analysis," Karma Geiger and Rob Walther, Campus Ecology Research Project Report No. 6, University of Wisconsin-Madison, 1994.

University and College Solid Waste Reduction and Recycling, Hegberg, Brenniman, Hallenbeck, University of Illinois Center for Solid Waste Management and Research, 1992. (Available for the time being at no charge from the Illinois Department of Energy and Natural Resources Information Clearinghouse (217) 785-0310. This especially useful report includes: university waste characterization studies and comparisons; sample recycling budgets; statistical methodology for estimating waste generation from samples; blank forms for building waste assessments, waste disposal inventory, waste composition, and material recycling estimation; and sample contracts and letters of agreement.)

Waste Prevention, Recycling, and Composting Programs: Lessons from 30 U.S. Communities, Brenda Platt et al., Institute for Local Self-Reliance, 1994. (202) 232-4108.

Worms Eat My Garbage, Mary Appelhof, Kalamazoo, MI, Flower Press, 1982.

NETWORKING

Campus

This is only a partial listing, mostly of campuses with paid recycling coordinators, but reflects some of the diversity of type, region and size of higher education recycling programs in the U.S.. Contact Campus Ecology staff for other contacts in your region.

Appalachian State University
Attn: Jim Rice
Environment & Safety
Boone, NC 28608
(704) 262-4007
FAX: 262-4017
Tailors newsletter and recycling program to staff and office needs; serves as a contact point for the statewide Collegiate Recycling Coalition; also contact about award-winning furniture recycling program in residence halls.

Arkansas State University
Attn: Starr Fenner
Environmental Safety
P.O. Box 1530
University, AR 72467
(501) 972-3803
Comprehensive recycling program.

Arkansas Tech University
Attn: Dr. Robert Allen
ATU Box 7500
Russellville, AR 72801
(501) 968-0310
e-mail: psba@atuvm.atu.edu
Students and faculty operate community drop-off center; are creating video-documentation of recycling process.

Bates College
Attn: Betsy Kimball
Lewiston, ME 04240
(207) 786-6251
Local composting arrangement.

Birmingham-Southern College
Attn: Roald Hazelhoff
Office of the Environment
Birmingham, AL 35254
(205) 226-4934
Runs one of the most comprehensive institutional recycling programs in Alabama; their new Environmental Center includes solid waste and other environmental exhibits and programs for local school children.

Brigham Young University-Hawaii
Attn: Kenneth Kamiya or Alan Cheung
Physical Plant
1949 BYU, Hawaii
Laie, HI 96762
(808)293-3444 or
(808)293-3445
Unique recycling and composting video produced in spring, 1994; physical plant hires students to help coordinate paper recycling and composting programs.

Brown University
Attn: Kurt Teichert
Box 1941
Providence, RI 02912
(401) 863-7837
e-mail: kurt_teichert@brown.edu
Teichert administers "Recyc-l," a discussion group on Internet meant especially for campus recycling coordinators (see below). Also of note: Brown's solid waste/recycling contracts were revised in 1991 to facilitate cost-avoidance accounting; comprehensive recycling program includes scrap metal and wood; food waste is collected by a local pig farmer; student interns are frequently hired to evaluate and improve waste reduction efforts.

If you find that an organization listed here has moved or a contact has been replaced, let the Campus Ecology Program staff know. We'll help match you with the latest source for the information you need.

California State University-Fresno
Attn: Robert Fischer
Peace and Conflict Studies
Fresno, CA 93740
(209) 278-2891
Remarkable recycling start-up story.

Claflin College
Attn: Dr. Betty Stokes
Biology Department
Orangeburg, SC 29115
(803) 535-5249
Small volunteer program.

Dartmouth College
Attn: Bill Hochstin
McKenzie Hall
Hinman Box 6111
Hanover, NH 03755
e-mail:
william.a.hochstin@dartmouth.edu
Composting permits and regulations, use of compost in vegetable gardens, cost-benefit analyses, waste reduction, cooperation with dining services, materials exchange.

Duke University
Attn: Stephanie Finn
Recycling Office
Durham, NC 27708-0251
(919) 684-3362
A contact person for Collegiate Recycling Coalition; does own hauling and commodities brokerage.

Georgetown University
Attn: Jon Miller
B-24 Harbin Hall
37th & O Sts., N.W.
Washington, D.C. 20057
(202) 687-2033
Does own hauling and commodities brokerage; introductory recycling manual, Enchiridion Renovandi, *including maps of separation sites, is distributed to new students; contact person for the College and University Recycling Caucus.*

Highline Community College
Attn: Kari Lopez
Recycle, MS 10-2
PO Box 98000
Des Moines, WA 98198
(206) 870-3761
Recycling program in operation since 1991.

Johnson State College
Attn: Frank Fortin
ARA Food Service
Johnson, VT 05656
(802) 635-2235
Composts pre-consumer food scraps.

Lander University
Attn: Beth Davis
Physical Plant
Lander University
Greenwood, SC 29649
(803) 229-8361
Very impressive waste diversion rates even though there is no tipping fee for waste in Greenwood.

Missouri Valley College
Attn: Stacy Galary
Student Life Office
Marshal, MO 65340
(816) 886-6924
Institutionalized recycling at a small college, heavy volunteer and work-study involvement.

Montgomery College
Attn: Don Campbell
51 Mannakee St.
Rockville, MD 20850
(301) 279-5000
Community college recycling program run by building services has been in operation since 1991.

North Carolina A&T University
Attn: Mary Barbee
Housekeeping Administration
1601 East Market Street
Greensboro, NC 27411
Housekeeper-run recycling program; Ms. Barbee gives motivational talks on the "whys" and "hows" of investing housekeepers and custodians in campus recycling programs; contact point for the Collegiate Recycling Coalition.

Northland College
Attn: Tom Wojciechowski
Ashland, WI 54806
(715) 682-1699
Composting, Great Lakes "Zero Discharge" pilot campus.

Ouachita Baptist University
Attn: Dr. Tim Knight
OBU Box 3705
Arkadelphia, AR 71998
(501) 245-5528
e-mail: knight@obu.arknet.edu
Paper vendor distributes paper and back-hauls used office paper for recycling.

Paul Smiths College
Attn: Karen Smith
Paul Smiths Library
P.O. Box 265
Paul Smiths, NY 12970
(518) 327-6313
ksmith@sescva.esc.edu
On-line waste exchange program; composting permitting and coordination with county; Paul Smiths was recognized by the Adirondack North County Association as a model business in the local Saranac Lake area for the promotion of waste reduction on a large scale.

Prairie View A&M University
Attn: Dr. Ronald Humphrey
Biology Department
Prairie View, TX 77446
(409) 857-3913
*Volunteer recycling program
funds community service
groups.*

Rutgers University
Attn: Kevin Lyons
Procurement and Contracting
Division
P.O Box 6999
Piscataway, NJ 08854
(908) 445-5192
*Offers consultation on contract
writing and commodities
brokerage; Department of
Environmental Science, which
has conducted composting
research and development since
1970, will bring a pilot
composting research and
education facility on line in
1995–96.*

San Jacinto College-South
Attn: Andrea Norfleet
Science Club
Department of Biology
13735 Beamer Road, Houston,
TX 77089-6099
(713) 484-1900
Outstanding recycling video.

Seattle Central Community
College
Attn: Jeff Watts
Physical Plant
1701 Broadway
Seattle, WA 98122
(206) 587-5439
*Model institutional recycling
program.*

South Carolina College
Attn: Dr. James Stukes
Biology Department
Orangeburg, SC 29117
(803) 536-5208
*Volunteer recycling program
funds community service
groups.*

Spokane Falls Community College
Attn: Gary Blevins
Box 3180
3410 W. Fort George Wright Rd.
Spokane, WA 99204
(509) 533-3661
*Recent move from aluminum to
paper and institutionalization,
interesting tale of sustaining
recycling at a community
college.*

University New York-Buffalo
Attn: Matt Deck
B1 Helm Building
Buffalo, NY 14260
(716) 645-5962
e-mail:
deck@ubvms.cc.buffalo.edu
*Comprehensive recycling
program, especially impressive
recovery rates for office paper:
despite emphasis on high-grade
paper, Deck's program has been
able to accommodate, and has
in fact encouraged, increased
use of post-consumer recycled
papers, including those with
some groundwood content.*

St. Charles Community College
Attn: Dr. Arlan Hinchee
Biology Department
P.O. Box 76975
St. Peters, MO 63366
(314) 922-8000 ext. 4340
*Reusable mug video, aggressive
reusable mug program
supported by many area
businesses.*

St. Lawrence University
Attn: Dr. Alan Schwartz
Environmental Studies Program
Canton, NY
(315) 379-5357
e-mail: asch@slumus
*Hired student monitors to
facilitate aggressive source
separation programs in
recycling rooms opened during
set hours in 11 residence halls.
Food and paper waste
composting program was
dismantled, but is an instructive
case study.*

University of California-Davis
Attn: David G. Orr
Office of Environmental
Services
Davis, CA 95616
(916) 752-6970
dgorr@ucdavis.edu
*Contact person for composting
and other campus waste
reduction efforts as well as for
College and University Recycling
Caucus.*

University of Colorado-Boulder
Attn: Jack DeBell
Recycling Office
Campus Box 207
Boulder, CO 80309
(303) 492-8307
FAX: (303) 492-1897
*Consultation covering custodial
collections and cart design,
contracting, life-cycle cost
accounting, training student
staff and volunteers, design and
planning for recycling. DeBell is
a contact person for the College
and University Recycling
Caucus.*

University of Arizona Recycling
Attn: Sharon Aller
Bldg. 49, Facilities Management
Tucson, AZ 85721
(602) 621-1264
*Contact person for "Garbage
Project," junk mail elimination
program, comprehensive
environmental audit, graywater
recycling, chemical waste
exchange, and recycling.*

University of Georgia
Attn: John Ayoob
Housing Department
Athens, GA 30602
(706) 542-1421
*Installed high-rise recycling
system in nine-story residence
hall in spring 1995.*

University of Iowa
Attn: Carol Casey
100 Physical Plant
Iowa City, IA 52242-1000
e-mail: cdcasey@pps1-
PO.phyp.uiowa.edu
*Contact person for College and
University Recycling Caucus.*

University of Michigan
Attn: Erica Spiegel
Recycling Office
326 E. Hoover
Ann Arbor, MI 48109
(313) 763-5539
e-mail:
erica.spiegel@um.cc.umich.edu
*Contact person for College and
University Recycling Caucus;
contact person for information
on week-long "Student Move-
Out" project held each spring,
collecting furniture, loft wood,
clothing, food, household items,
notebooks and mixed paper,
return-deposit cans and bottles,
etc.*

University of Minnesota
Attn: Dana Donatucci
Como Recycling Facility
3009 Como Ave., S.E.
Minneapolis, MN 55414-2804
*Model materials exchange
program for furniture,
computers and other office
equipment, precious metals,
and other resources.*

University of North Carolina
-Chapel Hill
Attn: Charles Button
CB #1800
Chapel Hill, NC 27599-1800
(919) 962-1442
-Charlotte
Attn: B.J. Tipton
Recycling Dept., Physical Plant
Charlotte, NC 28223
(704) 547-2137
-Greensboro
Attn: John Bonitz
Physical Plant
Greensboro, NC 27412-5001

University of Vermont
Attn: Dennis Clark
Physical Plant
622 Main St.
Burlington, VT 05405-0098
(802) 656-3385
e-mail: dennisc@ppuax.uvm.edu
*Composts animal bedding made
from shredded paper waste,
manure and other materials.*

University of Oregon
Attn: Karyn Kaplan
Physical Plant
Eugene, OR 97403-1276
(503) 346-1529
e-mail:
karyn_kaplyn@ccmail.uoregon.edu
*Fruitful collaborations with the
printshop, bookstore, and other
areas on campus.*

University of Wisconsin-Madison
Attn: Neil Michaud or Daniel
Einstein
Environmental Management
1069 WARF, 610 Walnut Str.
Madison, WI 53705
(608) 265-3417
e-mail:
nmichaud@students.wisc.edu
*Developing materials exchange
program, contact person for
solid waste and procurement
analyses.*

Vanderbilt University
Attn: Brenda Gilmore
Resource Conservation Advisory
Committee
Nashville, TN 37235
(615) 343-6923
*Coordinates "clothing moun-
tain," office paper recycling,
waste reduction in mail services.*

Yale University
Attn: C.J. May
Physical Plant
New Haven, CT 06520
(203) 432-6852
cj-may@quickmail.yale.edu
*Aggressive junkmail reduction,
various other source reduction
efforts.*

Regional and National

Collegiate Recycling Coalition, NCRA
Attn: Bobbi Tousey,
7330 Chapel Hill Road, Suite 207
Raleigh, NC 27607
(919) 851-8444
This is a model wide recycling network which holds an annual conference in the fall attended by campus recycling coordinators from North Carolina and many other states; campus contacts include Jim Rice at Appalachian University (704) 262-3190 ext. 108, Stephanie Finn at Duke University (919) 684-3362; B.J. Tipton at UNC-Charlotte (704) 547-2137; and Charles Button at UNC-Chapel Hill (919) 962-1442.

College and University Recycling Caucus
This is a growing network of campus recycling professionals; Brown University administers its discussion group "Recyc-l" on Internet (see below); see contact campuses listed above.

Institute of Scrap Recycling Industries
Paper Stock Institute
1627 K St., NW Ste. 700
Washington, D.C. 20006
(202) 466-4050

National Recycling Coalition (NRC)
101 30th St., N.W. Ste. 305
Washington, D.C. 20007
(202) 625-6406
Holds national conference; operates Peer Match Program; hosts the College and University Recycling Caucus.

National Office Paper Recycling Project
The U.S. Conference of Mayors
1620 Eye St., NW
Washington, D.C. 20006
(202) 293-7330

National Wildlife Federation
Campus Ecology Program
1400 16th St., N.W.
Washington, D.C. 20036-2266
(202) 797-5435 (general information)
(313) 769-9970 or midwest@nwf.org (M.W.)
(202) 797-5468 or noreast@nwf.org (N.E.)
(404) 876-2608 or soeast@nwf.org (S.E.)
(503) 222-1429 or western@nwf.org (West)
Ask for Campus Composting, Procurement or 4Rs Issue Packet which includes updated recycling contacts list, video ordering and recycled product info. The Campus Year in Review also describes recycling and waste reduction initiatives of member campuses.

"RECYC-L"
Kurt Teichert, Listowner
Brown is Green
Box 1941
Brown University
Providence, RI 02912
(401) 863-7837
e-mail: kurt_teichert@brown.edu
"Recyc-l" is a "listserv" or electronic correspondence group on the Internet. It was established primarily for campus recycling professionals connected with the College and University Recycling Caucus. To subscribe to the list, send the following message to LISTSERV@BROWNVM.BROWN.EDU: subscribe RECYC-L "your name".

United States Environmental Protection Agency
Region V (HRP-8J)
Attn: Paul Reusch
Solid Waste Section
77 West Jackson Boulevard
Chicago, IL 60604
(312) 886-3585
Contact for "Recycling and Procurement Survey of Midwestern Colleges and Universities" or for recycled paper/copy machine compatibility studies by Susan Mooney.

CHAPTER 8

Hazardous Waste Minimization

Thanks to tireless grassroots lobbying, Congress has passed a series of laws that encourage manufacturers to cut the quantity of hazardous waste they produce—and thus the extent to which they pollute the air, water, and soil. Using a combination of "carrots" and "sticks," these federal initiatives have helped convince many businesses that reducing waste and preventing pollution are better long-term financial and public-relations strategies than merely managing their waste.

These laws include the Clean Air and Clean Water Acts, passed in 1970 and 1972 respectively, which now include outright bans on certain ozone-depleting compounds and which regulate treatment and emissions of certain other chemicals; the Toxic Substances Control Act (TOSCA), passed in 1976 to establish new requirements for identifying and monitoring toxic chemical hazards; the Comprehensive Environmental Response, Compensation, and Liabilities Act (or "Superfund"), first authorized in 1980, which increases corporate liability for environmental damage and for cleanup; the 1984 Hazardous and Solid Wastes Amendments to the Resource Conservation and Recovery Act (RCRA), which dramatically increase disposal and incineration costs; the Emergency Planning and Community-Right-to-Know Act of 1986, which for the first time gives citizens access to information on the hazardous chemicals stored, used, and released in their communities; and the Pollution Prevention Act of 1990, which encourages prevention of pollution at the source over recycling and disposal of hazardous waste.

The idea that pollution prevention pays, a concept now revolutionizing enterprise worldwide, is catching on in academia. Gone, for the most part, are the

University of Washington's Harriet Ige works full-time to minimize hazardous waste by helping lab and physical plant staff identify safer substitutes for commonly used chemicals.

days when academic laboratories disposed of hazardous chemicals down sink drains or dumped barrels of toxic waste into nearby oceans with impunity.[1] Today, in the worst case, institutions may allow old chemical stocks to linger in lab and facility closets, but most campuses have improved labeling of chemicals and pay dearly for proper waste disposal. And a few colleges and universities have begun to eliminate hazardous waste altogether.

The effort of Bowdoin College in Brunswick, Maine, to reduce chemical use in student labs in the early 1980s helped spark a nationwide re-engineering of undergraduate chemistry courses, and serves as a classic example of how much one department, working autonomously, can accomplish. Print shops, landscaping, fleet maintenance, and other operations described more fully in other chapters provide additional examples of initiatives at the departmental level.

Most large campuses, however, rely on environmental health and safety (EH&S) offices to coordinate efforts like those at Bowdoin. Ranging in size from one individual to dozens of staff, EH&S offices, no matter how well staffed or funded, can seize only a fraction of the pollution prevention opportunities in the hundreds of labs and dozens of departments at an institution. But they can provide the framework, support, and staff training which are indispensable to safety and waste minimization in large settings. The environmental health and safety department at the University of Washington, for instance, is one of the most strongly oriented towards pollution prevention in the country. Their chemical tracking systems, waste minimization procedures, and training programs have been emulated by campuses across the state and in other parts of the country.

Campus pollution prevention efforts also help enhance community relations. Students at Dickinson College in Carlisle, Pennsylvania, use Community-Right-to-Know laws to investigate the pollution records of industries in Carlisle and in their home towns. Many of the students then go on to work in local and national pollution prevention programs.

🌿 MICROSCALE: STARTING SMALL

The Bowdoin College Initiative

Reducing waste—not recycling, reusing, diluting, deactivating, or concentrating it, but instead radically diminishing the quantity of hazardous substances used in experiments, manufacturing, and routine cleaning—is the next frontier of waste management in academia. Sometimes waste reduction involves the relatively simple substitution of one product for another. More often, however, it

> *Each year, U.S. educational institutions collectively generate up to 4,000 metric tons of a wide variety of hazardous wastes, according to the U.S. EPA's 1990* Guides to Pollution Prevention.

---

[1] "Hazardous Waste," *In our Backyard*, p. 146. See bibliography.

necessitates the development of new equipment and the altering of approaches that have remained constant for decades. Initiating these changes, as Bowdoin College demonstrates, requires a confluence of the right impetus, the right personalities, a supportive atmosphere, and sufficient resources.

The Impetus

An outdated ventilation system, a fast-growing undergraduate chemistry enrollment, and one particularly vocal student inspired some creative problem-solving by Bowdoin's chemistry faculty. Enrollment in chemistry programs began to rise significantly in the 1970s. By the mid-1980s, Bowdoin was graduating more chemistry majors than any other undergraduate institution in the country. But the college used lab ventilation systems so antiquated that students, especially in the organic chemistry classes, began to complain; eventually, a student whose father headed California's Occupational Safety and Health Administration visited the president. Shortly after that, Chemistry Chair Samuel Butcher was asked to do whatever was required to update the labs. But when he discovered that new ventilation hoods, ducts and blowers would cost the college more than $300,000, Butcher turned to Professor Dana Mayo, the resident organic chemist, issuing what Mayo recalls as a mildly-phrased but seminal challenge: "Gee, it is too bad you fellows can't teach that lab some other way."

Key Personalities

"After suffering through the agony of having to shed the poor technique . . . developed as an undergraduate by working with much larger quantities," recalls Mayo, he learned as a graduate student and throughout much of his research career to conduct organic chemistry experiments involving very small amounts of materials. With Butcher's challenge hovering over him, he asked himself if it made sense to develop microscale experiments for undergraduates. "I figured out on the back of an envelope how far we would have to go," says Mayo, "and it was in the milligram level—down to material that you can see comfortably, where you are just this side of being required to magnify it."

But there was a lingering sense of doubt. Mayo anticipated that microscale experiments would not adapt well to the undergraduate level—that they would be too instructor-intensive and would frustrate students. However, his friend, Prof. Ron Pike of Merrimack College in North Andover, Massachusetts, who was a visiting professor at the time, ardently supported the concept. "I think without his encouragement," Mayo reflects, "I might have been less enthusiastic, because at that stage I took a very pessimistic view of it." Together, they approached Butcher, who in turn presented the administration with a choice: either pay

Prof. Dana Mayo of Bowdoin helped engineer the microscale revolution in higher education.

$300,000 for new ventilation systems or provide Mayo with a $20,000 loan to explore microscaling—a strategy intended to make ventilation hoods obsolete. The administration took the $20,000 gamble.

Getting Started

A talented student named Caroline Foote stayed for a year after graduating to develop the first few experiments and test them on a group of 10 volunteers. Staff initially designed just enough experiments for the first half-semester of the introductory organic lab. After modifying dozens more experiments, Mayo, Pike, and Butcher, with the help of Foote and other students, published their first textbook: *Microscale Organic Laboratory*. Now in its third edition, the volume includes more than 90 experiments, of which "you would normally do more or less 30 in a year," says Mayo—"maybe 35 if you are really pushing it hard."

Mayo, Pike, and students collaborated with the Ace Glass Company in Vineland, New Jersey, to develop new apparatus. "They had a local representative in our area," recalls Mayo, "and when he walked in, his eyes lit up." Mayo had previously approached several other glass companies, he says, before finding a receptive one. "But this guy was right on to it; he saw the potential . . ." says Mayo, who quickly began sending Ace designs which would be "instantly transformed into glass and back to [him] by Federal Express, helping [Mayo and students] tremendously in developing the equipment."

Mayo's inventions have since been featured in *Chemical & Engineering News* and elsewhere. And one of Mayo's students, Robert Hinkle, patented a spinning band distillation column that is used in research and to teach fractional distillation inexpensively.

Initial Results

Even with only the first, skeletal set of experiments developed by Foote, the results amazed the Bowdoin faculty: students were more focused throughout experiments. "Usually the lab is just a lot of commotion, a lot of noise, and people chitchatting and kind of running around," says Mayo, "but I went into this lab and it was quiet." Within three weeks, it was obvious the students had adapted rapidly, finding they could perform more experiments in an afternoon and repeat experiments if necessary. "Instead of sitting around chewing the fat while something comes up to boil," Mayo noticed, "they were working. Consequently, they learned the techniques much more quickly . . . they really learned the right way to handle stuff, and they were much more concentrated on what they were doing."

> I figured out on the back of an envelope how far we would have to go, and it was in the milligram level—down to material that you can see comfortably.
>
> — Dana Mayo, Bowdoin College

The use of hazardous substances, and of solvents in particular, dropped dramatically. Where 300 to 400 milliliters of solvents per student had been used in the past (some eight liters total for a class), only 100 milliliters were now used for everyone. Experiments such as the Grignard Reaction, named after the Frenchman who invented the routine method of converting one organic material into another, became safer and more pleasant to run. With the Grignard Reaction, recalls Mayo, "you could smell the ether before you ever got to the building, let alone to the hallways and the lab; it was just pervasive. Now, when you walk into the building you don't smell any ether. In fact, if you walk right up to the student's reaction and sniff the equipment, you won't smell any."

Annual costs to run organic labs at Bowdoin declined from $8,000 per lab to less than $1,000, primarily due to reduced disposal fees. The costly ventilation upgrade proved unnecessary, saving the college an additional $280,000.

Bowdoin students' rate of acceptance to graduate chemistry programs, though high to begin with, now skyrocketed. Average students of the sort who had previously won acceptance to one or two graduate schools, reports Mayo, now got in almost everywhere they applied. "In the end," he says, "that is the thing that we have tended to pitch a lot to our colleagues—the pedagogic advantages of teaching the program in this fashion far outweigh those of the older methods."

The Microscale Revolution

In 1984, Prof. David Brooks of the University of Nebraska, then chair of the American Chemical Society Committee on Education, heard about microscale developments at Bowdoin, and he predicted: "This will be the way that everybody does it within the next ten years." Mayo and Pike thought that an incredibly optimistic prognosis, but time has proved Brooks right. Mayo estimates that 50 percent of undergraduates in U.S. chemistry labs learn some micro-procedures, if not on Bowdoin's scale then on a slightly larger one. Numerous institutions began converting to microscale techniques within the last few years, bringing the approach to fruition on a national scale almost exactly a decade after its inception.

Rice University is phasing in microscale experiments for its 250 undergraduate chemistry students. At the University of Washington, Chemistry Department Chair Ruth Levy has transformed most organic experiments to microscale and has begun using products from some experiments as reagents for others. Purdue University, with the largest chemistry program in the country, started microscaling in the 1993–94 academic year, and the University of Michigan, which adopted the microscale approach in 1990, recently designed a new building around the program. UCLA, New York University, North Carolina State, UNC, Duke, the

> In the end, we have tended to pitch to our colleagues [the fact that] the pedagogic advantages of teaching the program in this fashion far outweigh those of the older methods.
>
> —Dana Mayo
> Bowdoin College

University of Washington, and the Arizona state system have all begun microscale programs within the last five years. "The whole 23-campus unit at Wisconsin went micro," reports Mayo, "because a guy at one of the smaller campuses got excited about it and sold everybody on it; even Madison went microscale."

One prominent institution—whose faculty did not attend the microscale lecture Mayo gave at the university during the early days of Bowdoin's conversion—was later hit with a $20,000 disposal fee for waste from one semester-long lab, and promptly sent laboratory instructors to Bowdoin's summer institutes on microscale.

Mayo reports that a growing number of institutions now benefit from microscale's dramatic reductions in disposal costs and use of hazardous materials. The University of Wisconsin at Madison generated 110 liters of waste in 1987, for example, and only 14 liters in 1988, after only partial conversion to micro-procedures. The University of Minnesota converted only two freshman chemistry experiments and saved $35,000. Because as many as 3,000 students take freshman chemistry, explains Mayo, the savings from scaling down even one experiment can be impressive. Mayo recalls a conversation with staff at the University of Arizona:

> The question was: "If we converted . . . how much could we save?" We said, "How much waste are you processing?" And they said, "Well, we take our solvents and redistill and repurify them, and are distilling about 400 liters a week . . . . How much will we have to distill if we converted to your program?" We said, "About 4 liters." And there was silence at the other end of the line. It wasn't very long until both [the University of] Arizona and Arizona State converted.

Calls from hundred of colleges and universities, combined with the difficulty of getting papers on microscale published in prominent journals at the time, prompted Mayo and his students to start the *Smaller is Better* newsletter. This provided a clearinghouse for microscale developments for five or six years, until the *Journal of Chemical Education* established a column on microscale in 1991. This came as a relief to Mayo and staff who, he recalls, "were frantic with the amount of paperwork [we were] handling."

Microscale techniques are spreading overseas. Mayo knows of programs in Sweden, Australia, and Israel, and on several campuses in England. Mayo's collaborator, Ron Pike, has a Merrimack College colleague who plans to conduct trainings on microscale in Mexico. Pike himself has established summer training programs and developed a text for high school teachers.

Research Applications: The Next Threshold

Dr. Tamae Maeda Wang, study director for the widely-read National Research Council publication *Prudent Practices*, agrees that microscale techniques have

Introductory organic labs at the University of Wisconsin at Madison generated 110 liters of waste in 1987, but only 14 liters in 1988, after only partial conversion to micro-procedures.

advanced considerably in the last decade, but cautions against complacency. "There is still quite a lot of work to be done," says Wang, who continues to see chemistry departments "slapped with fines" for improper hazardous waste management. Mayo is optimistic, believing that disposal fees, if not health and environmental concerns, will prompt undergraduate chemistry departments to switch over. "I think the educational battle is all over; it is just a question of time before everybody is into this scale. But at the research level, it is just beginning to take hold and I think that is where the next real revolution is going to happen."

Mayo sees great potential for the application of microscaling to research. He asked student Chris Dinsmore to synthesize an exotic material through a process that involved running three reactions on successive amounts of materials. Within two weeks (an astonishingly short time), Dinsmore had synthesized the first product and was working on the second; ultimately, he created six products instead of the two or three Mayo had expected. Using microscale techniques, Dinsmore was able to run as many as five reactions at once under different conditions, quickly discerning the optimum conditions for best yields. He took those conditions, explains Mayo, scaled them up, ran them on research-grade quantities (grams of material), and got a very good yield for the first step. He then ran a series of reactions on the first product to discern optimal conditions for creating the second product, and so on, until he had synthesized six products. The implications were obvious to Mayo:

> That, to me, drove it home that the strategy for doing research at this level is not appreciated by those people who work with larger quantities. They say, "You need to have larger quantities in order to carry these reactions out." That is it. I agree with that entirely. But your exploratory reactions, if you do them on a small scale, can be much more efficiently done . . . and, in the end, you use a lot less material, and so your operational costs are less.

But old habits die hard. Although Mayo has been contacted by several drug companies and industries (many of which are facing huge cleanup costs), he has encountered general resistance to microscale among research chemists accustomed to larger scale. Mayo once received a call from a distraught chemist who was left with very little product after the purification stage outlined in Mayo's text. It turned out the chemist had substituted crystallization for chromatography, thinking chromatography would take too long to do. "All of a sudden in a gleam," Mayo recalls, he realized the flaw in the chemist's reasoning: "Sure, if you do it on a large scale you might even take several days to do chromatography, but for us it is done in ten minutes. So I said, follow what it says in the book and let me know. An hour later came his phone call saying, 'You were right.'"

Sure, if you do it on a large scale, you might even take several days to do chromatography, but for us, it is done in ten minutes.

—Dana Mayo
Bowdoin College

The best advertisements, it turns out, are the graduates of Bowdoin and other institutions where good microscale techniques are taught. These chemists bring coveted insights and skills to research labs. "We are beginning now to see requests," says Mayo, "for people to run laboratory programs or teach who have had microscale training."

☙ COORDINATION AT LARGE INSTITUTIONS

The Lab Safety System at the University of Washington

The Bowdoin microscale program illustrates what one innovative department can accomplish, as well as how ideas can percolate up from smaller to larger institutions, and *vice versa*. But environmental health and safety offices at large universities often find the task of waste reduction compounded by their wide-ranging responsibilities, which include assuring chemical safety across dozens of departments; enforcing compliance with numerous, evolving regulations; estimating total quantities of specific chemicals used on campus; creating chemical inventories; and assisting in chemical recycling and waste reduction. The fact that the chemical industry often supports research through endowed chairs, fellowships, research contracts, and direct donations hardly makes the job of scaling back chemical use any easier.

A team in the EH&S department at the University of Washington has developed a tool for solving the myriad problems associated with hazardous waste management on campuses: a computer-based chemical inventory and Material Safety Data Sheet program called the Lab Safety System (LSS). Campus environmentalists have long agitated for reforms in the handling of hazardous wastes. The LSS system has quietly made meeting these demands possible by facilitating comprehensive and systematic programs for the sharing of surplus chemicals and the recycling and substitution of hazardous materials campus-wide.

Several factors prompted the University of Washington to invest time and money in such a prototype chemical inventory system. One of the most salient factors, recalls Erin McKeown, UW's industrial hygienist and database manager, was compliance with the Hazard Communication Standard (OSHA, CFR 1910.1200) enacted by Washington state in 1985. The standard requires that chemical manufacturers supply Material Safety Data Sheets (MSDSs) to everyone who purchases potentially hazardous products. Employers must then provide their employees with these MSDSs, along with training in how to analyze them. Each MSDS contains information on the health hazards, physical hazards, protective

Erin McKeown works on the pioneering Lab Safety System at the University of Washington.

measures, storage guidelines, reactivity, spill response, fire safety, and waste guidelines for a particular chemical.

Like many campuses that manage thousands of MSDSs, UW initially kept these documents in hard-copy files. Staff received "long lists of MSDS requests from all over the campus," recalls McKeown, and "it took weeks to find, photocopy, and replace these documents. It was time to make a change, utilizing newly available technology." UW could have purchased several MSDS collections on CD-ROM from various manufacturers, but that would not have solved the accessibility problem. A database available to all employees via the campus network was needed. Otherwise, EH&S staff would continually retrieve MSDSs and distribute them all over the campus, as before; distributing *updated* MSDSs would have been impossible.

Because of the Emergency Planning and Community-Right-to-Know Act passed by Congress in 1986 as Title III of the Superfund Amendments and Reauthorization Act (SARA), UW, like many large public research institutions in certain states, explains McKeown, must report their total quantity of any chemical classified "extremely hazardous" by the EPA—as well as the storage, emission or disposal of 10,000 pounds or more of certain other chemicals. To generate these reports (called the Tier II), UW needed not only a way to inventory each chemical on campus for MSDSs, but also a system with which to aggregate the *total* quantity of each Tier II chemical used in multiple sites on campus.

IS YOUR LAB A GREEN LAB?

adapted from the University of Wisconsin-Madison
"1993 Chemical Safety and Disposal Guide"

A Green Laboratory is one that understands its impact on the environment and tries to minimize it. Since laboratory operations differ, there is no standard for a Green Laboratory. The following actions, however, indicate that a laboratory is a leader in pursuing sound environmental practices. A Green Laboratory will:

- Train personnel in chemical and environmental safety, including methods for preventing pollution and minimizing wastes.

- Assess laboratory air emissions, waste water discharges and waste generation to understand environmental effects.

- Buy only the chemicals and quantities needed.

- Use redistributed surplus chemicals whenever possible.

- Review chemical inventories and routinely make usable surplus available to other laboratories.

- Review the chemicals in use to understand their hazards (e.g., reading Material Safety Data Sheets) and search for safer substitutes.

- Keep caps on ontainers of volatile chemicals.

- Prepare for leaks and spills by using secondary containment and by stocking spill control supplies.

- Take responsibility for waste disposal by neutralizing acids and treating other chemicals.

- Remind colleagues and new personnel to keep waste types separate, and devise a system of separate waste collection that works for their laboratory.

But for Don Brown, the director of EH&S when the LSS was first implemented, the biggest impetus behind the system was the need to comply with newly adopted building and fire codes. The Washington State Department of Construction and Land Use and the Seattle Fire Department enforce some of the most stringent codes in the country; they require hazardous material inventories and management plans for all areas in which hazardous chemicals are used. And fire fighters want information on the quantity of each type of hazard within each fire-control zone. "We are seeing, increasingly, a reluctance by fire fighting staff to enter a burning structure in laboratories," says Brown, "because they don't know the types and quantities of chemicals that are in those labs and the hazard represented by them."

The Inventory System

To satisfy all three requirements—OSHA's HazCom, Community-Right-to-Know, and the local fire and building codes—in an efficient and affordable manner, UW needed an integrated database system. On a campus with 36,000 students, 17,000 staff, 282 buildings, and 4,000 projected chemical-use areas, the system had to be decentralized; fortunately, a network already connected campus computers. Hundreds of faculty and researchers would need access to the LSS from their terminals in order to maintain their own chemical inventories and to edit and update information. Users would gain electronic access to MSDSs, eliminating the lag time and extensive staffing inherent in the old central storage system. The LSS would also accommodate hazard classification information prepared by UW staff to supplement existing MSDSs, which McKeown says have not been standardized and are sometimes incomplete.

Although substitution with a safer chemical is one of the best ways to prevent pollution, the authors of this table note that some substitutions do not work as well and that some substitutes, though less dangerous, are still unsafe.

SAFER SUBSTITUTES FOR COMMON LABORATORY CHEMICALS

adapted by the University of Madison-Wisconsin from a study conducted by the University of Illinois at Urbana-Champaign

Hazardous Chemical	Safer Substitute	Used For
Acetamide	Stearic Acid	Freezing point depression
Benzene	Xylene or hexane	Many solvent uses
Benzoyl Peroxide	Lauryl Peroxide	Some polymer catalysts
Carbon Tetrachloride	Cyclohexane	Qualitative test for halides
Formaldehyde (Formalin)	Ethanol	Specimen storage
Halogenated solvents	Non-halogenated solvents	Some extractions and other solvent uses
Sodium Dichromate	Sodium Hypochloride	Some oxidation reactions
Toluene-based Scintillation Cocktail	Non-ignitable Scintillation Cocktail	Studies using radioactive materials

After months of adapting the system in late 1993 and early 1994, the LSS has begun meeting all these and other needs. Six hundred users are online; 1,949 chemical inventories out of a projected 4,000 are established; 170,000 MSDSs (purchased in ASCII on disk or tape) are in the system, and 14,500 hard copies of MSDSs, not available online, are indexed on the LSS.

UW staff now plan to share the LSS with other academic institutions in the state of Washington. An electronic correspondence group on the Internet called "Safety," administered by the University of Vermont, disseminates news of UW's innovations to professionals elsewhere. The UW staff hope eventually to form a nationwide consortium for adapting the system to the needs of other institutions. Campuses with central laboratory purchasing, for instance, may want to track chemicals throughout their life cycle—from the source of manufacture through purchase, laboratory use, and ultimate disposal—an approach known as documenting the "chain of custody" of hazardous materials.

Minimizing Waste

Beyond keeping chemical inventories and generating reports, the LSS will help the university further minimize hazardous waste. Waste minimization is one of the topics of greatest interest today in campus EH&S circles, says Wendy Phippen, hazardous waste manager at the University of Washington. This interest, however, is just beginning to translate into commitment of staff and resources on most campuses. Though campus EH&S offices sometimes employ as many as 70 people, few campuses have devoted full-time staff to waste minimization. But with two full-time staff who focus on waste minimization, one of whom specializes in source reduction, UW is an exception. (In general, waste minimization encompasses a broader set of options—such as recycling and deactivation of waste—than source reduction, which entails finding less-hazardous substitutes and/or reducing the use of hazardous materials.)

Phippen describes UW's policy as an effort "to minimize the amount of chemical waste that is going into the environment—whether it enters through incineration, landfill or discharge into the water system." Where necessary, minimization at UW includes chemical recycling, but Phippen says: "Our number one goal is source reduction. We don't generate hazardous waste in the first place, so we don't have to worry about finding a disposal facility or recycling."

The LSS requires facility managers and laboratory directors alike to document chemical storage in their departments. Generation of hazardous waste increased 100 percent between 1990 and 1994, despite UW's aggressive efforts to stem the tide. This increase, according to Phippen, tracks closely to increases in

Wendy Phippen poses beside the 55-gallon drums in which the University of Washington ships out hazardous waste for disposal. Efforts to share, reduce, and recycle these chemicals cut disposal fees and minimize environmental damage.

funding for research—not an unusual phenomenon in higher education. At UW, 75 percent of hazardous waste emanates from research laboratories. Student labs generate a relatively small portion of this, and of approximately 2,000 labs at UW, only about 40 are intended for undergraduate use. Physical plant operations and other services account for the other 25 percent of the hazardous waste. Although a small proportion of the waste stream, this non-lab waste amounts to 70,000 pounds annually, and is an area ripe for reform on every campus.

Recycling Solvents

Solvents are to the campus hazardous waste stream what paper is to the solid waste stream. They dominate laboratory and non-laboratory waste and are used in numerous applications: for laboratory experiments and cleaning; in print shops to clean printing plates; in maintenance and art departments to clean paint brushes and thin paint; and in machine and automotive shops to degrease carburetors, gears, and other machinery. Naptha, mineral spirits, and other petroleum-based solvents are commonly used in physical plant settings, says Phippen, while acetonitrile, toluene, xylene, and other petroleum-based solvents, as well as the more hazardous chlorinated solvents such as methylene chloride and chloroform, are common in labs. Many of these chlorinated substances are suspected carcinogens, mutagens, or teratagens (capable of causing birth defects), and a few deplete stratospheric ozone.

UW's EH&S department runs a chemical distillation redistribution program to reduce the quantity of laboratory solvents entering the waste stream. Staff identified high-volume, high-purity solvents coming from research laboratories and now collect and distill roughly one 55-gallon drum of xylene every month and another 55-gallon drum of acetone every three months. The distilled chemicals are returned to the labs, reducing both disposal costs and the need to purchase new solvents. As with the chemical surplus exchange program, demand for the chemical distillation redistribution services far exceeds original expectations.

Solvent wastes from facilities are more often recyclable than the complex solvent waste mixtures generated by the labs. Recycling impure solvents helps reduce waste, says Phippen, but results in significant quantities of hazardous sludge. One solution lies in the use of non-chlorinated and non-petroleum-based solvents whenever appropriate in facilities maintenance, says Phippen, whose staff is currently evaluating such alternatives—many of the best of which are citrus and aqueous-based. But existing substitutes for petroleum-based solvents cannot always do the job. "Certain metal parts at the machine shop, for example, need to be cleaned in a petroleum base," explains Phippen, "because if they go into an aqueous-based solvent they will rust."

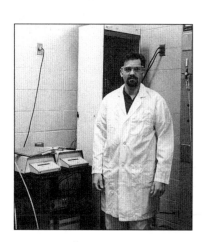

David Wick coordinates chemical distillation and redistribution, heavy-metal recovery, and other waste minimization programs at UW.

The UW staff has chosen substitute solvents for art classes and many physical plant needs, but they are still seeking biodegradable solvents for certain laboratory applications and the print shop. These products are developing so rapidly that there may be substitutes soon for print shops, as well as for machinery that cannot be degreased in aqueous- or citrus-based solutions. (See the networking section at the end of this chapter.)

The Research Lab Challenge

The three biggest obstacles to change in research laboratories are lack of financial incentive, dated research procedures, and manufacturers' resistance to reform. Most campuses, including UW, do not bill individual laboratories for the disposal of their hazardous waste, says Brown, so they reduce the labs' incentive to cut waste. Disposing of the chemicals usually costs far more than obtaining them—especially since chemical purchases are itemized within research grants and are seldom charged directly to the institution, says Brown.

UW, Notre Dame and a handful of other campuses have or are in the process of invoking surcharges to offset disposal costs. Notre Dame, in fact, charges the *full* cost of disposal when chemicals are acquired. But while progressive, these surcharges are billed upon purchase of the chemicals. "As long as the steps that we have taken on the surcharge and Notre Dame's more drastic step is hidden from the department through the campus budgeting process . . ." admits Brown, "the incentive is obviously reduced." Brown thinks the reluctance to charge labs the full cost for disposal stems from fear of tacitly encouraging improper disposal, though his experience with surcharges suggests little correlation.

Dated research procedures pose another obstacle to minimizing research lab waste. While microscale techniques make inroads, most of the academic research establishment, says Phippen, continues to use "protocol that was developed 10 to 15 years ago. Change is occurring" she believes, "but slowly."

Manufacturers also impede waste minimization by requiring minimum purchases of chemicals that often far exceed researchers' needs—or by charging high per volume prices for small quantities. The University of Minnesota has addressed this problem by centralizing laboratory purchasing, thus enabling the university to purchase in bulk and distribute small quantities of chemicals to individuals (see Chapter 1, Purchasing).

Surplus Chemical Exchanges

One of the most compelling waste minimization features of the LSS is the chemical surplus exchange. Managing surplus chemicals presents a challenge in academia, where Brown says that unused and even unopened containers often

> The University of Notre Dame charges the *full* cost of disposal when chemicals are acquired.

enter the waste stream. As research directions shift and researchers move to other institutions, chemical stocks (some of them very old and unlabeled) pile up in chemical supply closets all over the country. "It is a consequence," reflects Brown, "of the granting mechanism that exists for funding research." It is fairly common, says Brown, to overestimate the quantity of chemicals that will be needed when applying for research funds that include a category for chemical acquisition. "If they are doing various research projects over periods of time, maybe five or 10 years," says Brown, "you can see [how] significant stocks of surplus chemicals build up in a laboratory."

Administrators often assume that researchers will not use someone else's chemicals for fear of contamination, but the UW program dispels this myth. "We find that people are very willing to use free surplus chemicals rather than buy them," notes McKeown. At UW, the EH&S department's formal waste reduction program increases campus awareness, and the LSS system makes chemical surplus exchange possible campus-wide, rather than just within individual departments or through informal channels, as at many campuses. On the LSS, users can check the availability of surplus chemicals and add their own surpluses to the list. The surplus viewing screen indicates the quantity, location, and container condition of the surplus; staff can then trade among themselves or have chemicals delivered to them.

EH&S was overwhelmed by demand for storage and delivery of surplus chemicals, having redistributed more than 5,000 pounds in 1993 alone. Recycled solvents are now delivered and sold by UW's Central Store. That, combined with the posting of weekly chemical surplus updates on the university's Information Network (UWIN)—an electronic network with a broader campus audience than the LSS—has dramatically increased participation in the chemical surplus exchange. In summer of 1994, one researcher requested more than 200 chemicals from surplus stock.

Cradle to Grave Accountability

The LSS, surplus chemical exchange program, fire codes, building codes, audits, trainings, and other assistance EH&S staff provide make waste minimization easier at the University of Washington than at just about any other campus in the country. Support from the top has also helped. The provost and vice president for academic affairs sent a letter to all deans, department chairs and principal investigators, requiring researchers to inventory chemicals on the LSS in order to comply with fire and building codes. Individuals have been fired for repeated failure to dispose of hazardous substances properly. As a result, UW pollution prevention efforts have a relatively high rate of participation by the campus community.

The Chemical Surplus Exchange Program is one of the most compelling waste minimization features of the UW's Lab Safety System.

But until more faculty, students, and staff are similarly motivated at campuses nationwide, hazardous waste will continue to follow the path of least resistance—ending up in Arkansas, Texas, Louisiana, and other, mostly southern states (California, Ohio, Illinois and New York are also major waste receivers) where large incinerators burn the hazardous waste and landfills house the resulting ash. Incineration is attractive to many institutions, says Phippen, in that, though controversial, it is generally considered more environmentally sound than other existing disposal options, and institutions are no longer liable for the hazardous waste once it has been incinerated. "However," she acknowledges, "people don't want the incinerators within their own neighborhood . . ." because of concern about dioxin and other newly synthesized chemicals that can leach into water and pollute the air. "Ultimately," Phippen reasons, "we need to concentrate on not generating hazardous waste; that's number one. Number two, we need to then find new and better ways to manage waste once we have it, and I think we need to find a better way than incineration."

🦋 BRIDGING TOWN AND GOWN

Dickinson's "Science by the People, not Just for the People"

Like Bowdoin, Dickinson College in Carlisle, Pennsylvania, is a prime example of an innovative small, liberal arts institution unencumbered by the pressure to fund large research labs and projects. Since the late 1980s, Professors Michael Heiman and Candie Wilderman have taught students to use a tool crafted by Congress in 1986 to help citizens evaluate environmental health and safety in their communities—and prevent such disasters as the methyl isocyanate release in Bhopal, India, in 1984.

Introduction to Accountability

In introductory environmental science classes, Dickinson students learn to use the Emergency Preparedness and Community-Right-to-Know Act (EPCRA), passed by Congress as part of the Superfund Amendments and Reauthorization Act of 1986. Title III of the Community-Right-to-Know Act requires all manufacturing plants with more than nine employees to submit toxic release inventories (TRIs), consisting of a "Form R" for each of 320 chemicals listed by the EPA, if the chemical is manufactured or processed onsite in amounts greater than 25,000 pounds a year or shipped offsite to waste management firms or sewage treatment plants in quantities of 10,000 pounds or more. Firms must also detail their chemical waste minimization efforts and the quantities of hazardous chemicals they discharge into the air and water.

We need to concentrate on not generating hazardous waste; that's number one. Number two, we need to then find new and better ways to manage waste once we have it, and I think we need to find a better way than incineration.

— Wendy Phippen, University of Washington

Using data collected by the EPA and available in a CD-ROM format or online via the Right-to-Know Network (RTK-Net) operated by the nonprofit OMB Watch and the Unison Institute, students locate and interpret TRI data from manufacturers across the country. Some students also tour facilities and meet with union officials and community residents. Students then use a variety of references to prepare environmental and epidemiological profiles on the chemicals they track.

Approximately 75 students participate in the introductory program each year, making Dickinson's effort the largest campus-based audit program in the nation.

In the spring of 1994, several Dickinson students audited the complex of chemical companies on Neville Island, in the Ohio River just below "The Point," where the Monongahela and the Allegheny rivers join in Pittsburgh. This area only a few hundred acres large, they discovered, generated the vast majority of reported chemicals released to the Ohio River watershed. None of the audited firms in this case, however, would meet with the students—much less discuss their releases or their efforts to reduce their use of toxins.

Dickinson professor Michael Heiman (second from left) and his students use toxic release inventories to identify local environmental threats.

Other students have met with more cooperation. "Once the students are actually in the companies' offices," says Heiman, "the plant managers are typically enthusiastic about the exercise and more than willing" to share information. It helps, admits Heiman, if students emphasize their interest in toxic waste reduction efforts and not toxic emissions when requesting to tour a plant.

Industry is responding to public inspection of its hazardous chemical use and emissions. For example, in the year following a student tour of waste reduction efforts at the Grasselli DuPont Plant in Linden, New Jersey in 1990, DuPont verbally committed to emission reductions of 50 percent for TRI chemicals. "DuPont itself was by far the largest emitter of TRI chemicals nationwide in 1988," says Heiman, "with some 319 million pounds of listed chemicals either released or transferred—accounting for more than 5 percent of the nation's total TRI release and transfer that year." By 1991, however, DuPont reported releases of 76 million pounds below its 1988 levels, and the amount has since continued to fall.

Students have audited pulp and paper mills, lead battery recyclers, a soup company, marine boat manufacturers, oil refineries, petrochemical companies, and many others. They have also used the database to help affected communities identify toxic waste by plant, chemical, and amount shipped offsite to specific named waste incinerators and landfills, as well as to track toxic emissions into specific bodies of water and sewage treatment plants.

Heiman believes that the Dickinson tours and audits contribute, along with citizen efforts across the country, to a "good neighbor" ethic in communities. Industries see that citizens use the information made available by the Community-Right-to-Know Act, voice concern about their findings, and encourage waste reduction efforts, thereby contributing to pressure on industry to "clean up its act."

Advanced Activism

In an upper-level course, students monitor environmental quality themselves, rather than relying solely on TRI data and site visits. Through the Alliance for Acid Rain Monitoring (ALLARM) founded by Dr. Wilderman and based at Dickinson, students assist some 500 community activists in testing water from more than 450 sites throughout the state of Pennsylvania. Dickinson now has the largest database of water quality levels in Pennsylvania. Aided by new equipment supplied through a grant from the National Science Foundation, Wilderman's lab can supply a "toxic fingerprint" for heavy metals and hydrocarbons based on water tests, and help communities identify the source of any emissions unreported on TRIs.

In addition to water testing, upper-level students assist Heiman with workshops in which they teach community activists how to use the TRI databases. During the summer of 1994, for example, students helped residents audit the Chevron and Sun Oil refineries in Southwest Philadelphia. According to Heiman, these refineries generate "by far the

ZERO DISCHARGE
A Campus Initiative to Protect Lake Superior

The Zero Discharge Campus Working Conference, the first of its kind in the Great Lakes region, was held on February 24, 1995, at Northland College in Ashland as part of the National Wildlife Federation's Zero Discharge Campus Initiative. Participants devised techniques and policies to progressively eliminate the discharge of various toxic chemicals from their campuses into the waters of Lake Superior. The combination of these techniques is described as "zero discharge."

According to Elena Takaki, based in the Federation's Great Lakes Regional Resource Center and co-coordinator of the conference, "Our campuses are an ideal setting for testing and implementing zero-discharge mechanisms; they're like miniature cities, with the same pollution and waste management challenges. They also have a tremendous impact on their host communities through increased consumption and waste production, traffic, chemical usage, and energy consumption."

The Zero Discharge Working Conference is in the process of developing and publishing a report summarizing the participants' chosen strategies for achieving zero discharge, which will be used as a blueprint to guide Lake Superior Basin campuses in eliminating the use of toxic chemicals in their operations. Northland College has agreed to be the lead school in developing a model program based on conference findings.

majority of all toxic air emissions—a situation already suspected by the predominantly African American and Latino residents of the surrounding neighborhoods . . . ." Reports Heiman:

> It is amazing to see a group of local residents who may have had no prior training whatsoever, come together and—with the TRI database and their own initiative and tireless research—actually stand up to countless expert witnesses, trained geologists, chemists, and other "hired guns" for the other side, and . . . shoot holes through their testimony . . . eventually defeating the project in question or securing the desired outcome, such as emissions reduction.

Recognizing the community empowerment aspect of this project, the EPA (Region 3) awarded Dr. Heiman and his students a grant in 1994–95 to conduct 18 TRI data-access workshops for local grassroots environmental groups from low-income neighborhoods and communities of color. These are areas where the toxic emissions are often greatest, as in South Philadelphia with its oil refinery and Institute, West Virginia, with its chemical plants.

"Despite the fact that many students and community residents are science-phobic to start out with," says Heiman, "they soon are able to use this database and, in the process of conducting the audit, educate themselves about chemicals and their environmental and epidemiological health properties." Consulting firms, private industry, government agencies and non-profits have hired Dickinson graduates specifically because of their skills in the use of the TRI database and their comfort with site interviews. "Almost every major full-feature environmental consulting firm in the nation now has at least a TRI-trained audit team that consults for industry," says Heiman, "helping it fill out the data forms and interpreting this and similar databases."

Dickinson students perform water testing for the Toxic Fingerprints Project.

One Dickinson graduate who started out with an environmental consulting firm performing TRI audits soon advanced to the booming field of environmental insurance, where he helps firms acquiring new property avoid old waste sites—and the liability for other companies' neglect. The company was so impressed with his broad training and flexible skills, reports Heiman, that they funded a masters degree in environmental engineering and later supported his study at law school. Several graduates have been hired by the Virginia-based consulting firm Booz Allan to help maintain the EPA's EPCRA hotline. They field questions from across the nation on the TRI database reporting requirements, Superfund, and RCRA issues.

Many Dickinson students volunteer for local nonprofits. Juliane Bowman, for example, gave workshops on TRI access to the Pennsylvania Environmental Network and state science teachers. Jamie Baxter used the RTK-Net to help the Chesapeake Bay Foundation estimate the watershed's toxic load—focusing on the Susquehanna River, the primary tributary of the bay. Baxter and another student, Todd Shively, assisted Heiman with Community-Right-to-Know workshops in Southwest Philadelphia during the summer of 1994 and have since conducted community workshops on their own in rural Union County, where a large commercial hazardous waste incinerator was proposed.

What students have learned at Dickinson, they are giving back to their communities. In the end, explains Heiman, "we are dedicated to bringing science to the typical citizen and especially to those who might not have had the chance to go to college." With unparalleled computer and informational resources, campuses are often particularly well-suited to the sort of community outreach carried out at Dickinson. And as pollution prevention efforts make campuses cleaner places in which to live, their moral grounds for encouraging neighborhood businesses to follow suit become more solid. As reflected by their motto "Science by the People, not Just for the People," Heiman and Wilderman's environmental science courses offer applied learning opportunities to students, as well as a model for extending such opportunities to those beyond campus borders.

Despite the fact that many students and community residents are science-phobic to start out with, they soon are able to use this database and, in the process of conducting the audit, educate themselves about chemicals and their environmental and epidemiological health properties.

— Michael Heiman
   Dickinson College

MINIMIZING CHEMICAL HAZARDS ON CAMPUS

The following list was compiled based on conversations with Wendy Phippen, hazardous waste manager, and Erin McKeown, industrial hygienist, at the University of Washington (UW); materials from the University of Wisconsin-Madison's safety department, and discussions with Bill Hochstin, environmental manager at Dartmouth College. Staff were asked which hazardous-waste-generating products and practices are especially troublesome on campus and what alternative products or practices they recommend. See also the chart reprinted here from UW-Madison's *1993 Chemical Safety and Disposal Guide* for a list of the substitutes for commonly used laboratory chemicals, based on recommendations in a 1992 study conducted at the University of Illinois at Urbana-Champaign.

Chromic Acid: Chromic acid solution, a mixture of concentrated sulfuric acid and potassium dichromate or chromium anhydride, cleans laboratory glassware by oxidizing residues and removing a thin layer of glass surface, UW-Madison safety staff report in "Part F: Pollution Prevention and Waste Minimization" of their *1993 Chemical Safety and Disposal Guide.* It is a strong corrosive as well as a strong oxidizer, they write, that has been known to explode when combined with oxidizable materials. It is also a known human carcinogen and is toxic in other ways to humans, flora and fauna. The safety department "strongly encourages labs to stop using chromic acid solutions," and provides a list of the many commercially available alternatives.

Chloroform: When UW's McKeown discovered that chloroform, an identified carcinogen, mutagen, toxicant, and irritant, is widely used in schools of dentistry, she searched the Internet and spoke with dentists, finding just one alternative—thermal softening. Chloroform is typically used to soften gutta percha, a sap-like natural rubber product used to fill the holes left by root canal drilling and extraction. Until the thermal method of softening gutta percha is improved, McKeown recommends that chloroform only be used in fume hoods.

Cleaning and Disinfecting Products: Many institutional cleaning products are toxic and corrosive. Dartmouth College has moved away from phenol-based antiseptic (commonly called carbolic acid), in particular, because of its extreme toxicity and corrosivity—as well as from bleach, iodine, and alcohol. Material safety data sheets (MSDSs), which should be available for each cleaning product on campus, can aid in the identification and substitution of hazardous with less-hazardous products. Al Lewis, head of custodial services at Rutgers University, is working with Senior Buyer Kevin Lyons and vendors to identify appropriate substitutes for the university.

UW's EH&S staff encourage employees to buy cleaning and other hazardous products in small quantities, rather than in bulk, and to use them up completely. "It is probably more expensive in the short run to purchase small quantities," notes Phippen, "but in the long run, it is less expensive because you will have less hazardous waste; you pay almost twice as much for disposal as for purchase of many cleaning products." Eliminating spray cans, since their contents cannot be removed when nozzles malfunction, is another recommended and cost-saving strategy for minimizing hazardous waste. Instead of paying more than $3 per 12-ounce can, Dartmouth spends about 14 cents per gallon by mixing their own cleaning solutions and using reusable pump bottles, which also cut down on waste.

Chlorofluorocarbons (CFCs): "Campuses consume an amazing amount of CFCs in vehicle and building air-conditioning units, and as refrigerants," says Phippen. Ozone-depleting compounds are also found in solvents, foam insulation, and packaging. CFCs deplete stratospheric ozone and contribute to global warming. Alternative refrigerants containing less harmful CFC compounds, although less ozone-depleting, remain potent greenhouse (or heat-trapping) gases. As required in 1990 Amendments to the Clean Air Act, most campuses are now phasing out certain CFCs and recycling others. April Smith, author of *Campus Ecology,* highlights the University of Kansas at Lawrence for its effort to identify all ozone-depleting compounds used on campus—including freon, halon, certain solvents (such as carbon tetrachloride), and preservative sprays.

Contaminated Rags: Rags used to apply hazardous materials are ubiquitous in campus settings. They are used by maintenance staff to clean, absorb spills, and polish furniture; by the print shop to wipe ink off plates; in laboratories to clean apparatus and absorb spills; in art departments to apply stains and solvents; and in machine and fleet maintenance shops to absorb oil and clean parts.

UW's largest user of rags, the physical plant, contracted with a laundry service and expects to recoup their costs within three months, thanks to reduced disposal costs, as well as reduced costs for new rags. The EH&S department audited prospective launderers for the physical plant, settling on a company with a permit to treat cleaning effluent before discharging it to the sewer.

Fungicides and Wood Preservatives: Designed to control mildew and prevent rot, fungicides and wood preservatives are often extremely toxic. Dartmouth uses cloth or untreated shower curtains, says Bill Hochstin, and "tries to stay away from fungicides in general." When working with wood preservatives, workers are instructed to wear masks, ensure proper ventilation, and take other precautions. "Treated wood won't rot and insects won't eat it," explains Hochstin, "because it is treated with very hazardous materials such as benzene and pentachlorophenol."

Mercury: Breakage of monometers and thermometers is one of the largest sources of hazardous mercury waste on campuses. The rags used to wipe up spills, along with lab coats and any other absorbent materials the liquid mercury touches, also become hazardous waste. Liquid mercury can be recycled, but it is difficult and expensive to safely dispose of contaminated debris. Lab purchasing staff at the University of Washington, the University of Wisconsin-Madison, and the University of Minnesota have begun strongly encouraging the use of alcohol thermometers, thermocouples, and other alternatives to mercury thermometers.

Mercury compounds, especially those containing a halogen such as fluorine, bromine, chlorine, or iodine, are especially hazardous.

University of Washington staff must use an

COMMON HAZARDOUS WASTES
(continued)

ion-exchange treatment to precipitate mercury sulfide from mercury halides in order to get a reputable retorter to take the waste. The University of Wisconsin-Madison encourages laboratories to use a less toxic substitute (such as copper sulfate instead of mercury as a catalyst in Kjeldahl analyses). EH&S staff at many campuses are challenging researchers to curtail their use of mercury halides.

 **Motor Oil, Transmission and Brake Fluids:** After solvents, motor oils are the second largest category of non-laboratory hazardous wastes at most campuses, but many campuses successfully recycle these substances. (See the case study on fleet management at the University of Kansas in Chapter 3, Transportation.) Oils contaminated by carbon tetrachloride and other solvents become an even more hazardous waste, so UW's EH&S department instructs all campus operations to store spent oils and solvents separately.

Paints: In their audit of fine and applied arts courses at the University of Washington, EH&S staff found almost no paint waste, due, they suspect, to the extremely high costs of pigments. And students at the UW now use mostly citrus-based alternatives to hazardous solvents for cleaning brushes and pallets.

Paint waste remains a prominent issue, however, in the physical plant. Whenever possible, custodial and maintenance staff at UW use latex instead of the more toxic and combustible oil-based paints. They also separate latex paint from oil-based paint waste, rather than pouring them into the same 55-gallon drums. Separation makes recycling possible and lowers disposal costs. "There is a business in Oregon that will take in latex paint, reblend it, and then sell recycled paint," says Phippen, "and we will probably be buying some of that recycled paint."

As with cleaning products, the EH&S department at UW encourages maintenance staff to curtail their use of paint spray cans, which often lose propellant or become clogged before the paint runs out. EH&S has purchased equipment to pierce and drain spray containers so that the metal can be recycled and only the paint waste must be disposed of as hazardous waste.

PCBs: Polychlorinated biphenyls (PCBs), along with other halocarbons described previously, such as polychlorinated dioxins and chlorobenzene, are highly toxic and environmentally persistent chemicals. PCBs were designed to prevent fires associated with such electrical equipment as transformers and ballasts, explains Phippen, but the Toxic Substances Control Act now requires that transformers be drained of PCB-containing insulation oil or replaced. Proper PCB handling becomes especially important as campuses replace old fluorescent lamps and fixtures with more efficient lighting. Kevin Lyons, senior buyer at Rutgers University has contracted with a company that recycles old lamps and ballasts after removing PCBs (see Chapter 1, Purchasing).

Pesticides (Indoor and Outdoor): Several campuses—including Seattle University, Nebraska Wesleyan, Davidson College, Georgetown University, and Purdue University—have adopted integrated pest management (IPM) techniques to remove undesired insects, weeds, and other wildlife in ways that generate less hazardous waste and protect human health and wildlife. Ciscoe Morris's success with IPM at Seattle University is described in detail in Chapter 2, Landscaping.

Ink: Campuses that use copious quantities of ink in their print shops and office equipment are beginning to opt for newly formulated inks with soy bases and lowered heavy-metal content. These are less hazardous than their petroleum-based, high heavy-metal counterparts. Oregon State and the University of Oregon have begun to increase the amount of soy-based inks they use, and Ecoprint, together with Alden & Ott Inks, has created a line of inks with nontoxic pigments (see Chapter 6, Communication Services).

Photoprocessing Chemicals: Three photochemical wastes commonly used in print shops and student newspaper photo labs are considered hazardous: photographic fixer, developer and stopbath. Staff at the University of Washington, Tufts University and many other campuses have begun to recover silver from photofixer, which cannot otherwise be safely disposed in sewer systems. Photo developer contains hydroquinone in concentrations beyond some states' sewer limits and many brands of stopbath are also hazardous. The automation of film development in two labs at the University of Washington, reports EH&S staff, has considerably reduced these wastes. And photochemical companies have begun to develop less-hazardous and biodegradable alternatives.

Solvents: The most significant hazard, in terms of volume, on campuses is solvent waste. UW's Phippen describes some of these wastes, emanating primarily from science laboratories and the physical plant, on p. 170.

BIBLIOGRAPHY

Alternative Landscaping Issue Packet, Campus Ecology Program, National Wildlife Federation.

Art Hazard News, Center for Safety in the Arts, 5 Beekman St., Suite 820, New York, NY 10038. (212) 227-6220.

"Hazardous Wastes in Academia," Peter Ashbrook and Peter Reinhardt, *Environmental Science and Technology*, No. 19, 1985, pp. 1150–1152.

"Can Superfund Get on Track, Karen Schmidt, *National Wildlife*, April/May, 1994, 10–17.

Case Studies in Environmental Health and Safety, Association of Higher Education Facilities Officers (APPA), 1446 Duke St., Alexandria, VA 22314-3492. (Topics include radioactive wastes, sick building syndrome, medical waste, and PCBs.)

Catalogue of Hazardous and Solid Waste Publication, 7th Ed., Solid Waste and Emergency Response (5305), United States Environmental Protection Agency, EPA/530-B-93-002, May, 1994. (800) 553-7672.

Determination, Implementation and Evaluation of Laboratory Waste Minimization Opportunities, Peter C. Ashbrook, Cynthia Klein-Banay and Chuck Maier, Division of Environmental Health and Safety, University of Illinois at Urbana-Champaign, 1992.

Directory of Pollution Prevention in Higher Education: Faculty and Programs, Nandkumar Bakshani and David Allen, National Pollution Prevention Center for Higher Education, University of Michigan, 1992.

Does Your Business Produce Hazardous Waste?, Solid Waste and Emergency Response (OS-305), United States Environmental Protection Agency, EPA/530-SW-90-027, Jan, 1990. (800) 553-7672.

Fertility on the Brink: Legacy of the Chemical Age, National Wildlife Federation, 1994. (202) 797-6800.

Guide to Waste Minimization in General Medical and Surgical Hospitals, Jacobs Engineering Group, Inc., Pasadena, CA 91101-3063.

Guides to Pollution Prevention: Research and Educational Institutions, Office of Research and Development, U.S. Environmental Protection Agency, 1990. (Includes hazardous waste audit of a large university, research institute, and small college.)

Hazardous Materials and Solid Waste Management, Association of Higher Education Facilities Officers (APPA), 1446 Duke St., Alexandria, VA 22314-3492.

Household Hazardous Waste Wheel, Environmental Hazards Management Institute, 10 Newmarket Road, P.O. Box 932, Durham, NH 03824. (603) 868-1496.

"Hazardous Waste," *In Our Backyard: Environmental Issues at UCLA, Proposals for Change, and the Institution's Potential as a Model*, April Smith et al., Department of Architecture and Urban Planning, University of California at Los Angeles, 1989, pp. 146-194. ($30 through UC Regents, Publications Coordinator, UCLA Graduate School of Architecture and Urban Planning, 1317 Perloff Hall, 405 Hilgard Ave. 90024-1467.)

Layperson's Guide to Reading MSDSs, Massachusetts Department of Environmental Quality, One Winter St., Boston, MA 02108. (617) 292-5993.

Microscale General Chemistry Laboratory, Zvi Szafran, Ronald M. Pike, and Judith C. Foster, John Wiley & Sons, Inc., 1993.

Microscale Organic Laboratory: with Multistep and Multiscale Syntheses, 3d Ed, Dana Mayo, Ronald Pike and Peter Trumper, John Wiley & Sons, Inc., New York, 1994.

National Directory of Citizen Volunteer Environmental Monitoring Program, 4 Ed., U.S. Environmental Protection Agency, Jan, 1994. (202) 260-7018. (Contains information on 519 citizen/campus environmental monitoring programs across the nation.)

"The Playground that Became a Battleground," David Thigpen, *National Wildlife*, Feb/March, pp. 14–17.

Pest Control in the School Environment, Office of Pesticide Programs (H7506C), United States Environmental Protection Agency, EPA/735-F-93-012, Aug, 1993.

"Part F: Pollution Prevention and Waste Minimization," *1993 Chemical Safety and Disposal Guide*, Safety Department, University of Wisconsin-Madison, pp. 1F–14F. (608) 262-8769.

Preventing Industrial Toxic Hazards: A Guide for Communities, Marion Weis and Lauren Kenworthy, INFORM. (212) 689-4040. ($25.00/$15.00 non-profits; primary manual used by Dickinson College students in conducting toxic waste audits.)

Prudent Practices, National Research Council, 2101 Constitution Ave., Washington, D.C. (202) 334-2154.

Regulatory Compliance for Facilities Managers, Association of Higher Education Facilities Officers (APPA), 1446 Duke St., Alexandria, VA 22314-3492. (Includes summaries of regulations such as EPCRA/RCRA/Superfund, clean air, clean water, and instructions for compliance, sample forms and bibliography.)

"Resources and Hints for Accessing the SARA Title III 'Community-Right-to-Know' Database (The Toxic Release Inventory)," Michael Heiman, Environmental Studies, Dickinson College, Carlisle, PA 17013. (717) 245-1338.

"Serious Reduction of Hazardous Waste," John H. Gibbons, et al., Office of Technology Assessment, OTA-ITE-318, September, 1986. (Order through: OTA Publication Request Line (202) 224-8996, Congressional and Public Affairs Office, Office of Technology Assessment, U.S. Congress, Washington, D.C. 20510-8025.)

"Solid Waste Reduction in Colleges and Universities: A Status Report," Sarah Hammond Creighton, et al., Center for Environmental Management, Tufts University, Curtis Hall, 474 Boston Avenue, Medford, MA 02155. (617) 627-3486.

"Superfund Reform on the Move," *National Wildlife EnviroAction*, National Wildlife Federation, July/Aug, 1994, p. 6.

Toxics Issue Packet, Campus Ecology Program, National Wildlife Federation.

Using Your Community Right to Know, Brian Lipsett and Karen Stults, Citizens Clearinghouse for Hazardous Waste, P.O. Box 6806, Falls Church, VA 22040. (703) 237-2249.

The Volunteer Monitor, Eleanor Ely, Ed., 1318 Masonic Ave., San Francisco, CA 94117. (415) 255-8049.

"Waste Reduction in Your Business," Washington State Dept. of Ecology, publ. #89-56, Feb, 1991.

NETWORKING

Campus

Bowdoin College
Department of Chemistry
Brunswick, ME 04011
(203) 725-3000
Helped catalyze a nationwide move to microscale procedures in higher education.

California State University
Attn. Michael Ceser
Environmental Health and Safety
Long Beach, CA 90840
(310) 985-9013
e-mail:
michael_ceser@qm.calstate.edu
For information on regional and national discussions on waste minimization in higher education.

Dickinson College
Attn. Drs. Heiman and Wilderman
Environmental Studies
Carlisle, PA 17013
Developed community toxic waste auditing, water testing, and toxic "finger printing" curricula.

If you find that an organization listed here has moved or a contact has been replaced, let the Campus Ecology Program staff know. We'll help match you with the latest source for the information you need.

Indiana University
Attn: Jim Gibson,
Dean of Student Activities
Bloomington, IN 47408
(812) 855-IUSA
*Students in the Student
Environmental Action Coalition
(SEAC) organized a campaign
to prevent the university from
selling land near an African-
American community in
Mississippi to a company
intending to build a hazardous
waste landfill and incinerator.*

Pennsylvania School of Art &
Design
Attn: Brenda Witmer
Lancaster, PA 17603
(717) 396-7833
Turpentine recycling.

University of Washington
Attn. Erin McKeown
Environmental Health and Safety
Hall Health Center, GS-05
Seattle, WA 98195
(206) 543-0467
FAX: (206) 543-3351
e-mail:
mstoxic@u.washington.edu
*Coordinates the LSS, a fully
integrated chemical inventory
and Material Safety Data Sheets
(MSDS) database which is being
emulated by other campuses.*

University of Illinois at
Urbana-Champaign
Division of Environmental
Health and Safety
Urbana, IL 61801
(217) 333-6548
*Prepared extensive waste
minimization opportunities
report, listed in references
section, in 1992.*

University of Wisconsin at
Madison
Safety Department
Madison, WI 53706
(608) 262-8769
*Prepared useful guide to campus
hazardous waste minimization
listed in bibliography section.*

Regional and National

Campus Safety Association
(for more information, contact:
Univerisity of Massachusetts,
Attn: Don Robinson, Environmental Health & Safety, Box
35710, Amherst, MA 01003-5710)

EPA POLLUTION PREVENTION
INFORMATION SERVICES

Electronic Network:
Office of Air Quality Planning
and Standards (OAQPS)
Technology Transfer Network
(TTN)
(919) 541-5384
*The TTN is a network of
electronic bulletin boards
developed and operated by
OAQPS. The network provides
information and technology
exchange in various areas of air
pollution control, ranging from
information on the Clean Air
Act amendments of 1990 to
current coarse offerings on air
pollution. Call the help desk
listed above for assistance in
accessing the system.*

The EPA's On-Line Library
System (OLS)
Internet Access:
EPAIBM.RTPNC.EPA.GOV
Dial-in Access via Modem:
(919) 549-0720 (select OLS at
prompt)

EPA National Computer Center:
(800) 334-2405

EPA Public Information Center:
(202) 260-2080
*The OLS is a computerized list of
bibliographic citations. It can be
used to locate books, reports,
articles, and information on
myriad environmental topics. If
you need help getting online,
call the EPA's national Computer
Center. For the OLS Users Guide,
call the EPA Public Information
Center.*

EPA SOLID AND HAZARDOUS
WASTE HOTLINES

EPCRA/Superfund/RCRA
(800) 424-9346

Air Quality Hotlines:

Indoor Air Quality:
(800) 438-4318

National Air Toxics:
(919) 541-0850

National Radon:
(800) SOS-RADON

Stratospheric Ozone:
(800) 296-1996

EPA WATER QUALITY
HOTLINES

Clean Lakes
(800) 726-LAKE

National Small Flows
Clearinghouse
(800) 624-8301

Safe Drinking Water Act
(800) 426-4791

Green Seal
1730 Rhode Island Ave., NW,
Ste. 1050
Washington, D.C. 20036-3101
(202) 331-7337
Publishes Environmental Standard for Household Cleaners including performance, toxicological (e.g. carcinogens, reproductive toxicity, biodegradability, phosphate levels, volatile organic compounds, etc.), and packaging specifications.

The "Lab Safety—Chemical Exchange Conference" run out of the University of Vermont's safety office, is a "listserv" or electronic correspondence group on the Internet. It is very active (i.e. 50+ postings a day) and recommended primarily for higher education safety professionals. To find out if this forum would be appropriate for your needs, send an e-mail query to: safety@uvmvm.uvm.edu.

National Pollution Prevention Center for Higher Education
University of Michigan, Dana Building
430 E. University
Ann Arbor, MI 48109
(313) 936-2195
Established by EPA in October 1991 to develop and disseminate pollution prevention curriculum modules to colleges and universities in a variety of disciplines. The NPPC is a collaborative effort between academia, industry, government, and public interest groups.

National Wildlife Federation
Campus Ecology Program
1400 16th St., N.W.
Washington, D.C. 20036-2266
(202) 797-5435 (general information)
(313) 769-9970 or midwest@nwf.org (M.W.)
(202) 797-5468 or noreast@nwf.org (N.E.)
(404) 876-2608 or soeast@nwf.org (S.E.)
(503) 222-1429 or western@nwf.org (West)
Contact for Toxics and Alternative Landscaping Issues Packets; National Wildlife EnviroAction which has updates on toxics and hazardous-waste legislation; the NWF report Fertility on the Brink: Legacy of the Chemical Age; *and information about the Campus Zero Discharge Campaign coordinated by NWF's Great Lakes Natural Resource Center and Campus Ecology staff.*

OMB Watch/Right-to-Know Network
Attn. John Chelen
1742 Connecticut Ave., N.W.
Washington, D.C. 20009-1171
(202) 234-8494
Maintains on-line access to TRI database—free for academics and non-profits.

Working Group on Community-Right-to-Know
Attn. Paul Orum
215 Pennsylvania Ave., S.E.
Washington, D.C. 20003
(202) 546-9707
Dickinson College's expert on Toxic Release Inventory Database.

Other Resources

AFM Enterprises
1140 Stacy Court
Riverside, CA 92507
(909) 781-6860
Bulk quantities of nontoxic dishwashing detergents, furniture polishes, mold and carpet cleaners, etc.

Inland Technologies Products
2612 Pacific Highway East
Tacoma, WA 09424
(206) 922-8932
Specializes in environmentally responsible industrial solvents.

Medina Agricultural Products Co.
Box 309
Hondo, TX 78861
(210) 426-3011
55-gallon drums and five gallon containers of nontoxic septic tank, pipe and drain cleaners.

National Chemsearch Products
2727 Chemsearch Blvd.
Irving, TX 75062
(214) 438-0211
Nontoxic solvents.

CHAPTER 9

Evaluating Campus Stewardship Programs

12 Benchmarks of Success

The eight preceding chapters document environmental stewardship in various campus operations. In these generally decentralized, grassroots efforts, dedicated staff, students, and faculty worked with few allocated resources and without much compensation. And although most of the programs were well-received and strongly supported by senior management, some have endured while others have not.

As described in earlier chapters, a few remarkable efforts either are struggling or have disappeared, despite widespread appreciation on campus for the benefits they do, or did, provide. Grants run out; visionary senior managers retire; innovators take jobs elsewhere or graduate. And as Walter Simpson at SUNY-Buffalo and others have pointed out, large institutions are frequently riddled with disincentives to conserve resources and save money. The absorption of a department project's savings into general funds, changes in utility rate structures, and the emphasis on short-term returns on investment obstruct the work of many dedicated staff and students.

Most of the programs in this book, however, merit discussion precisely because they endure—after five years, a decade, or even longer—and, in several cases, because they have reshaped larger aspects of their institutions. Such programs blossom in a variety of campus settings, from community colleges to the largest universities. Brevard Community College, for instance, continues to build upon the energy conservation program it launched in the early 1980s, and its main campus will soon co-host the New Energy Center, one of the most energy efficient office buildings in the world. Over its 16-year history, the University of Colorado-Boulder's recycling program has shaped purchasing, accounting, and planning policies university-wide. SUNY-Buffalo's energy conservation program, which will begin its 15th year in 1996, set the precedents for campus-wide

The jump from individual initiative to campus-wide policy ultimately involves an ethical commitment of senior administrators who formulate, or at least must approve, policy.

—Tom Kelly, Director, Secretariat of University Presidents for a Sustainable Future

recycling, energy-efficient buildings, green computing, and a campus-wide conservation committee.

How have these and other programs endured, improved, and ultimately achieved campus-wide, regional, and even national significance? The incorporation of environmental stewardship into the very framework of an institution is a crucial component of their success. These programs enjoy executive-level support, for example, and most are codified in official policy. The managers of most successful programs have lobbied for and won sufficient resources and have dismantled financial disincentives. Many have tied their programs to the curriculum and provide hands-on experience for students. Some of the most popular programs foster a sense of investment in the campus and surrounding community. They generate good public relations and are typically well-documented. They frequently provide leadership development opportunities and training for the staff, faculty, and students involved. And, ultimately, these programs result in an appreciable reduction of cost and waste.

If institutions of higher education are to guide the way toward a sustainable future, successful environmental programs must not only endure, they must serve as catalysts for change throughout their institutions. While they alone cannot make a campus sustainable, successful stewardship initiatives do help build institutional will and momentum, spurring the redesign of buildings, resource systems, and curricula.

There is no template for making an environmental program an irrevocable part of the structure and policy of an institution. But the characteristics which distinguish the most

BREVARD COMMUNITY COLLEGE
Policy Regarding Protection of the Environment

The Board of Trustees recognizes that the educated and responsible use of natural resources and protection of the environment is consistent with the standards of Brevard Community College and all its students and work family, and the Board recognizes a tremendous potential exists for improvement which is more in harmony with the ideals of the College. Therefore, Brevard Community College reaffirms these principles by adopting this policy related to sound environmental management and encourages all staff and students to be aware that:

- All buildings will be constructed with the utmost concern for their environmental impact.

- The College will pursue a sound program for energy efficiency and conservation.

- The College will ensure that proper handling and disposal be conducted for all hazardous waste materials.

- The College will seek alternatives to products which are environmentally detrimental.

- The College will initiate recycling programs for all recyclable products.

- All faculty and staff are encouraged to implement and update periodically an awareness program of education in the conservation of energy, the recycling of materials and the handling of hazardous waste.

successful and enduring programs can serve as a guide to broadening and institutionalizing environmental stewardship—and as benchmarks for measuring the success of that effort. Although several of the 12 benchmarks which follow measure successes on the policy level, policy changes often result from initiatives at the grassroots. Many comprehensive programs, for example, trace their beginnings to a small-scale recycling effort or a recycling committee. There is no established order in which campus environmental programs grow stronger, broader, and more comprehensive. Typically, staff and students start with the evident strengths of their institutions and expand from there in all directions.

1. EXECUTIVE SUPPORT

In many of the most successful stewardship initiatives, executive staff play crucial roles. Presidents, vice presidents, business officers, chancellors, vice-chancellors, and trustees have helped make possible a broad range of initiatives on campuses, including the development of environmental policy; the establishment of a committee or other structure to encourage environmental accountability and innovation; the development of new specifications for purchasing, investment, and research; and the incorporation of ecological criteria into plans for new buildings and infrastructure. They have also allocated funds, staff, and other tangible resources to environmental coordination, training programs, leadership development, and the advancement of ecological literacy.

Forging partnerships with their counterparts around the globe, more than 200 university presidents and chancellors from 42 countries have now signed the Talloires Declaration. Drafted in Talloires, France, in 1990, the declaration outlines the role of university leadership in global environmental management and sustainable development. Signatory institutions become members of the Secretariat of University Presidents for a Sustainable Future, dedicating their academic leadership to the advancement of global environmental literacy. University presidents who sign the Talloires Declaration commit to a series of comprehensive actions, including:

- reshaping the curriculum and pedagogy through faculty training in environmental literacy;

- fostering interdisciplinary research that is both ecologically and socially responsive;

- minimizing the impact of the institution on the environment through such practices as resource conservation, recycling, energy efficiency, and waste reduction; and

One essential part of the president's role is to support new initiatives that cannot, at least at first, be financially self-supporting, but which promise to make important contributions to society and the college.

—Douglas North,
President,
Prescott College

🐦 expanding the scope and outreach of environmental initiatives through public- and private-sector international partnerships.

The Secretariat supports the signatories in their efforts through such programs as the Tufts Environmental Literacy Institute, the Institutional Ecology Program, and the Global Partners Program. And for its far-reaching agenda, the Secretariat is winning international recognition. In its first report to the Parliament in January 1995, the British Government Panel on Sustainable Development called on all institutions of higher education to "subscribe to the Talloires Declaration," thereby effectively launching a nationwide campaign for education on the environment and sustainable development.

Refusing to settle for symbolic roles, many of these senior administrators have shown an outstanding degree of personal commitment. For instance, at Paul Smith's College in upstate New York, where staff in virtually every campus operation have launched environmental initiatives, Dean of Administration Susan Kinneston provides resources and guidance, helps develop the campus environmental newsletter, organizes environmental planning meetings, and otherwise sustains campus-wide commitment. "We have to do ecologically sound things better than anybody else," she explains, "because we are wearing the flag, and our students are very good consciences for us."

2. POLICY

When it is supported by senior administrators, written environmental policy can help ensure that commitment to ecology survives among competing priorities, limited funds, and perpetual turnover in campus leadership. The Tufts CLEAN! program ended after five enormously successful years, but its coordinator, Sarah Hammond Creighton, can proudly point to the university's adoption of an environmental policy as a sign of potentially lasting success. She and her assistants brought together faculty, staff, administrators, and students in several meetings in which they asked participants to draft and review components of the policy before it was presented to the president for approval. (See boxes on pages 188, 191, and 194 for examples of campus environmental policies.)

Policies and guiding principles may also be adopted at the departmental or division level. Duane Hickling, the assistant vice-chancellor for facilities planning and management at the University of Wisconsin-Madison, incorporated a broad statement of environmental commitment—"We will strive to be good citizens of society, recognizing our duty to protect the environment in all various aspects"—into the mission and guiding principles of his division. This is a general statement, but it has helped set a receptive tone, encouraging such specific initiatives

> Writing on a piece of paper is not a sign of lasting success. Without the commitment of those in authority, the policy may not be worth the paper it is printed on.
>
> —Tom Kelly,
> Tufts University

TUFTS UNIVERSITY ENVIRONMENTAL POLICY

We, the Tufts University community, affirm our belief that university faculty, staff and students have a responsibility to take a leadership role in conducting activities as responsible stewards of the physical environment and using educational activities to promote environmental awareness, local action and global thinking. In our university functions, Tufts University will strive to:

- Conserve natural resources and support their sustainable use;
- Conduct affairs in a manner that safeguards the environmental health and safety of students, faculty, staff and communities;
- Reduce the use of toxic substances and the generation of wastes and promote strategies to reuse and recycle those wastes that cannot be avoided; and
- Purchase renewable, reusable, recyclable and recycled materials.

In our education and research missions, Tufts University will strive to:

- Foster an understanding of and a responsibility for the physical environment;
- Ensure that individuals are knowledgeable about the environmental and health issues that affect their discipline;
- Encourage environmental research;
- Conduct research and teaching in an environmentally responsible way; and
- Provide a forum for the open flow of information among governments, international organizations, industry, and academia to discuss and study environmental issues and their relationship to other social issues.

In our student and employee relations, Tufts University will strive to:

- Delineate individual responsibility and guide action for ensuring safety and minimizing adverse environmental impacts in the implementation of this policy.

Tufts will consider full compliance with the law to be the minimally acceptable standard and will exercise whatever control is reasonable and necessary to avoid harm to public health and the environment, whether or not such control is required by regulations.

Tufts will initiate, promote and conduct programs that fully implement this policy throughout the university and the global community.

as the transportation demand management, environmental management, and campus ecology research programs.

General environmental policies may be further defined at the department level. Rutgers Senior Buyer Kevin Lyons has rewritten specifications for paper, construction materials, and innumerable other products that Rutgers purchases in large quantities. He is thus furthering the university's broad goals—increasing markets for recycled-content products, reducing waste, and supporting the local economy—in ways specific to his division.

3. RESOURCES AND INCENTIVES

The provision of resources and incentives, both for launching new programs and to increase participation in existing ones, has helped ensure the success of many campus stewardship initiatives. Executive staff, division managers, and department chairs have created new staff and work-study positions; provided office space, phones, and access to office equipment; and allowed departments to keep all or part of the savings that result from their conservation programs.

People are one of the most important resources campuses can allocate. In North Carolina, a state with progressive waste reduction laws (including a ban on aluminum in landfills), almost every campus in the state system boasts a designated recycling coordinator, as do many of the private colleges and universities. The resources these campuses devote to sharing information, whether via newsletters or at the Annual Collegiate Recycling Conference, make theirs one of the strongest statewide collegiate recycling networks in the country.

On several campuses, an environmental coordinator has been hired on a permanent basis to solve a range of problems beyond recycling and waste reduction. The University of Kansas, Birmingham-Southern College, and the University of Wisconsin-Madison, as well as Brown, Harvard, and Tufts Universities, each have full- or part-time environmental coordinators. These positions allow the coordination of efforts throughout the campus and beyond. For example:

- At the University of Kansas, one full-time and several part-time "environmental ombudsmen" manage environmental research and educational outreach, reporting directly to the executive vice chancellor.

- As director of Brown is Green, Kurt Teichert not only coordinates Brown's on-campus environmental research, education, and projects, but also facilitates campus networking nationwide through two correspondence groups and a hypertext resource on the Internet.

We [made people feel invested in the program] by interviewing them— not just the people in power, but the people who clean floors and make sandwiches . . . . We got managers' permission first. People were usually willing to talk with us if we said, 'I talked with your boss and you were suggested.'

—Sarah Creighton, Coordinator of Tufts CLEAN! 1989–1994

✍ At Birmingham-Southern College in Birmingham, Alabama, Professor Roald Hazelhoff manages an environmental office which coordinates such community efforts as watershed restoration, a food-share project, and the development of an on-campus environmental education center for elementary school children.

Start-up capital is also important. Launched with a half-million-dollar bond from the university, UC-Boulder's recycling program grew to include dozens of work-study students, as well as two full-time staff. The program has already retired most of its debt through avoided tipping fees and other savings to the university.

Grants and other funds from outside organizations may help get a program off the ground, but outside money is no substitute for university commitment and a guaranteed line in the campus budget. Campuses have dismantled several exemplary programs when outside funding expired. Based on her experience managing the Tufts CLEAN! program, Sarah Hammond Creighton advises, "If you do get an outside grant, seek matching funds or more commitment from the university." During the program's tenure, Creighton and work-study students conducted studies of pollution prevention opportunities on campus, launched several cost-saving programs, assisted with legal compliance issues, and encouraged an exchange of ideas among campuses throughout New England. Despite its many successes, however, the program lasted only as long as its outside funding.

4. STRUCTURAL FRAMEWORK

Creating a structure for environmental planning, such as an environmental committee or a recycling task force, is often one of the first steps staff and students take to strengthen and broaden their initiatives. Structures may be as simple as a small committee or as complex as several intersecting committees and task forces to facilitate communication between departments. For example, Chapter 1, Purchasing, described the value of overlapping membership on waste abatement and lab oversight committees at the University of Minnesota.

To launch the Green University program announced by President Trachtenberg in the fall of 1994, The George Washington University has established one of the most comprehensive structures to date. GW's task force and its four subcommittees are charged with developing "a comprehensive, integrated, 'deep green' orientation, covering all areas of university activity, including curriculum, research, infrastructure, and outreach."

Let's face it: it's very hard to even imagine a college or university of any size being sustainable. We need to address that, not cover it up. Misleading the campus community or the general public about how far we have to go to achieve sustainability is a disservice and will ultimately be self-defeating.

—Walter Simpson,
Energy Officer,
SUNY-Buffalo

5. CURRICULUM

When woven into the curriculum, environmental responsibility becomes part of the fabric of academic life. By encouraging staff and faculty in an array of disciplines and operations to involve students in stewardship initiatives, colleges and universities can increase environmental literacy among *all* graduates. At several institutions, students assist staff with the research and operation of environmental projects, either as course work or for independent study credit, and faculty receive training support for including environmental issues and experiences in the curriculum.

The Tufts Environmental Literacy Institute (TELI) offers interdisciplinary professional development on environmental issues for university and secondary school faculty. Recognized as an international model, TELI was launched in 1990 by Environmental Dean Anthony Cortese to bring educators from around the world together for an active exploration of the workings of the environment and development. The TELI training equips faculty to teach environmental issues, in all their complexity and interrelatedness, both from an interdisciplinary perspective and with specific reference to their own fields. (Other environmental literacy initiatives in higher education are listed in the networking section of this chapter.)

Environmental courses that link the classroom to campus operations and to natural areas enjoy great success. Those in which students conduct campus environmental profiles (baseline studies of resource consumption and its impact on the environment) and suggest ways to redesign services, buildings, and infrastructure prove especially fruitful. Prof. David Orr has written extensively about the pedagogical value of this approach. His environmental studies course entitled "Oberlin and the Biosphere" requires students to inventory the flow of resources as "part of the longer-term effort," reads the syllabus, "to adapt institutions to the post-petroleum era. The 'curriculum' for the course is this campus and its connections to the region and to the farms, feedlots, forests, mines, wells, and dumps somewhere else."

ABOUT THE GEORGE WASHINGTON UNIVERSITY GREEN UNIVERSITY MISSION STATEMENT

The George Washington University, in its desire to contribute its resources and expertise in the service of creating an environmentally sustainable future, commits itself to the development of a new and comprehensive environmental ethic.

In pursuit of this mission, The George Washington University has developed the Green University Program—a unique program intended to comprehensively "green" curricula for all GW students; create a wide and interdisciplinary program of research at the university; and launch an ongoing program of environmental evaluation and remediation for university facilities and procurement. Administration, faculty, and students have joined together in the design and implementation of the Green University Program and, in this effort, express a strong commitment to protecting the environmental resources that sustain our nation and our planet.

By involving students in research, administrators and staff not only educate, but also foster collaboration in place of divisiveness, and reduce their research and consulting costs. Dozens of research projects result from the "IES 600" seminars taught by doctoral candidate David Eagan at the University of Wisconsin-Madison. The success of his collaborative model prompted Assistant Vice-Chancellor Duane Hickling to hire Daniel Einstein as a full-time environmental manager. In this role, Einstein tracks environmental projects within the facilities planning and management division, and also coordinates campus ecology research projects in which faculty advisors and student researchers are matched with staff clients. "These programs," says Einstein, "have paid for themselves many times over in reduced costs to the university." Similar programs, Tufts CLEAN! and the University Student Environmental Audit Research Program (USEARCH) at the University of Minnesota, also proved successful.

New approaches to environmental education often emphasize the process of learning as much as course content. At Prescott College in Arizona, ecological literacy and ecologically designed buildings are central to the college mission. In a 1993 letter to Campus Ecology staff, President Douglas North refers to Prescott's approach as the "garden" model of teaching and learning. As opposed to a "factory" model that emphasizes grades, tests and not making mistakes, he says, the "garden model emphasizes risk and supports making errors . . . through experiential forms of education, which place the faculty more in the position of guide, counselor, challenger, co-evaluator, and co-planner. . . . As long as environmental education is seen only as a content issue and not a process issue, much of the potential effect of education to achieve a society more in harmony with the biosphere will be lost."

Campuses just beginning to evaluate their curricula might look to George Washington University's initial efforts. As part of its Green University program, GW has established an academic subcommittee to evaluate the existing environmental curriculum in all university schools and departments and to investigate environmental curricula at other universities. The subcommittee will also assess the environmental holdings of the libraries. These evaluations will inform the development of an environmental curriculum encompassing environmental majors and degree programs, as well as all other academic programs.

6. RESEARCH

An institution can make great contributions to pollution prevention and ecology through its academic research. A handful of notable examples include the precedent-setting sustainable agriculture program at Cornell University;

> The goal of environmental literacy requires that all students, regardless of major, develop the fundamental awareness, knowledge, skills and values to carry out their professional activities in a sustainable manner. It also requires that interdisciplinary teaching and learning become a permanent part of university education.
>
> —Tom Kelly,
> Tufts University

renewable energy research and development programs at the University of Delaware, University of South Florida, and other campuses; native grasses research at the University of Nebraska; transportation demand management research at the Georgia Institute of Technology, UCLA, the University of Wisconsin at Madison, and other campuses; research on integrated pest management and on ecological architecture at the University of California at Berkeley; and research and development of efficient office equipment and buildings at MIT.

Because evaluating university research agendas is both sensitive and complex, campuses may want to start with a nurturing approach, providing support for research that explores environmental policies and values. George Washington University, for example, has announced that a research subcommittee appointed by the president will develop a mechanism by which researchers can draw on the university's environmental expertise across departments, schools, and disciplines; explore the establishment of an environmental research publication; develop communication links to environmental researchers at other universities; gain expanded access to GW's Center for Applied Environmental Technology; and participate in a coordinated program of environmental research, complete with its own priorities and "seed funding."

7. ECOLOGICAL PLANNING AND DESIGN

Incorporating ecological concerns into the design of buildings and campuses is a new challenge for most campuses. But some colleges and universities have set exciting precedents for putting environmental theory and research into practice. Such projects (several of which are covered in earlier chapters) include campus provisions for renewable energy and energy efficiency, nontoxic and recycled-content building materials, native landscaping, appropriate siting of buildings and plants, bicycle parking, water recycling and conservation, and ease of recycling.

Ecological design and planning on campuses occurs on a number of levels. Ambitious students, staff, and faculty sometimes implement their own designs on the periphery of the central planning processes. At Humboldt State University, Dickinson College, Tufts University, Hampden-Sydney College, and several other institutions, staff and students have established green residences or "eco-houses." More than a dozen of these alternative centers nationwide provide an environmental base-camp for those interested in extending ecological design principles to other buildings. Indeed, what was once considered alternative—recycling and water- and energy-efficiency—has now become commonplace, so that eco-houses must now compost, recycle water, run on solar power, and otherwise expand

Our proposal to establish the University Student Environmental Research Program was approved in about 48 hours. We had a phone, desk, budget and place to be.

—Karen Linner, USEARCH Coordinator 1993–94, University of Minnesota

their repertoire in order to provide environmental leadership.

At one of the more advanced green residences, the Campus Center for Appropriate Technology (CCAT) at Humboldt State University, photovoltaic panels power lights, a personal computer, and other electric necessities; water is solar heated; and organic waste is composted (kitchen and landscape trimmings outside, sewage in compost toilets). Live-in student staff manage a greywater reclamation system that collects water drained from sinks and the bathtub, filtering it through a marshlike plot on the property. The water collected at the other end of the marsh is used to water the fruits and vegetables in CCAT's organic garden. Co-directors also publish their own newsletter, offer regular trainings and lectures, and conduct tours.

Ecological concepts may influence the design of new buildings and the restoration of habitat or, on the many campuses where no new developments are planned, they may inform improvements in existing infrastructure. The New Energy Center at Brevard Community College/University of Central Florida and the xeriscape garden at Mesa Community College showcase ecological architecture and landscaping. They serve as regional models, cost less to operate and maintain, and provide a living laboratory for students, staff, and faculty.

Where ecological design principles have influenced long-range, comprehensive planning, it is often thanks to the efforts of executive staff who have brought campus experts with relevant experience into the process. As environmental responsibility becomes recognized as an intrinsic part of sound management and academic integrity, advocates of sustainable development are finding more room for themselves at the planning table. For instance, with funding and backing from Executive Vice Chancellor Judith Ramely (now president of Portland State University), Prof. Stephen Hamburg created the Environmental Ombudsman Program (EOP) at the University of Kansas at Lawrence. Within three years the EOP had founded several green projects and more than paid for itself each year through savings to the institution. By 1993–94, after a bit of lobbying, EOP staff participated in the university's long-range planning process. "Becoming parties to the university's planning," emphasizes Hamburg, "meant establishing a successful track record and having a credible presence on campus."

EOP staff subsequently lent their expertise to the earliest stages of the design of new buildings for the campus. "That made a big difference in how much we could do," says former EOP staffer Susan Ask, who says she "[had] seen many opportunities for resource efficiency lost once initial drawings and decisions [were] made." At UC-Boulder, Recycling Coordinator Jack DeBell reports that it is now university policy to consult with the recycling office before a building is designed. Both DeBell and EOP staff at the University of Kansas have helped

We have not thought of academic buildings as pedagogical, but they are.
—David W. Orr,
Earth in Mind

design "recycling-friendly" buildings that meet fire codes while allowing for easy emptying of recycling bins and dumpsters.

Students, too, have earned seats at the planning table. Members in the Earthkeeping Club at Dordt College in Sioux Center, Iowa, for example, spent 1993-94 preparing suggestions for the Campus Development Plan (a long-range plan for the development of buildings and grounds) and were invited by the president to make a presentation before the cabinet.

(This chapter's bibliography and networking sections list sources of information on sustainable building and design.)

8. SENSE OF PLACE

Many campus environmental groups struggle desperately to galvanize student and staff support and involvement. Although there are no pat solutions to this problem, the programs that lure people into natural areas on campus and in the community often elicit the most enthusiasm and the highest levels of participation. Connecting the campus to the community, these programs extend campus stewardship projects beyond one institution to examine broader community and regional contexts. Whether urban, suburban or rural in location, these undertakings instill in students and staff a deeper appreciation of the local ecology, economy, and natural history—in short, a deeper sense of place.

Reflecting on the stewardship initiative he coordinated at the University of Wisconsin-Madison, in which 48 seniors from his environmental studies seminar and students from other classes examined the impact of the university on the environment, David Eagan writes in *The Campus and Environmental Responsibility*: "Some of those who studied Muir's Woods, the marsh, and other natural areas of the campus expressed strong feelings toward those places and counted the time spent there as a highlight of their semester."[1] These initial research forays into Muir Woods, an oak-basswood woodland in the central campus, later spawned the "Campus Keepers" program, in which students and staff volunteers spend many hours removing alien and otherwise detrimental plants.

Ron Dinchak's xeriscape gardens and landscape restoration projects at Mesa Community College, Ron Jerido's Adopt-a-Plot program at Texas Southern University (see Chapter 2, Landscaping), and Professors Heiman and Wilderman's community waste-auditing and water-testing programs at Dickinson College (see Chapter 8, Hazardous Waste) prompt similar stories of growing community involvement and participants' enhanced understanding of the local natural history and ecology.

5. 1992, p. 73. See bibliography.

The programs that lure people into natural areas on campus and in the community often elicit the most enthusiasm and the highest levels of participation.

Through the Office of the Environment at Birmingham-Southern College, Prof. Roald Hazelhoff runs programs unique in their emphasis on community service. The community food-share program, Environmental Center, and various ecological restoration projects unite student volunteers and work-study students with diverse community leaders, residents, and elementary school children, bridging the gap between campus and community. The Environmental Center is a small, interactive environmental museum to teach children about energy conservation, solid and hazardous waste management, and water conservation.

The college's Watershed Restoration Program focuses on Village Creek, once a source of drinking water and a gathering place for Native Americans from throughout the Southeast. Today, says Hazelhoff, the creek collects residues from mine drainage and industrial emissions, as well as runoff from small businesses that use large quantities of paints, solvents, and other toxic chemicals. By identifying sources of pollution and tailoring educational programs to them, BSC's program seeks to prevent pollution in the creek. "We are adopting neighborhood associations and small businesses in the watershed, like the neighborhood dry cleaners and gas stations," explains Hazelhoff, "giving them positive reinforcement and setting up all kinds of educational programs . . . to instill a sense of ownership over that watershed."

9. MEASURABLE REDUCTION OF COST AND WASTE

As their programs begin to reshape the campus and the world beyond it, environmental stewards are becoming increasingly savvy about analyzing their results. Rigorous analysis buttresses "feel-good" programs with the quantifiable results necessary to win institutional support. By measuring their success in ways which dramatize connections between individual actions and the larger world, program managers can give participants campus-wide a crucial sense of efficacy and accomplishment. Although many benefits of campus ecology programs are qualitative (boosting morale and teamwork, improving aesthetics, etc.), many others can be quantified. Some improvements lend themselves easily to measurement: waste reduction and recycling, energy and water conservation, pesticide reduction, and decreases in campus carbon dioxide emissions and hazardous wastes, to name a few. Even some improvements to campus habitats can be measured—in terms of an increase in native plant diversity or sightings of specific species of birds, beneficial insects, and other wildlife.

Methodologies for measurement, especially in the field of solid waste management, have improved tremendously. In the early years of campus recycling, participants simply monitored the volume of various items recovered (aluminum

By measuring their success in ways which dramatize connections between individual actions and the larger world, program managers can give participants campus-wide a crucial sense of efficacy and accomplishment.

cans, glass, paper) or the revenues generated by their program. Today, many campuses track the percentages, by weight and volume, of material diverted from the waste stream. They can then set recovery goals and measure their improvement. Financial benefits can be calculated to include tipping-fee reductions and other savings, which almost always outstrip actual revenues. UC-Boulder's recycling staff worked with campus accountants to track such savings and allocate them back to their recycling program. (See Chapter 7, Solid Waste.)

The preceding chapters highlight many creative ways of measuring a program's success. Recyclers have calculated the trees saved through paper recycling programs and more generally tried to depict the global significance of local efforts. From commuting to air-conditioning, campus activities can be defined in terms of carbon dioxide emissions, allowing campuses to estimate their contribution to the greenhouse effect. At SUNY-Buffalo, Biophysics Professor Fred Snell and Energy Officer Walter Simpson determined that electrical use accounted for 221,900 tons annually, or 71 percent, of campus carbon dioxide emissions, while commuters accounted for approximately 51,000 tons, or 16 percent. UB's energy conservation projects are expected to reduce carbon dioxide emissions by thousands of tons by the end of the 1990s.

10. PUBLIC RELATIONS AND DOCUMENTATION

Hand in hand with measuring the impact of a program comes publicizing the results. Yet the documenting of programs and their progress is an often overlooked component of securing a place for environmental stewardship within an institution. To assure the permanence and effectiveness of any program, participants must take the time to detail their efforts for the benefit of others on their campus and beyond. Model case studies are now available on dozens of environmental projects at numerous colleges and universities. These include an account of the green office equipment initiative at SUNY-Buffalo, a solid waste management report from the University of Illinois, contract specifications and purchasing documents from Rutgers, and a cost-benefit analysis of the switch from reusable to disposable dishware at Bowling Green State. These and many other studies are listed in the bibliographies which follow each chapter of this book.

In addition to the two "listservs" or electronic correspondence groups formed specifically for campuses ("Greenschools," and "Recyc-l"), Internet provides numerous ecology resources applicable to campuses. (For a listing of electronic bulletin boards, "listservs," gopher, ftp, and http sites, see the EnviroNetworks Directory on the EnviroGopher. Instructions appear in the resources section of this

As The George Washington University endeavors to become an international model of excellence for leadership and stewardship in environmental management and sustainability among institutions of higher learning, we benefit greatly from the collective knowledge and experiences of our colleagues.

—Stephen Joel Trachtenberg, President, The George Washington University

chapter.) Less high-tech approaches also spread the word of campus trials and successes. Many campuses host tours of their "eco-houses" and open some environmental lectures and programs to local schoolchildren and members of the community, as well as to experts and interested novices from farther afield. (See networking section or call the Campus Ecology staff for more information.)

11. FINANCIAL ACCOUNTABILITY

As colleges and universities form environmental policies and put them into practice on campus, they are beginning to extend these expectations to the companies with which they do business. Shifts in college spending often begin with purchasing. Rutgers University, the University of Minnesota, the University of Wisconsin-Madison, and others have created environmentally sensitive specifications for dozens of contracts, including paper, construction, and office equipment. The nonprofit organization Green Seal has simplified this effort by testing equipment, cleaning supplies, paper, and other products, and developing standards that manufacturers must meet in order to qualify for the Green Seal logo. (See Chapter 1, Purchasing.)

A few campuses have begun to sign contracts which cost more initially but save money and resources over time. These schools consider the full cost of a product—including the environmental cost of manufacturing, transporting, using, and disposing of it, as well as the price of installation, operation, and maintenance, which often are not reflected in its purchase price. Examples include the switch from disposables to dishware and from commercially produced foods to local, organic foods (see Chapter 5, Dining Services), as well as the move from landfilling organic materials to composting (see Chapter 7, Solid Waste). Campuses have also begun to use life-cycle analysis, a more limited method of evaluating cost that leaves out some environmental factors but includes maintenance and operational expenses. Cornell University has developed a model software program that tracks life-cycle expenditures for preventative maintenance in facilities departments; Kurt Teichert is evaluating similar systems for Brown University's Brown is Green program.

Applying the principles of environmental stewardship to a college or university's investment portfolio requires a larger psychological leap. This often results when students call for divestment from such controversial projects as Hydro-Quebec's James Bay II (which would dam the Great Whale River in Northern Quebec, flooding more than 1,000 square miles of wilderness and Cree lands) and the Mount Graham Telescope Project (in a biologically diverse habitat containing the endangered red squirrel, as well as sites sacred to San Carlos Apaches). In both

A few campuses have begun to consider the full cost of a product—including the environmental cost of manufacturing, transporting, using, and disposing of it, as well as the price of installation, operation, and maintenance, which often are not reflected in its purchase price.

cases, students launched high-profile campaigns to educate trustees, administrators, and others at dozens of campuses. Both Tufts and Dartmouth sold their Hydro-Quebec bonds, and as many as 20 colleges and universities withdrew from the observatory project, thanks in part to the coordinated efforts of the Student Environmental Action Coalition (SEAC). When they sold their $2 million-worth of Hydro-Quebec bonds, Tufts trustees explained: "In reaching this decision, the trustees recognize that promoting increased awareness of environmental issues and educating students and others about their responsibility for preserving or improving our environment is a core value of the university."[2]

Many colleges and universities caught up in these time-consuming and expensive controversies have begun to recognize the need for comprehensive investment policies. In a fascinating analysis of environmental divestment on campuses, Robert Anderson writes in a March 1994 issue of *Investor's Environmental Report* (*IER*) that some campuses "are beginning to explore ways to establish consistent investment guidelines on environmental issues to provide early warning of investment situations affecting the environment." As a first step, some administrations have granted faculty and students some access to investment information and the decision-making process. The *Stanford Daily* student newspaper serves as a lively forum for discussion of Stanford University's $3 billion investment portfolio. Williams College created an advisory committee on shareholder responsibility, and Tufts runs a socially responsible investing committee.

After broadening campus participation in investment decisions, staff and students wrestle with how to establish environmental standards for investment in land, stocks, and bonds. This is a challenging process, but one for which there is growing precedent. According to Eric Packer of Prudential Securities' Socially Responsible Investing Program, "investments made according to some social criteria grew from $40 billion in 1984 to approximately $625 billion in 1992."[3] Socially and environmentally responsible investing consultants report to Campus Ecology staff that they have begun meeting with higher education business officers. A 1993 survey of financial officers at 395 colleges and universities conducted by the Investor Responsibility Research Center found that the environment ranked as the second largest area of student concern (after South Africa at the time), but that campus investment and proxy-voting policies had yet to reflect these priorities.[4]

Students and staff are consulting five key sources when establishing investment policies for corporate environmental accountability: (1) the Council on Economic

In reaching this decision, the trustees recognize that promoting increased awareness of environmental issues and educating students and others about their responsibility for preserving or improving our environment is a core value of the university.

—Tufts University Trustees, after divesting of $2 million in Hydro-Quebec bonds in February, 1994

2. *Investor's Environmental Report*, March/April, 1994, p. 11.

3. "Socially Responsible Investing," 1993, p. 2.

4. *Investor's Environmental Report*, Nov/Dec, 1994, p. 8.

Priorities, which conducts an annual ranking of corporate polluters; (2) the Coalition for Environmentally Responsible Economics (CERES), which established the globally recognized CERES Principles for corporate environmental responsibility; (3) Green Seal, which sets environmental standards for a wide variety of products; (4) investment consultants who specialize in environmentally responsible investment; and (5) their campuses' own central purchasing departments, whose environmental specifications and experience with vendors can help shape similar shifts in investments.

Once guidelines are established, reports Packer, institutions generally take a three-pronged approach, screening portfolios to determine which companies engage in practices most consistent with or divergent from the guidelines; identifying and investing in companies whose practices best meet environmental requirements, and whose performance is consistent with other investment criteria; and using their leverage as shareholders to influence a corporation's philosophy and practice.

12. LEADERSHIP DEVELOPMENT AND TRAINING

Campus environmental stewards must remember to invest close to home, too. If the lessons learned on campus are to be applied in the larger world, leaders must be trained for the task. The influx of new leaders also gives campus efforts welcome vigor; recycling and other programs which require broad and diverse participation likewise benefit from broad and diverse leadership. Some of the most outstanding environmental programs take particular care to include students and staff of diverse ethnicities, cultures, and disciplines, not just as participants but as designers and decision-makers. To nurture this diversity, campuses should invest the time and money necessary to offer training programs on environmental skills and leadership development.

The University of Colorado-Boulder's recycling program illustrates the benefits of such investment. Specialized collection carts, one of the centerpieces of the Boulder effort, were developed with guidance from the custodial staff, who helped design all phases of the recycling program. Custodians also helped translate recycling literature into Spanish and Hmong, the two languages most commonly spoken by CU custodians. Jack DeBell, the program's coordinator, recruits students from varied academic disciplines and cultural backgrounds by offering training and certification programs. These programs give students an edge in the job market and provide an incentive for those who otherwise might not participate in the programs.

> Some of the most outstanding environmental programs take particular care to include students and staff of diverse ethnicities, cultures, and disciplines, not just as participants but as designers and decision-makers.

Increasingly, staff and students recognize skills and leadership training as an incentive for volunteer participation and innovation. An increasing number of student activities offices, career planning and placement centers, student governments, facilities departments, and other offices and departments on campuses provide environmental and leadership training. These offerings take many forms, including environmental career fairs, campus ecology trainings, workshops at national association conferences, professional environmental auditing or issue seminars, and regional and national environmental stewardship conferences.

🐾 LOOKING FORWARD

Surveys consistently show that college and high school students feel enormous concern about clean air, clean water, endangered species, and other issues of community health. Students even express a willingness to pay more for more environmentally sound products, to forego convenience in order to conserve resources, and to take personal action to improve the environment.[5] Those whose efforts are described in Ecodemia share these values. Regardless of cultural background, age, or political affiliation, the staff and students interviewed for this book repeatedly expressed the view that protection of public health and the environment must not wax and wane with fashion or with fluctuations of the economy; these issues, they feel, require ardent and sustained effort.

Although their visions of a sustainable future vary slightly, staff and students show few differences in the intensity with which they are redefining their jobs and activities in pursuit of a healthy planet. Motives differ from person to person, but the outcomes are the same: lowered costs, increased biodiversity, and reduced pollution and waste.

Environmental responsibility creates common ground. At the dawn of the 21st century and beyond, higher education will probably assume ever greater levels of ecological responsibility—in teaching and in learning, in theory and in daily practice—in response to a strong and sustained public mandate for environmental stewardship. *Ecodemia* was written to encourage this effort.

Although their visions of a sustainable future vary slightly, staff and students show few differences in the intensity with which they are redefining their jobs and activities in pursuit of a healthy planet.

5. *Planet in Peril: A View from the Campus*, National Wildlife Federation, Nov., 1989; *Environmental Attitudes and Behaviors of American Youth*, Roper Starch, 1994; "College Students Believe the Condition of the Environment is Worsening," Veryfine, Dec. 1, 1995; "Lifestyle-Attitudes," Strategic Marketing Communications, Inc., 1995 showed 17% of students "strongly agreed" and 55% "agreed" that they "give up convenience to save resources."

BIBLIOGRAPHY

Accounting for the Environment: The Greening of Accountancy, Part II., Rob Gray with Jan Bebbington and Diane Walters, London, Paul Chapman, 1993.

Audubon House, National Audubon Society and Croxton Collaborative, American Society of Landscape Architects, 1994. (800) 787-2665.

"Blueprint for a Green Campus: The Campus Earth Summit Initiatives for Higher Education," Heinz Family Foundation, January, 1995. (202) 939-3316.

"Business-Environment Learning and Leadership (BELL) Conference Summary," *EnviroLink*, Winter, 1994, p.5.

The Campus and Environmental Responsibility, David J. Eagan and David W. Orr, No. 77, Spring, 1992, Jossey-Bass Publishers, 350 Sansome St., San Francisco, CA 94104.

Campus Ecology: A Guide to Assessing Environmental Quality and Creating Strategies for Change, April Smith and the Student Environmental Action Coalition, Living Planet Press, 1993. (available through SEAC at (919) 967-4600 and the Campus Ecology Program (202) 797-5467.)

The Campus Environmental Yearbook, Campus Ecology Program, National Wildlife Federation, 1989–90, 1990–91, 1991–92, 1992–93, 1993–94, 1994–95. (202) 797-5435.

Campus Green Buying Guide, 1994, Green Seal. (202) 331-7337.

The Campus Green Pages: 1995 Directory, Campus Earth Summit, Heinz Family Foundation, January, 1995. (202) 939-3316 or shadow@igc.apc.org.

"Colleges Going Green: A Guide to Environmental Action for Further Education Colleges," Shirley Ali Khan and Dr. Christopher Parkin, 1992, Further Education Unit and the Council for Environmental Education, Citadel Place, Tinworth St., London, SE11 5EH.

Conservation Directory, National Wildlife Federation. (800) 432-6564. $20.00/regular, $16.00/student (published annually; comprehensive listing of local, regional and national environmental/conservation organizations, agencies and officials with brief outlines of their areas of interest and contact information).

Dumping in Dixie, Robert D. Bullard, Westview Press, 1990.

Earth Ethics, Center for Respect of Life and Environment, Humane Society, Washington, D.C. (202) 778-6133. (newsletter covers developments in higher education curricula and other environmental initiatives.)

"Environmental Initiatives in British Universities," Katharine Willis, *Greening Universities*, Greening of Higher Education Council (GHECO), March, 1994.

"Environmental Movement Booming on Campuses," Julian Keniry, *Change*, Sep/Oct, 1993.

"Defining Sustainable Development Principles for Higher Education," *Second Nature*, Fall, 1994, p.5.

Earth in Mind: On Education, Environment and the Human Prospect, David Orr, Island Press, 1994.

EC Study Guide to Environment-Related Courses, Institut fur Europaische Umweltpolitick, Luxembourg: Office for Official Publications of the European Communities, 1993.

Ecological Literacy: Education and the Transition to a Postmodern World, University of New York Press, 1991.

Envirolink: A Newsletter for Educators in the Fields of Business and the Environment, Management Institute for Environment & Business, 1101 7th Street, N.W., Suite 502, Washington, D.C. 20036 (202) 833-6556.

"Environmental Responsibility: an Agenda for Further and Higher Education," Summary of the Report of an Expert Committee chaired by Professor Peter Toyne, 1992, Department for Education, Publications Centre, PO Box 2193, London E15 2EU.

The Green Guide: A User's Guide to Sustainable Development for Canadian Colleges, National Roundtable on the Environment and the Economy, 1 Nicolas St., Ste. 1500, Ottawa, Ontario K1N 7D7, Canada.

Greening Universities, Greening of Higher Education Council (GHECO), 120a Marlborough Road, Oxford OX1 4LS. (0865) 204244.

"Hannover Principles: Design for Sustainability," William McDonough, *Interiors*, March, 1993, p. 54.

"The Greening of American Universities," T. Cortese and S.H. Creighton, *The American Association of Governing Boards Report*, March/April, 1991.

"How to Plan Meetings That Don't Cost the Earth," Ecological Environment Communications, 1170 Waimanu Street, Honolulu, HI 96814. (808) 528-2297.

"Life Studies: Student Greens Get Practical at the University of Wisconsin," Steve Lerner, *The Amicus Journal*, Summer, 1994, pp. 36–41.

"Meeting Planners Going Green," Ted Saunders and Liz Kay, *Convene*, Nov, 1992, pp. 31–33.

The New Complete Guide to Environmental Careers, Environmental Careers Organization, Island Press, 1993.

"New Courses at CEM's Environmental Management Institute Address Changing Technologies and Strategies,", Warren Goldstein-Gelb, *CEM Report*, Vol. 12, Fall, 1992, pp. 1, 10. (617) 627-3531.

The Politics of the Solar Age: Alternatives to Economics, Hazel Henderson, Knowledge Systems, 1988.

A Primer on Sustainable Building, Rocky Mountain Institute, 1739 Snowmass Creek Road, Snowmass, CO 81654-9199. (970) 927-3851 or (e-mail: orders:@rmi.org).

Regenerative Design for Sustainable Development, John Tillman Lyle, American Society of Landscape Architects, 1994. (800) 787-2665.

SEAC Organizing Guide, Student Environmental Action Coalition. (919) 967-4600.

The Student Environmental Action Guide: 25 Simple Things We Can Do, The Student Environmental Action Coalition, 1991, Earth Works Press, 1400 Shattuck Avenue #25, Berkeley, CA 94709. (415) 841-5866.

Talloires Declaration, University Presidents for a Sustainable Future, Tufts Environmental Literacy Institute, 1990. (617) 627-3486.

Threshold, Student Environmental Action Coalition. (919) 967-4600.

NETWORKING

If you find that an organization listed here has moved or a contact has been replaced, let the Campus Ecology Program staff know. We'll help match you with the latest source for the information you need.

Campus

(This is only a partial listing of campuses with institutionalized environmental programs or examples of ecological design/ appropriate technology; see previous chapters for additional contacts; also contact Campus Ecology staff for additional campus contacts in your area.)

Birmingham-Southern College
Attn. Roald Hazelhoff
Environmental Center
900 Arkadelphia Rd.
Birmingham, AL 35254
(205) 226-4934
Children's environmental museum, community watershed restoration project, comprehensive environmental planning and coordination on campus.

Brevard Community College
Attn. Public Relations
1519 Clear Lake Road
Cocoa, FL 32922
(407) 632-1111
Award-winning energy conservation and efficiency programs.

Brown University
Attn. Kurt Teichert
Box 1941
Providence, RI 02912
(401) 863-7837
e-mail: kurt_teichert@brown.edu
Runs Brown is Green Program; contact for information on "Greenschools" and "Recyc-l" campus electronic correspondence groups or the new campus earth hypertext site.

California State Polytechnic University-Pomona
Attn. John Lyle
Center for Regenerative Studies
3801 W. Temple Ave.
Pomona, CA 91768
(909) 869-POLY
A community in which students live and work with life support systems that function in the self-renewing ways of natural ecosystems.

Connecticut College
Attn. Peter Esselman or Randall Lucas
Office of Environmental Activities
New London, CT 06320
(203) 439-2303
Office of environmental activities; runs "Environmental Model Committee," guiding policy, IPM, and other campus ecology programs.

Dickinson College
Student Activities
Carlisle, PA 17013
(717) 245-1231
In addition to community waste auditing and water testing, Dickinson runs an ecological residence called "the green-house."

George Washington University
Attn. Irwin Price, Assoc. Vice President
2121 Eye St., N.W., Ste. 603
Washington, D.C. 20052
(202) 994-0742
Launched multi-faceted "Green University" program in fall of 1994.

Humboldt State University
Attn. Campus Center for Appropriate Technology
Buck House #97
Arcata, CA 95521
(916) 826-3551
Students staff/residents live with and give tours of greywater recycling system, composting toilets, solar energy systems, thermal curtains, organic garden and more; they also publish the AT Transfer *newsletter.*

Miami University
Attn. Orie Louks/Sustainability Project
Zoology Department, 134 BSB
Oxford, OH 45056
(513) 529-1677
Ongoing committee plans campus ecology projects and forums.

Northland College
Attn. Students Activities
Ashland, WI 54806
Northland College is the host campus for the Zero-Discharge Campaign co-coordinated with the National Wildlife Federation's Great Lakes Natural Resource Center; residents of their eco-residence known as the "CUD" for "Conceptual Urban Dwelling," use efficient fixtures and appliances, purchase food (primarily organic and local) in bulk, recycle and compost waste, and run tours; they hope to install photovoltaic paneling for electricity.

Quinnipiac College
Attn. Keith Woodward
555 New Rd.
Hamden, CT 06518
(203) 281-8780
Comprehensive environmental programs.

Slippery Rock University
Attn. Larry Patrick
Slippery Rock University
Slippery Rock, PA 16057
Solar and other ecological design applications and curricula; the Homestead is one of the leading campus "eco-residences."

State University New York-Buffalo
Attn. Walter Simpson
Conserve UB
John Beane Center
Buffalo, NY 14260
(716) 645-3636
Comprehensive energy conservation and efficiency program, large solid waste recycling program, Green Computing Campaign, *building conservation contacts program, environmental policy and planning processes and guidelines.*

Tufts University
Attn. Tom Kelly, Director
Secretariat of University Presidents for a Sustainable Future (Secretariat)
Center for Environmental Management
474 Boston Ave.
Medford, MA 02155
(617) 627-3486
Contact for information about Tufts Environmental Literacy Institute (TELI), campus ecology initiatives, and Talloires Declaration.

University of Kansas-Lawrence
Attn. Environmental Ombudsman Program
Haworth Hall
Lawrence, KS 66045-2106
(913) 864-3208
Student research projects, environmental planning and policy.

University of Virginia
Attn. William McDonough, Dean
School of Architecture
Charlottesville, VA 22903
(804) 924-2678
One of the nation's leading advocates and practitioners of ecological design in higher education.

University of Waterloo
Attn. Waste Management
Coordinator
Waterloo, Ontario
Canada N2L 3G1
(519) 885-1211 ext. 3246
e-mail:
gbwright@watserv1.uwaterloo.ca
*WATgreen initiative has
sponsored dozens of student
campus environmental research
projects.*

University of Wisconsin-Madison
Attn: Daniel Einstein
Environmental Management
Rm. 120 WARF Bldg.
610 Walnut St.
Madison, WI 53705
(608) 265-3417
(or)
Attn. David Eagan
Institute for Environmental
Studies
70 Science Hall
(608) 263-3985
djeagan@students.wisc.edu
*Contact Eagan for information
related to IES seminars and
resulting student research
projects, curricular initiatives,
and ecological restoration
projects on campus; contact
Einstein for information about
university environmental
management initiatives, such as
transportation demand
management, materials
exchange and other solid waste
initiatives, and campus ecology
research projects.*

Regional and National

Campus Ecology Program
(see National Wildlife
Federation)

Campus Green Vote
Center for Environmental
Citizenship
Attn. Chris Fox
1400 16th St., NW, Box 24
Washington, D.C. 20036
(202) 939-3316

Campus Outreach Opportunity
League (COOL)
1511 K St., N.W., Ste. 307
Washington, D.C. 20005
(202) 637-7004
*The umbrella organization for
national student community
service; many excellent
community service resources
as well as a national
conference.*

Ecological Building Concepts
290 California Road
Morgantown, PA 19543
(215) 286-6456

EcoNet
(415) 442-0220
modem: (415) 322-0162
*EcoNet is one of many services
which provide access to the
Internet, though EcoNet is
specially tailored to environmental research and networking. See phone directory for
other providers.*

EnviroLink
Attn: Josh Knauer, Director
4551 Forbes Ave.
Pittsburgh, PA 15213
(412) 681-8300
fax: (412) 681-6707
e-mail: admin@envirolink.org
*Envirolink is a free service on
the Internet through which
one may obtain a list of
electronic correspondence
groups or "listservs," bulletin
boards, ftp, gopher, and
hypertext sites serving campus
ecology and other environmental work. Access
Envirolink by typing "telnet
envirolink.org" at the Internet
gateway (requiring EcoNet or
another Internet service). At
the menu of options, select #5
for the Environmental Gopher.
Within the EnviroGopher, one
can also access environmental
publications, environmental
law and government information, environmental organizations, and environmental
computer networks.*

Environmental Careers
Organization
286 Congress St.
Boston, MA 02210
(617) 426-4375

Environmental Protection
Agency
Attn. David Smith
National Green University
Program
401 M St., S.W.
Washington, D.C. 20460

Green Corps
1109 Walnut, 3rd Floor
Philadelphia, PA 19107
(617) 426-8506
*Interns, hired annually, work on
regional/state environmental
campaigns.*

"Greenschools"
Kurt Teichert, Listowner
Brown is Green
Box 1941
Brown University
Providence, RI 02912
(401) 863-7837
e-mail: kurt_teichert@brown.edu
*"Greenschools" (formally
"GRNSCH-L") is a "listserv" or
electronic correspondence group
on the Internet. It has become a
dynamic forum for discussion of
energy efficiency and other
issues of environmental
responsibility in higher education. To subscribe to the list,
send the following message to
listserv@brownvm.brown.edu:
subscribe GRNSCH-L "your
name".* The Blueprint for a
Green Campus *and other
campus ecology documentation
is available via Brown's World
Wide Web site: http://
www.envstudies.brown.edu/
environ.*

Institute for Conservation
Leadership
6930 Carroll Ave., Ste. 420
Takoma Park, MD 20912
(301) 270-3900
*"Trainings for trainers," these
folks help train new NWF
Campus Ecology staff every year.*

Investor Responsibility Research
Center
Attn: Peter Chines
1350 Connecticut Avenue, N.W.,
Suite 700
Washington, D.C. 20036-1701
(202) 833-0700
Publishes Investor's
Environmental Report.

Management Institute for
Environment and Business
1220 Sixteenth St., N.W.
Washington, D.C. 20036
Publishes EnviroLink, *a
newsletter for educators in the
field of environmental management.*

National Association of Colleges
and University Business Officers
(NACUBO)
One Dupont Circle, Suite 500
Washington, D.C. 20036-1178
(202) 861-2500
*Innovative Management
Achievement Awards (IMAA)
Program has recognized
numerous campus and resource-
saving programs on campuses,
such as paper elimination,
furniture recycling, etc. Contact
for entry forms.*

National Association of College
Stores (NACS)
Attn. Environmental Concerns
Committee
500 East Lorain St.
Oberlin, OH 44074-1294

National Association of College
and University Food Services
(NACUFS)
Attn. Environmental Committee
Chair
1450 South Harrison Road, Suite
303
Michigan State University
East Lansing, MI 48824
(517) 332-2494

National Wildlife Federation
Campus Ecology Program
1400 16th St.
Washington, D.C. 20036-2266
(202) 797-5435 (general
information)
(313) 769-9970 or
midwest@nwf.org (M.W.)
(202) 797-5468 or
noreast@nwf.org (N.E.)
(404) 876-2608 or
soeast@nwf.org (S.E.)
(503) 222-1429 or
western@nwf.org (West)
*Regional organizing staff
provide consultation on project
planning and organizing,
Campus Issue Packets on 14
topics, annual Environmental
Yearbooks, Campus Ecology
Connection, annual Campus
Ecology Video Contest, Campus
Ecology auditing manual,
speakers bureau, organizing
and issue workshops, case
studies, internships; also,
information on the Endangered
Species Program, EnviroAction:
legislative updates,* National
Wildlife *magazine, Campus
Habitat and Backyard Wildlife
Habitat Programs, regional and
state campaigns, business
curricula co-developed by NWF's
Corporate Conservation Council,
and the annual Washington
Action Workshops.*

Second Nature
17 Msgr. O'Brien Highway
P.O. Box 410350
East Cambridge, MA 02141-0004
*Train professors, teachers, and
trainers to incorporate environmental themes, problem solving,
and applied learning experiences into higher education
curricula.*

Secretariat of University
Presidents for a Sustainable
Future (Secretariat)
Attn. Tom Kelly, Director
Center for Environmental
Management
Tufts University
474 Boston Ave.
Medford, MA 02155
(617) 627-3486
Contact for Talloires
Declaration.

Sierra Club Student Coalition
223 Thayer St., #2
Providence, RI 02906
(401) 861-6012
*Coordinates high school
chapters.*

Society for College and
University Planning (SCUP)
2026 M, School of Education
Building
610 East University Avenue
Ann Arbor, MI 48109-1259
(313) 763-4776
*Calls for ecological design and
planning proposals from faculty
and students for annual
conferences.*

Student Environmental Action Coalition (SEAC)
PO Box 1168
Chapel Hill, NC 27514-1168
(800) 700-SEAC
The umbrella of the student environmental movement, offers organizing guides and organizer training weekends, Threshold *newsletter,* Campus Ecology *auditing guide, regional conferences, assistance with divestment, environmental justice and corporate accountability and other campaigns; contact for access to Alliance for Solidarity, Environment, Equality and Development (ASEED) and People of Color Caucus.*

United States Public Interest Research Group (USPIRG)
215 Pennsylvania Ave., SE
Washington, D.C. 20003
(202) 546-9707
Student chapters run various consumer-oriented, public health and enviornmental campaigns on the local and state level.

Student Pugwash USA
1638 R St., NW, Suite 32
Washington, D.C. 20009-6446
(202) 328-6555
Provides resources for organizing alternative career festivals, job guides, and college forums for dialog with and mentoring from senior scientists on issues of science and technology.

United States Student Association (USSA)
815 15th St., N.W., Suite 838
Washington, D.C. 20005
(202) 347-8772
Their grassroots organizing (GROW) trainings get rave reviews.

U.S. Green Building Council
7900 Wisconsin Ave., Ste. 404
Bethesda, MD 20814
(301) 657-3469

GREENING OUR OWN HOME
The National Wildlife Federation
Environmental Quality Task Force

Efforts to improve the environmental profile of NWF's operations began in a formal way with the establishment of the Environmental Quality Task Force (EQTF) in the fall of 1988. Since then, interns and staff representing the diverse activities of the Federation (from lobbying through purchasing), have met bimonthly to plan and implement more than 100 conservation initiatives.

But these measures represent only the first steps for us. To live up to our commitments as a member of the Coalition for Environmentally Responsible Economics (CERES) and signatory to its "Valdez Principles" of environmental responsibility, we had our operations and employee practices audited in the spring of 1993 by Science Applications International Corporation (SAIC), an employee-owned environmental consulting firm. SAIC helped us identify many additional opportunities for improving resource efficiency, employing new technologies and redesigning operations. SAIC suggestions, along with a constant influx of new ideas from interns and staff, keep us from becoming complacent about our accomplishments—or the challenges ahead.

Two spin-offs of the EQTF are our Workplace Conservation (WCP) and Vendor Certification Programs. Through the WCP, we send the members of our staff with the most experience and success in greening their operations to other institutions, where they share their stories and techniques with purchasers, print shop staff, facilities staff, landscapers, and others. Our Vendor Certification Program requires that our suppliers strive to meet the same environmental standards we have set for ourselves (see Chapter 1, Purchasing, for more information).

On the following page, we list some highlights of the EQTF's accomplishments and its ongoing projects at NWF. If you would like further information about these efforts, assistance in organizing similar programs, or to share success stories of your own, please contact our Campus Ecology Program staff at National Wildlife Federation, 1400 16th St., N.W., Washington, D.C. 20036-2266.

EQTF Accomplishments and Current Projects: A Few Highlights

- Introduced the "Conservation Commuters" program, offering ride-matching, vanpooling, guaranteed rides home, and a variety of incentives and awards, such as preferential parking for commuters and transit subsidies.

- Switched to unbleached envelopes and paper in print and copy centers.

- Switched to crushed egg cartons and high post-consumer recycled-content bags as packaging material.

- Adopted a new NWF reduced-emissions monitor standard for all future microcomputer and terminal purchases and provide alternative monitors upon request. (Exploring EPA Energy Star standards for computer and monitor efficiency.)

- Maintained 50 percent diversion rate (by weight) since 1990, recycling approximately 339 tons and saving approximately $30,000 annually.

- Established composting program in which kitchen waste at Laurel Ridge facility is composted using 5-pallet bins in the demonstration habitat used for education.

- Instituted annual community Christmas tree mulching program at Laurel Ridge facility, returning 1,200 trees to the soil each year.

- Switched to soy-based inks and alcohol-free, nontoxic fountain solutions for all print shop jobs. (Exploring use of alternatives to solvents for press cleaning, nontoxic inks and recycling inks.)

- Reached goal of 100 percent use of recycled content (with post-consumer content) for all tree-based products.

- Markedly improved lighting efficiency, received utility rebates, and became a member of the EPA's Greenlights program.

- Instituted numerous source reduction practices, including purchasing photocopying paper in strapping paper instead of boxes, switching to electronic mail for most internal memoranda, reusing of cardboard boxes for shipments, discontinuing the individual wrapping of t-shirts, elimination of polystyrene packaging, switching to bulk condiments and reusable items in the food service, and changing cleaning procedures to reduce solvent use.

- Discontinued use of ozone-depleting substances where possible and recycling of these substances when not.

- Developed guidance for housekeeping service providers on selection of nontoxic cleaning products and reusable materials. (Currently working on enforcement and follow-through.)

INDEX

A

B

C

D

N

O

P

ABOUT THE AUTHOR

Promoting campus environmental stewardship has been Julian Keniry's passion since she helped coordinate recycling and other environmental activities as a student at Agnes Scott College in Decatur, Georgia. She has authored several articles on the subject, and has lectured and conducted trainings nationwide since 1989, when she first joined the staff of the National Wildlife Federation. Currently based in Washington, D.C., Keniry coordinates youth urban ecology projects in her free time and works as a volunteer with the master gardening programs of the D.C. and Virginia Cooperative Extension Services.